WITHDRAWN

OCT 24 2022

DAVID O. McKAY LIBRARY
BYU-IDAHO

D0923837

The Treatment of Stuttering in the Young School-aged Child

APR 14 2006

The Treatment of Stuttering in the Young School-aged Child

EDITED BY

ROBERTA LEES MBE, MSc, MRCSLT

Division of Speech and Language Therapy,
University of Strathclyde, Glasgow

AND

CAMERON STARK MBChB, MPH, MSc, MRCPsych, FFPH

Consultant in Public Health, NHS Highland, Inverness

W

WHURR PUBLISHERS
LONDON AND PHILADELPHIA

© 2005 Whurr Publishers Ltd (a subsidiary of John Wiley & Sons, Ltd)
First published 2005 by
Whurr Publishers Ltd
The Atrium, Southern Gate, Chichester, West Sussex, PO19 8SQ, U.K
Telephone: (+44) 1243 779777
E-mail: cs-books@wiley.co.uk
Visit our Home page on www.wiley.com

All rights reserved. No part of this publication may be
reproduced, stored in a retrieval system, or transmitted in any
form or by any means, electronic, mechanical, photocopying,
recording or otherwise, without the prior permission of
Whurr Publishers Limited.

This publication is sold subject to the conditions that it shall
not, by way of trade or otherwise, be lent, resold, hired out,
or otherwise circulated without the publisher's prior consent
in any form of binding or cover other than that in which it is
published and without a similar condition including this
condition being imposed upon any subsequent purchaser.

British Library Cataloguing in Publication data

A catalogue record for this book is available from the British
Library.

ISBN 1 86156 486 4

Printed and bound in the UK by TJ International Ltd,
Padstow, Cornwall, UK.

Contents

Contributors

Nan Bernstein Ratner EdD
Chair, Department of Hearing and Speech Sciences
University of Maryland
USA

Willie Botterill Cert MRSCLT, MSc Counselling Psychology, Reg UKCP (PCT)
Consultant Speech and Language Therapist in Fluency Disorders
Michael Palin Centre for Stammering Children
London, UK

Frances Cook MSc Cert MRCSLT, Cert CT (Oxford), Reg UKCP (PCT)
Head of Speciality in Disorders of Fluency
Michael Palin Centre for Stammering Children
London, UK

Professor Ashley Craig BSc, PhD, Hon Doct (2002, SWU), MAPS
Department of Health Sciences, UTS
Broadway, Australia

Joseph Donaher MA
Center for Childhood Communication
Children's Hospital of Philadelphia
Philadelphia, USA

E Charles Healey PhD
Department of Special Education and Communication Disorders
University of Nebraska-Lincoln
Lincoln, USA

Roberta Lees MBE, MSc, MRCSLT
Division of Speech and Language Therapy
University of Strathclyde
Glasgow, UK

Kenneth J Logan PhD
Department of Communication Sciences and Disorders
University of Florida
Gainesville, USA

Robert Reid PhD
Department of Special Education and Communication Disorders
University of Nebraska–Lincoln
Lincoln, USA

Cameron Stark MBChB, MPH, MSc, MRCPsych, FFPH
Consultant in Public Health
NHS Highland
Inverness, UK

Yvonne Tran, BSc (Biomed), PhD
Research Fellow
University of Technology
Sydney, Australia

Roberta Williams MSc, MRCSLT
Department of Language and Communication Science
City University
London, UK

Foreword

In relating a lesson passed on to him by one of his own teachers, Wendell Johnson wrote that there are three stages to learning. In the first stage, the student says, 'Please help me'. Next, he says, 'I can take care of myself'. Finally, the learner becomes the teacher when she says, 'Please let me help you' (Johnson and Moeller, 1972).

The Treatment of Stuttering in the Young School-aged Child is intended for clinicians who strive to help children who stutter, and their families, to get to this final stage in learning to help themselves. It is clear that this journey must begin with two things: a willing child and family, and a clinician armed with a broad and deep understanding of the problem of stuttering and how to help. The purpose of this book is to provide students with the foundation to grow in this understanding, and to encourage experienced clinicians to continue their learning.

As Roberta Lees and Cameron Stark note in the introduction, clinicians often have to seek out relevant information about childhood stuttering from a variety of sources, resulting in a 'do-it-yourself' manual that best fits their needs. This is not necessarily a bad thing. Searching for and uncovering the pieces of the puzzle is a valuable learning experience in and of itself. It is also unquestionably a daunting task, especially for students. For clinicians in the making, the nature and treatment of stuttering is often a mystery and this is understandably so. I think I speak for all of us who have devoted our professional lives to the study of stuttering in saying that it is exactly this complexity that makes what we do simultaneously challenging and rewarding. What more could one ask for? That sentiment aside, this book offers an exceptional starting point for beginning clinicians who don't have the expertise or the time to 'do it themselves'; at the same time it contains enough new information and provocative discussion to challenge both newcomers and seasoned speech-language pathologists to dig deeper.

In these pages, Lees and Stark have assembled a slate of international clinician-researchers who together allow the reader to obtain a multidimensional view of stuttering in childhood. Chapter 1 sets the stage with a discussion of the who, what, where and when of stuttering, while Chapters 2 and 3 provide the backdrop and context for subsequent discussions of different therapy approaches (Chapters 4–8). These first eight chapters present a seamless transition from the nature of stuttering and general considerations for studying the effectiveness of intervention, to the specific pieces that clinicians need to help their young clients and their families along the road to meaningful change. Chapters 9 and 10 remind us that clinical work is never a one-size-fits-all proposition. Children who stutter, just like all children, come to us in different packages. Our understanding of the influence that their individual strengths and challenges have on their ability to make change deserves the careful attention that it receives in these pages.

As clinicians, we often find ourselves right smack in the middle of what Chodron (2001) calls 'the big squeeze': that uncomfortable place where we realize the discrepancy between our notion of the ideal therapy outcome and the reality of what occurs. An interesting characteristic of being 'squeezed' is that, at the same time as it feels impossible for us to accept that our clients are not changing the way we think that they should or hoped that they would, we know that we are in it for the long haul. We cannot accept the reality, but nor can we stop trying to help. As Chodron tells us: 'The big squeeze is one of the most productive places on the path . . . it humbles you, and at the same time, it has great vision' (Chodron, 2001, p. 122). When we are just beginning to work with a client, or are at a point in the clinical process where we (and the client) feel 'stuck', we rely on our knowledge, creativity, experience and collegial support to forge ahead . . . and, always, we read. The information in this text serves that dual purpose: it provides clinicians with a clear road map for planning and implementing treatment for children who stutter, and contains new and innovative ideas – the vision – to keep moving forward. No matter where you are on your professional journey, this book will help you to be a wise travelling companion to the children and families who accompany you. In return, they will teach you more than you could ever learn on your own.

Patricia Zebrowski
University of Iowa
Iowa City, Iowa, USA

Introduction

This book is intended to provide a resource for students and clinicians working with school-aged children. The opening chapters discuss the epidemiology of stuttering, review the measurement of effectiveness and the assessment process and provide a general overview of treatment. The core of the book is a series of chapters describing particular approaches to treatment. It is difficult to find good descriptions of the available treatment styles for this age group. When available, the information is spread between numerous papers and textbooks. The present volume presents these treatment approaches side by side to allow readers to identify the main features of each approach, and to consider their relevance to their own practice.

We set out to produce a text that would be useful to clinicians and to students. Texts on stuttering are often devoted to the very young child or the adolescent or, in some cases, to all age groups with a small section devoted to the school-aged child. For clinicians or student clinicians who treat school-aged children who stutter, it should be helpful to have one text that encompasses a number of ideas for this age group. In an age of evidence-based practice it is not sufficient to have a description of treatment; future clinicians will need to know how effective these treatments are. Clinicians are answerable to their employers and to their clients (and families). It is reasonable to assume that employers will expect the best value for money, and clients can assume that they are receiving the most effective treatment that is suitable for them.

Each contributor was invited to consider the same areas, to make it easier for the reader to compare the treatments, in an approach similar to the one taken by Gregory (1979). The authors of these chapters were asked to address the following topics.

- The theoretical models on which the treatment is based.
- Description of the treatment approach.
- Description of the length and type of maintenance activities.

- How closely do the authors follow their own protocols? Are there instances when this would be modified?
- The treatment setting.
- Useful outcome measures.
- When does treatment stop?
- For how long should the clinician maintain contact with the child after treatment has stopped?

In addition, a number of children who stutter have concomitant problems which may affect approaches to treatment and, indeed, treatment success. These concomitant problems may be linguistic, behavioural or physiological. In Chapters 9 and 10 Bernstein Ratner, and Healey, Reid and Donaher, respectively, discuss these problems and how they affect assessment and treatment, providing information on their approaches which can be used to supplement the other treatment chapters when a child presents with a complex mixture of problems.

We did not set out to produce information on an hypothesized aetiology of stuttering, but this is often included, where relevant, in relation to theoretical models of treatment.

This text reflects international perspectives from three continents. Eminent writers from each of these continents have contributed to produce a wide understanding of the issues involved in treating a school-aged child who stutters. As would be expected when a group of international authors contribute to the same text, there are differences in terminology between the three continents. Healey, Reid and Donaher (Chapter 10) discuss 'mental retardation' and clearly define its meaning in the USA, although the term 'learning disability' would normally be used in the UK in reference to intellectual impairment or resulting disabilities (Hogg, 1994). In the USA 'learning disability' refers to specific learning disabilities. Altering the terms would have made it difficult for interested readers to follow arguments across the authors' published papers, so we have left them unaltered. These terminological differences do not detract from the understanding of the text.

The aim of this text was to produce a clinically relevant book for students and for clinicians who are working with children of primary or elementary school age who stutter. It is impossible to be too rigid about age groups as stuttering is influenced by much more than chronological age. However, the text is intended to cover children in the age range of approximately 7 to 12 years. Treating the young child who stutters should be interesting, exacting and challenging. At the same time it should be an enjoyable experience for the child and the clinician. We hope this text will help to make it so.

Roberta Lees and Cameron Stark
January 2005

Chapter 1
Epidemiology of stuttering

ASHLEY CRAIG AND YVONNE TRAN

Introduction

Stuttering is a problem in all societies and it has the potential to be a socially and psychologically disabling disorder (Craig, 1990; Bloodstein, 1995; Craig et al., 2003). It is a disability that begins at an early age. In at least 20% of those stuttering at two years of age it will persist all through the lifespan (Craig, 2000). The major problem that presents in stuttering is the difficulty in speaking fluently when a child who stutters wishes to talk. It can be safely assumed that willingness to engage in social communication is important for personal growth, so this disorder has the potential to become a significant barrier to normal social and psychological development. For instance, from our own research we know that stuttering provokes anxiety (Craig et al., 2003), that stuttering may impede the vocation prospects of a child who stutters (Craig and Calver, 1991) and that stereotypes about stuttering in society may also limit the growth of a child who stutters (Craig, Tran and Craig, 2003). For these reasons it is very important that stuttering be well understood and managed, otherwise the future prospects of many children in our societies will be seriously disadvantaged.

Although the socioeconomic cost of stuttering is as yet unknown, it makes sense that health and social resources are strategically allocated to its treatment and management, especially for children and adolescents, as these age groups are conceivably most vulnerable (Bloodstein, 1995; Craig, 2000). To achieve the above, it is important that clinicians, researchers and health administrators have reasonable estimates of how common stuttering is, as well as estimates of how many people are at risk of developing stuttering, not only as children but throughout their entire lifespan. This is certainly true for the formative cognitive and physical development years (say 0–12 years) as stuttering is generally diagnosed as a developmental childhood disorder as described in the *Diagnostic and Statistical Manual for Mental Disorders, 4th edn* (DSM-IV: American Psychiatric Association, 1994). Exceptions to a developmental diagnosis would include those who have a sudden onset of stuttering in adulthood, say, as a result of a head injury. This is called 'acquired stuttering' (Bloodstein, 1995). However, acquired stuttering will not be considered in this chapter.

Estimating the quantity and quality of clinical resources needed to address the problem of stuttering adequately will be mere guesswork unless sophisticated studies of the distribution and determinants of stuttering are conducted. Unfortunately, there are few studies that have investigated this area with a high degree of scientific control. Most studies conducted and published during the past 50 years have limited investigation to the distribution of stuttering in children and adolescents (Bloodstein, 1995). However, the majority of such studies were conducted in a way that lowers confidence in their findings, such as a lack of randomized selection in the population, no careful validation of stuttering and so on. Furthermore, to our knowledge, only one study, conducted by the authors, has investigated the extent of the population who stutter over the entire lifespan (Craig et al., 2002). In order to gain an appreciation of the nature of stuttering as it occurs in society, this chapter presents a critical review of the natural history of stuttering for children and adolescents. In addition, this information will be described across the entire lifespan. Implications for treatment of the disorder are also discussed.

Definition of epidemiology

In order to study the health status of populations, or the frequency, risk and determinants of any particular disease, we must become involved in the discipline of epidemiology. Epidemiology is concerned with the natural history of diseases and health states in individuals and groups (Beaglehole, Bonita and Kjellstrom, 2002; Bhopal, 2002). Natural history involves the determinants (aetiology) of a disorder, its progression, frequency and risk in the population. It could also involve the outcomes of clinical intervention for a disease or disorder. Epidemiology has been defined by Last (2001) as:

> The study of the distribution and determinants of health-related states or events in specified populations, and the application of this study to control of health problems, p. 62.

Consequently, epidemiology is not only concerned with mortality rates or disease states, but also with well-being, health status and the improvement of quality of life (Beaglehole, Bonita and Kjellstrom, 2002). This approach to epidemiology has been favoured by the World Health Organization (WHO) in its global strategy for health for all in 1988 (Beaglehole, Bonita and Kjellstrom, 2002), in which member states of the WHO were encouraged to apply epidemiological data and methods in attempts to improve the quality of life of individuals in societies around the world (Beaglehole, Bonita and Kjellstrom, 2002). Because of the potential damage that untreated stuttering can inflict on children who stutter as they grow older (Beitchman et al.,

2001; Craig et al., 2003) it is important that epidemiological studies are conducted and that their findings are applied so that the quality of life of children who stutter is improved.

Measures used in epidemiology

Population at risk

To estimate reliably the natural history of stuttering in the community, it is essential that those at risk of stuttering be identified. Therefore, the section of the community that is susceptible to stuttering is defined as the 'population at risk'.

What section of the community is at risk of developing stuttering? As stuttering is predominantly a disorder that begins in early childhood, at the time when a child is learning to speak, all young children could be identified as the potential population at risk. However, the population at risk can be narrowed down. We have good evidence that suggests stuttering has a genetic aetiology (Yairi, Ambrose and Cox, 1996). We know, for instance, that children who have a parent who stutters have a substantially increased risk themselves of stuttering (Andrews et al., 1983). We also know that male children have an increased risk of stuttering compared to female children (Craig et al., 2002). Some evidence suggests that children with developmental disabilities have an increased risk of stuttering (Andrews et al., 1983; Ardila et al., 1994; Bloodstein, 1995). For example, Ardila et al. (1994) found that university students who stuttered had significantly higher risks of having an associated disorder such as dyslexia, minor brain injury and so on. The population at risk of stuttering (disregarding the population at risk of acquired stuttering) could therefore be defined as 'all young children who are developing speech, but especially those who have a history of stuttering in the family, who are male and who have a developmental disability'.

Prevalence

In epidemiology, it is crucial to obtain reliable estimates of the frequency of a disease in the population at risk. Prevalence is a measure of disease frequency and is, therefore, an important epidemiological concept. It has been defined by Last (1995) as 'the number of cases in a defined population at a specified time'. In our epidemiological research into the natural history of stuttering (Craig et al., 2002), we used point prevalence to estimate the frequency of stuttering in the population. Point prevalence can be defined as 'the number of confirmed cases in a sample at the time the sample is interviewed' (Slome et al., 1986; Beaglehole, Bonita and Kjellstrom, 2002).

The stuttering prevalence rate can be calculated by dividing the 'number of people who have been found to stutter at the time of interview' by the 'number of people in the population at risk at the time of interview'. The rate is generally expressed as cases per 100 or per 1000 of the population. Factors known to influence the prevalence of a disease are as follows.

- The number of people who die of the disease or how severe the disease is. Diseases with high mortality rates will have lower prevalence rates.
- The length of time the disease can last. If a disease lasts for a long time, the prevalence is increased, or, conversely, if there is a high recovery rate the prevalence will be reduced.
- The number of people who develop the disease. Prevalence rates will increase if many people continue to develop the disease (Beaglehole Bonita and Kjellstronm, 2002).

Measures of prevalence are crucial for assisting in the appropriate planning of healthcare services such as clinical services for stuttering.

Incidence

In epidemiology it is also crucial to estimate the incidence of developing a disease in the population at risk. A simple measure of incidence (or risk) is called the 'cumulative incidence rate' and it is usually defined as 'the occurrence of new cases of a disease during a specified period of time' (Slome et al., 1986; Beaglehole, Bonita and Kjellstrom, 2002). The cumulative incidence rate is computed by dividing the number of new cases of a disease during a specified period of time by the number of people free of the disease in the population at risk at the beginning of the period of time. Again, it is expressed as cases per 1000 of the population. Incidence research is usually conducted with prospective study designs; that is, a population at risk is identified and followed longitudinally over a period of time to determine the number of people who develop the disease.

Prevalence of stuttering

Stuttering prevalence in children and adolescents

It is not the intention here to review the large number of prevalence studies that have been conducted over the past century. For this, the reader is referred to Bloodstein (1995, pp. 105–107), who has provided a succinct review. The aim of this chapter is to analyse a smaller number of more recent studies that have contributed to the current understanding of the epidemiology of stuttering.

In a landmark study to determine the prevalence of stuttering in children, Andrews and Harris (1964) surveyed 7358 school children aged 9–11 years in a number of schools in Newcastle upon Tyne, England. They relied upon school teachers to identify children who stuttered, and then assessed each child selected by the teachers for the presence of stuttering. Although 86 children were identified by teachers as stuttering, only 80 children were subsequently confirmed as children who stuttered. Although Bloodstein (1995, p. 107) reports a prevalence of 1.2% for this study (based upon 86 children), the correct prevalence rate should have been based upon the 80 children, and thus the prevalence rate was approximately 1.1%.

Using a similar study design to that of Andrews and Harris (1964), Leavitt (1974) conducted two surveys among Puerto Rican school children. The first was conducted in 12 schools in San Juan, Puerto Rico (n =10 449 and included 5476 boys and 4973 girls); the second was conducted with Puerto Rican children from 19 schools in New York (n = 10 455; 5270 boys and 5185 girls). Leavitt (1974) also relied upon school teachers to identify the children who stuttered, and then conducted assessments to confirm the diagnosis. She found an overall prevalence rate of 1.5% among the Puerto Rican children living in San Juan (2.17% in boys and 0.76% in girls) and an overall prevalence rate of 0.84% among the Puerto Rican children living in New York (1.44% in boys and 0.23% in girls).

Aron (1962) conducted a survey of South African school children, also using teacher referral to select children who stuttered, although the diagnosis of stuttering was confirmed in a personal interview after the referral. Altogether, 6581 school children (3105 males and 3476 females, aged from 6 to 21 years) were surveyed, in 13 schools in Johannesburg, and an overall prevalence rate of 1.26% was found (83 children who stuttered, 62 males and 21 females). Unfortunately, Aron (1962, p. 120) used the term 'incidence' when really she was referring to prevalence – highlighting the importance of having a thorough understanding of epidemiology when researching in this area (Moscicki, 1984).

In order to determine the prevalence of speech problems in children, Gillespie and Cooper (1973) surveyed junior and high school students in Alabama, USA. They interviewed 5054 students from grades 7–12, consisting of 2359 males and 2695 females, with approximately half from junior high school. The children were selected using convenience (that is, non-random) sampling. Overall, Gillespie and Cooper (1973) found a 5.5% prevalence of speech disorders, with stuttering having a prevalence rate of 2.1%.

To determine the frequency of chronic childhood disabilities (including stuttering) Boyle, Decoufle and Yeargin-Allsopp (1994) used data from the National Health Interview Survey – Child Health Supplement (NHIS-CH), conducted by the National Center for Health Statistics. This large survey involved 17 110 children, aged from the very young to 17 years. Children were invited to participate from a register established by the NHIS. The NHIS involved an ongoing survey of households within the USA and used a sampling procedure believed to be representative of the civilian non-institutionalized population (Boyle, Decoufle and Yeargin-Allsopp, 1994). The study was designed to assess a number of disabilities, such as developmental disability, deafness, learning disability and stuttering.

Unfortunately, few details are provided about how stuttering was diagnosed and validated. Boyle, Decoufle and Yeargin-Allsopp (1994) found that 16.8% of children in the USA had at least one developmental disability, and almost 30% of these had more than one disability. Prevalence rates included those for cerebral palsy (0.2%), learning disability (6.5%), deafness (3.5%), emotional or behavioural problems (6.1%), and they found a stuttering prevalence rate of 1.89% (297 stuttering cases). In contrast, Brady and Hall (1976) conducted a survey on a very large convenience sample ($n = 187\ 420$) of schoolchildren in Illinois, USA, and found only a 0.35% prevalence rate for stuttering.

One way to make sense of the above prevalence data was to compute the mean prevalence rate of the above seven studies conducted on children and young adolescents. When this was completed the computed mean prevalence rate for stuttering in children was found to be 1.29%. However, Bloodstein (1995) lists 17 USA-based school-aged children prevalence studies that report a mean prevalence of 0.97% for stuttering, and 21 non-USA-based studies that report a mean prevalence rate of 1.28% for stuttering. Andrews et al. (1983) suggest the difference between the two rates may be attributed to the higher proportion of children in the USA who remain in school after puberty. Conversely, differences may also be due to error arising from the various sampling and diagnostic and assessment methods used in many of these studies. Another problem may be deriving prevalent estimates from samples that contain both younger children (say, aged 2–10 years) and adolescents (aged 11–20 years). Research suggests the prevalence is very different between these two age groups, so that the combined prevalence rate will not accurately reflect the true rate. Where randomization and stratification of the sample do not occur, the sample cannot be relied upon to be truly representative of the broader population. Although these studies correctly targeted the population at risk, only a minority employed objective strategies to identify and validate the presence of stuttering.

Stuttering prevalence rates in older adolescents have rarely been studied; however, Ardila et al. (1994) found a 2% prevalence rate in 1879 Spanish-speaking university students, whereas Porfert and Rosenfield (1978) found a 2.1% prevalence rate in 2107 students at a university in the USA. Unfortunately, both studies employed non-randomized sampling, thereby increasing the likelihood of obtaining unrepresentative samples, and both failed to confirm stuttering cases objectively.

Stuttering prevalence in disabled populations

Prevalence rates have varied widely in studies conducted on disabled populations. Stansfield (1990) conducted a non-randomized survey of adult psychiatric wards, and relied on medical staff to send back information on patients who had speech problems. Stansfield (1990) then assessed the speech of a percentage of those believed to have speech problems, and found a 6.3% prevalence rate of stuttering in the adult psychiatric population.

Montgomery and Fitch (1988) mailed survey forms to 150 schools for the hearing impaired. Only children who had been diagnosed as having a stutter by a qualified speech professional were counted in the survey. Just over half the schools replied. Only 12 children out of a total of 9930 were reported to have a stutter, and all but one were congenitally hearing impaired. They found a prevalence rate of 0.12% in hearing-disordered school-age children. Because of the non-randomized sampling methods used, these two studies do not provide reliable stuttering population rates among disabled people.

Stuttering prevalence across the entire lifespan

The only study that has investigated the prevalence of stuttering across the entire lifespan was conducted by Craig and colleagues (Craig et al., 2002). It is worthwhile discussing the method used in the study to illustrate the methods necessary to ensure the validity of the estimated prevalence rates. The study involved a random and stratified selection of households in New South Wales (NSW), Australia. The population comprised primarily city and urban dwellers (74%). Almost 77% of people in NSW are born in Australia, although the population is ethnically diverse with the most common regional groups in NSW (in rank order) being people of European or British descent, Asian, Middle Eastern and Indian. Families living in city, urban and rural areas across NSW were randomly selected, so that:

- all families had equal chances of being selected
- the distribution of people in the sample from these three types of areas was proportional to the known population spread in NSW.

The population at risk in the study by Craig et al. (2002) comprised the total population of NSW. The hypothesized proportion of people in the community believed to stutter was 1% or 0.01, and so it was planned to find up to 100 people who stuttered, as it was believed that this would provide sufficient and stable numbers of people who stuttered, so that a valid estimate of the epidemiology of stuttering could be determined. Seeking 100 people who stuttered required a sample size of 100/0.01 or 10 000 people from which to collect epidemiological data regarding stuttering. As stuttering is now believed to be genetic in origin (Ambrose, Cox and Yairi, 1997), the randomness of the selection process could be negatively influenced by cluster sampling (that is, stuttering tends to occur in families). Therefore, we aimed to collect a larger sample than 10 000 in order to overcome any possible influence of cluster sampling. The final number of participating families was 4689, consisting of 12 131 people. In accord with the population distribution across NSW (Australian Bureau of Statistics, 1998), three-quarters of the sample were from city or urban areas spread across NSW, while the remaining sample came from rural areas across the state of

NSW. It is known that if a survey is strategically conducted according to known distributions of a population, then regional coverage rates are higher and therefore are believed to be valid representations of the population (Cannell, 1985).

Households were contacted by telephone, and interviews were then conducted (either during this initial contact or at a convenient follow-up time). Since more than 95% of Australian households had a telephone in 1995/96, a high penetration rate in the community was assured. Therefore, only a small chance existed of introducing population bias into the sample. Telephone numbers that were disconnected, or where there was no answer after three attempts, were also noted and the same procedure followed. The time and day of interviews varied across the week and weekend to ensure a high penetration rate. The random procedure used to select subjects and interview procedure has been described in detail in Craig et al. (2002).

Stuttering was defined using the following definition (Craig et al., 1996): 'repetitions of syllables, part- or whole- words or phrases; prolongations of speech, or blocking of sounds'. If requested, the interviewer gave a demonstration over the telephone of a repetition and a block. If the person answering the telephone believed they or a member of their household stuttered, corroborative questions were asked directly of the person believed to stutter, or to parents if a young child stuttered. These questions included: 'Has the stuttering persisted for the last three months?', 'Has the stuttering caused fear and avoidance of situations?', 'Has the person consulted a speech professional?' and 'Has the person had therapy for stuttering?'. This information acted as corroborative evidence if one of the questions was affirmed. If someone in the family was believed to stutter, the interviewer asked for permission to speak to the individual and to tape their speech over the telephone for up to five minutes. In the case of a child, the interviewer asked the parents for permission to tape their child's speech for at least five minutes. The reliability of the telephone interview technique has been presented elsewhere (Aneshensel et al., 1982; Cannell, 1985; Quine, 1985; Paulsen et al., 1988; Craig et al., 2002).

An accurate determination of prevalence and risk depends upon a valid and robust method of detecting stuttering. All family or household members who were believed to stutter were consequently interviewed for up to five minutes until at least 500 syllables were taped for each subject. During this interview time, and based upon the above definition of stuttering, the interviewers decided whether the person stuttered. The interviewers then passed the tape to a co-researcher 'rater' who had more than 15 years' experience in treating and diagnosing stuttering. The rater evaluated the tape of the subject's speech qualitatively and quantitatively. If both interviewer and rater agreed that the individual stuttered, the frequency of stuttering (percentage of syllables stuttered, %SS) and speech rate (syllables per minute, SPM) were then determined. This was the primary measure of stuttering.

To ensure reliability, an independent rater (that is, not the interviewer or rater) assessed a proportion of the rated tapes for %SS and SPM. If stuttering was diagnosed from the tape, the corroborative evidence mentioned above was then used to confirm the diagnosis of stuttering. The rater and independent rater demonstrated over 96% agreement on the diagnosis of stuttering from the tape. When there was disagreement or no corroborative evidence, the case was not confirmed as a person who stuttered. Only confirmed stuttering cases were used in the analysis to determine prevalence and estimated incidence. Obviously, taping speech on the telephone will not assess secondary aspects of stuttering, such as facial grimace, etc. However, secondary symptoms are extremely variable and are not generally considered necessary to measure frequency of stuttering (Bloodstein, 1995).

Table 1.1 shows age and sex breakdowns in the sample. The sample of 4689 families consisted of 12 131 individuals (6023 males, mean age 35.5 (SD 21.6) years, age range <1–95 years; 6108 females, mean age 37.3 (SD 22.1) years; age range <1–99 years). There was an average of 2.9 members in each of the 4689 families interviewed. There was a total of 1638 subjects aged 10 years or younger (13.5%), although only children who were aged at least 2 years (on the basis that stuttering usually begins around 2 years of age) were included, resulting in a sample of 1622 subjects. There was a total of 1881 subjects aged 11–20 years (15.5%) and the majority of subjects ($n = 8612$) were aged 21 years or over (71%).

Table1.1 Stuttering cases and prior stuttering cases by age group			
Ages (years)	*SC*	*PSC*	*Total (no. of males)*
2–5	10	10	720 (389)
6–10	13	18	902 (465)
11–20	10	32	1881 (1006)
21–50	42	71	5405 (2607)
51+	12	45	3207 (1556)
All ages	87	176	12 131 (6023)

Note that there are 16 missing cases in the 2- to 5-year age breakdown as children aged less than 2 years were not included in the analysis. Children under 2 years of age are not included in this table.

SC = stuttering cases; PSC = prior stuttering cases.

The mean frequency of stuttering (%SS) for the sample of those who stuttered ($n = 87$) was 5.04 %SS (range 0.5–24.7 %SS, SD 3.8 %SS) and the mean speech rate was 169 SPM (range 88–218 SPM, SD 26 SPM). All the people who were confirmed cases of stuttering were asked if they had ever sought therapy (such as speech pathology, medical, psychological or hypnotherapy) for their stuttering, and a minority of approximately 30% replied that they had received therapy at some time in their life (just over 50% had never received therapy, and approximately 20% were unsure). Frequency of stuttering was shown to correlate significantly and positively with seeking therapy (point biserial $r = 0.23$; $p < 0.05$). This suggests that the more severe stutterers had sought therapy.

Table 1.2 shows prevalence rates across all ages, broken down for age categories. Prevalence was highest in the 2–5 (1.4%) and 6–10 (1.44%) year age groups, and lowest in the adolescent (0.53%) and older age (0.37%) groups. The overall prevalence rate for the entire sample was 0.72% (95% CI 0.57–0.87%). Bloodstein (1995) presented data on the prevalence of stuttering in school-age children (say, 5–18 years of age) of approximately 1%. The prevalence of stuttering in this same age group breakdown (5–18 years inclusive; $n = 2553$, with 23 individuals who stuttered) in this study was found to be 0.9% (95% CI 0.54–1.26%). This finding demonstrates the problem of reporting prevalence rates in these combined ages.

Table 1.2 Prevalence and incidence rates (per 100) and male:female stuttering ratios

Ages (years)	Prevalence (%) (95% CI)	M:F ratios	Risk (%) (95% CI)
2–5	1.4 (0.54–2.26)	2.3:1	2.8 (1.6–4.0)
6–10	1.44 (0.66–2.22)	3.3:1	3.4 (2.2–4.6)
11–20	0.53 (0.20–0.86)	4:1	2.2 (1.5–2.9)
21–50	0.78 (0.55–1.01)	2.2:1	2.1 (1.7–2.5)
51+	0.37 (0.16–0.58)	1.4:1	1.8 (1.3–2.3)
All ages	0.72 (0.57–0.87)	2.3:1	2.2 (1.3–2.3)

Sex ratios in the population at risk of stuttering

Male:female ratios in children who stutter were investigated by Aron (1962), who found a 2.9:1 male:female child ratio, while Andrews and Harris (1964) found a similar ratio. Gillespie and Cooper (1973) found a child male:female ratio of 2.7:1, whereas Porfert and Rosenfield (1978) found a male:female ratio of 2.4:1 in university students. The majority of studies have found child stuttering male:female ratios of approximately 2.5:1 (Bloodstein, 1995). The sex ratios, by age group, found in the epidemiological study by Craig et al. (2002) are shown in Table 1.2. Over the total sample, the male:female sex ratio was 2.3:1. The ratio was highest during adolescent years (4:1) and lowest in the older age group (1.4:1).

Cumulative incidence of stuttering

The incidence of stuttering is a major contributing factor to the prevalence of stuttering. It is crucial that we estimate the risk in the population by conducting research that follows a sample of the population longitudinally, in order to detect emerging new cases of stuttering. This study method is called a 'prospective design'. Unfortunately, there are very few such carefully designed studies that have investigated the incidence of stuttering (most are based on retrospective information). Furthermore, incidence studies are less common than prevalence studies (Bloodstein, 1995).

Two well-designed prospective studies are considered here. Andrews and Harris (1964) investigated the incidence of stuttering in a sample of 1000 children in England, followed up from birth to 15 years. They defined incidence as the percentage of the 1000 children who stuttered at any time in their life. However, there was a 25.8% attrition rate over the first five years. The resulting sample of 875 included 43 children who were thought to stutter, providing a 4.9% incidence estimate. Ingham (1976) questioned the reliability of the incidence data from this study because of, among other things, an uncertainty of whether 16 of the 43 children actually stuttered. If the 16 are removed, the estimate of the lifetime risk of stuttering in the study by Andrews and Harris (1964) is reduced to approximately 3.1%.

Mansson (2000) studied the incidence of stuttering in Denmark. All children born on the island of Bornholm in 1990 and 1991 were assessed for stuttering when they turned 3 years of age. The total population of this island was 45 000. Although 1042 children were born, only 1021 participated in the study at their third year. Fifty-one children were believed to stutter, and only two additional cases were isolated in surveys conducted two years later (at the age of 5 years) and four years later (when aged 9 years). As a result, Mansson (2000) suggested the incidence of stuttering for this group of children was 5.19%. This study is to be commended for its prospective design and sampling rate. However, Mansson acknowledged that the island's geographic isolation and homogeneous ethnic population limit the generalizability of the findings. Mansson (2000) also failed to report the reliability of the assessment of stuttering or a definition of stuttering.

The above two studies were prospective in design. Although the study by Craig et al. (2002) was not designed to follow prospectively the population at risk, it was thought possible to be able to compute from the data an estimate of the cumulative incidence of stuttering. The estimate was determined from the number of confirmed stuttering cases at the time of interview (prevalence), and the number of persons who stuttered in the past but who did not stutter at the time of the interview. This is possible as stuttering is not a terminal disease. In this study, incidence was therefore defined as 'the risk of the person ever stuttering in the sample population over the period of the person's lifespan' and was based upon confirmed cases of stuttering as well as cases who stuttered in the past.

In order to capture people who had stuttered in the past, participants were asked if someone in the household had ever stuttered at some previous time (that is, was not presently stuttering). If someone was thought to stutter in the past, permission to speak to this person was requested and similar corroborative questions were asked as in the prevalence study. Prior cases of stuttering are shown in Table 1.2, allowing an estimate of the incidence of stuttering. The cumulative estimated risk over the entire sample in the study by Craig et al. (2002) was 2.2%, with, as would be expected, the highest incidence in young children (2.8%) and older children (3.4%). The lowest risk was in those over 50 years of age (1.8%). The incidence in the 5–18-year-old group (n = 2553, with 71 stuttering and prior stuttering cases) was 2.8% (95% CI of 2.16-3.44%).

In summary, there are few studies from which one can obtain incidence data on stuttering. Based upon the few appropriate controlled studies available (though obviously not including the study by Mansson (2000)), Andrews et al. (1983) and Bloodstein (1995) concluded that the risk of stuttering was approximately 4–5%. Mansson's (2000) estimate also concurs with this figure. Craig et al. (2002), using a retrospective study design in which the risk was more than likely underestimated, found the incidence to be lower at around 3–3.5%, but with a 95% CI upper limit of approximately 4.5%. It seems then that cumulative risk of stuttering in children is somewhere between 3% and 5%. Notwithstanding this figure, the incidence of stuttering is obviously greater than the prevalence of stuttering. This fits with data, which suggests many who stutter in their early years recover so that they are no longer believed to be a child who stutters. This leads us on to the issue of spontaneous recovery.

Spontaneous recovery from stuttering

As said previously, the prevalence rate of stuttering will be influenced by the number of new cases who stutter in addition to the number who continue to stutter. Given the relatively high risk of stuttering in children (say, 3–5%), the question arises as to why the prevalence rate is less than 2% (Yairi and Ambrose, 1999). The answer lies in the spontaneous recovery that is believed to occur in children who stutter. Defining spontaneous recovery, however, has been difficult, and has been the topic of some debate (Yairi and Ambrose, 1992; Onslow and Packman, 1999; Yairi and Ambrose, 1999). It refers to those who cease to stutter in the absence of intervention or treatment. The problem occurs in defining ceasing stuttering, as some people who claim to have ceased may still stutter minimally (Onslow and Packman, 1999). Furthermore, those who cease stuttering when young may still be at risk later on in life (Bloodstein, 1995). Regardless of this, data do suggest that of those who begin to stutter at an early age, a majority will cease to stutter (Bloodstein, 1995). For example, Andrews et al. (1983) suggest that the chances of recovery depend upon the age of the child who stutters. Based upon well-designed research, these authors suggest that a child who stutters at 4 years of age will have a 75% chance of spontaneous recovery by the time he or she is 16 years old. A child who stutters at 6 years of age has a 50% chance of recovery by age 16, and a child who stutters at 10 years old has a 25% chance of recovery. Dickson (1971) showed that spontaneous recovery from stuttering was most likely to occur at the age of 3.5 years. Data on recovery rates were also elicited from the epidemiological research of Craig et al. (2002). Table 1.1 shows that there were 87 individuals identified as people who stuttered, and 176 identified as having stuttered in the past. This suggests a recovery rate of 67% (176/263).

Trait anxiety and stuttering in older children and adults

We have been exploring the natural history of stuttering with regard to its prevalence, risk, sex distribution and recovery. However, epidemiology can also explore other factors that may be associated with a disease. An important factor that will be discussed in this chapter is the influence of stuttering on levels of anxiety. The question as to whether people who stutter are more anxious than people who do not stutter has been debated over the years (Craig, 1990; Menzies, Onslow and Packman, 1999; Craig et al., 2003).

In children, few differences in trait anxiety have been found with non-stuttering control subjects matched for age and sex. Craig and Hancock (1996), for instance, found no differences in anxiety between 96 children who stuttered, aged 9–14 years, compared with 104 children who did not stutter, and who were similar in age, sex, education and cultural background. However, differences in communication fears were found, indicating that the group who stuttered had more negative attitudes concerning their communication. This has also been shown in research by Blood et al. (2001). Although the majority of children who stutter are unlikely to have abnormal trait anxiety levels, a qualification must be made. Research has consistently found that children with speech disabilities have an increased risk of anxiety disorder in early adulthood (Baker and Cantwell, 1987; Beitchman et al., 1996; Beitchman, et al., 2001). Presumably, the above research suggests that as we grow older the continued negative influence of a chronic speech disorder such as stuttering can be debilitating socially and psychologically. We argue that this potentially negative influence throughout childhood and adolescence, and into adulthood, can result in raised trait anxiety levels.

Whilst children who stutter are generally not more highly anxious about life than non-stuttering children (though they may have more worries about speaking), anxiety levels in adults have been much more controversial. This is demonstrated by the varying results of research projects that have attempted to compare anxiety levels with non-stuttering adult control subjects. Some have found no significant differences (Miller and Watson, 1992), whereas others have found significant differences (Craig, 1990; Fitzgerald, Djurdjic and Maguin, 1992).

Other than research conducted by ourselves (Craig et al., 2003), no studies have been published that have measured the anxiety levels of people who stutter in the community using random selection procedures. Such a sample is more likely to be representative of the population of people who stutter. Our study involved a random selection of people in 4689 households (see our prevalence results for details on this sample). A definite case of stuttering was based upon:

• a positive detection of stuttering from the person's taped speech
• at least one of the corroborative questions supporting the diagnosis.

A total of 87 people were identified as definite cases of stuttering across all ages, and 63 participants who were aged 15 years or older completed a trait anxiety questionnaire over the telephone. Mean trait anxiety levels using the Spielberger State-Trait Anxiety Inventory (STAI) (Spielberger et al., 1983) were significantly higher than levels generally found in society. The stuttering sample was shown to have significantly higher chronic anxiety levels (mean trait anxiety level 38.5, SD 9.6) than the non-stuttering control subjects (mean trait anxiety level 35.8, SD 7.0). This suggests that older people who stutter are at risk of developing higher levels of anxiety than expected, regardless of whether or not they have had treatment or not. Other researchers have reached similar conclusions (Stein, Baird and Walker, 1996).

The study by Craig et al. (2003) also examined differences in anxiety between those who received therapy for their stuttering (not within the 3 months prior to the study) and those who had never received therapy. The majority of people in the sample who stuttered had never sought or received therapy (n = 33; 52.4%), whereas a minority had received some form of therapy (n = 18; 28.6%). The remaining people were unsure of whether they had ever received therapy (19%). Those who had received therapy at some time in their life were significantly more anxious than the non-stuttering control subjects (12% higher levels of anxiety). This group's anxiety level (mean 40.1) is similar in trait anxiety to that of the Craig (1990) pre-treatment stuttering group level of trait anxiety (mean 43.1). It is also relevant to point out that abnormal levels of trait anxiety begin around the mean +1 SD, and, in this case, abnormal anxiety would constitute a trait score of approximately 44 (USA mean 35; SD 9) (Spielberger et al., 1983). Clearly, the more severe stutterers who seek therapy are more likely to be more anxious. The group who had sought therapy also had a higher frequency of stuttering than those who had never received therapy, so a reasonable interpretation of these results is likely to involve their stuttering severity. More severe stuttering is likely to be associated with greater levels of social and psychological concern (such as embarrassment, frustration or shyness) leading to higher levels of anxiety. Consequently, their worries and concerns led them to seek professional help for their stuttering.

Summary and implications for treatment of children and adults

It will help to summarize the epidemiology of stuttering presented in detail above so that we can draw out important clinical implications. Table 1.3 presents the summary data. The prevalence of stuttering over the entire lifespan (from 2 years to older age) is approximately 0.7% of the population, and males have at least a 50% higher prevalence rate of stuttering. In addition, epidemiological data suggest that a higher prevalence rate of 1.4% exists in children (aged 2–10 years), with male children, again, having a higher prevalence of stuttering (at least twice as likely to stutter). Due, no doubt, to spontaneous recovery as well as treatment, the prevalence falls in adolescence (aged 11–20 years) to around 0.5%, with boys still more likely to stutter (4:1 male:female ratio). As perhaps expected, because of relapse following treatment, the prevalence rate rises again into early adulthood and then falls substantially from late middle to older age (0.37%), with males still stuttering more frequently than females (ratio of 1.4:1). It is important to note that the 95% CI for the prevalence of stuttering in school-aged children found in the study by Craig et al. (2002), that is, aged 5–18 years, 0.9% prevalence, CI range 0.54–1.26%, covers the estimates given by Bloodstein (1995), who suggested that the prevalence in the USA was 0.97% and that outside the USA it was 1.28%.

Table 1.3 Summary of the epidemiological data for people who stutter

Factor	Children (2–10 years)	Adolescents (11–20 years)	Adults (21–49 years)	Older adults (50+ years)
Approximate prevalence (%)	1.4	0.5	0.8	0.4
Cumulative incidence (%)	3–5	about 2	about 2	<2
Male:female ratio	2–3:1	4:1	2:1	1.4:1
Spontaneous recovery rate (%)	50–75	<50	<25	<25
Anxiety levels	Normal	Slightly above normal	Abnormal	Abnormal
Communication fears	Slightly raised	Abnormal	Abnormal	Abnormal

The findings of our epidemiological research indicate that a more realistic estimate of the prevalence of stuttering in children is around 1.4%, rather than 1%, of the population at risk. This prevalence rate is substantially higher than the estimates of Andrews et al. (1983) and Bloodstein (1995), and is closer to the mean prevalence rate of 1.3% derived from the seven studies critiqued in this chapter. The prevalence of stuttering in children should not be confused with the prevalence in adolescents, and, if it is, the combined prevalence rate acts to lower the actual rate in children. Therefore, we argue that a higher stuttering prevalence rate of approximately 1.4% in children should be accepted as the most reliable current estimate.

What are the clinical implications of this difference in the accepted child prevalence rate? Well, for example, the acceptance of the lower estimate will have a potentially negative impact on the clinical services and management of stuttering in younger children. In effect, we are underestimating the prevalence of the disorder in children. For example, assuming a population of 200 million people has 15% of its population in the age range of 2-10 years, a 1% prevalence rate of the number of children who stutter at any one time is 300 000. However, if the prevalence is at least 1.4%, then the number of children stuttering is underestimated by 120 000 (420 000 rather than 300 000 children may be expected to stutter). If this underestimation of prevalence were the case, then the client load for clinicians treating children who stutter would be high, with long waiting times. Public services for adults who stutter will be severely reduced as a result, forcing adults to seek more expensive and possibly less credible private services (in terms of the evidence base for the treatment efficacy). We believe this clinical scenario is already a reality in Australia and no doubt it is also the case in many other countries.

The lower stuttering prevalence rate in adolescents should not have been a surprise, given that the current thinking in treating children who stutter is that it is best to treat the stutter early rather than wait (Lincoln and Onslow, 1997). In addition, 50-75% of children who stutter at an early age will possibly recover spontaneously before adolescence (Andrews et al., 1983; Yairi and Ambrose, 1992). In addition, an estimated recovery rate of almost 70% was found in the study by Craig et al. (2002). This presumed recovery rate does help to explain the large drop in the prevalence of stuttering from childhood (say 2-10 years) to adolescence (11-20 years). Epidemiological evidence suggests that recovery is more likely to occur in females (Ambrose, Cox and Yairi, 1997).

Although there may be problems in proposing that many children who stutter will recover by the time they are 16 years old, important clinical issues and implications arise from the tension between whether a child will recover naturally or whether a child should be treated. For example, should a clinician treat a young child who stutters when referred, or should the clinician allow time to see whether the child will recover without treatment? To resolve this difficult question, we believe that clinicians should judiciously consider all factors that influence the case, such as the following.

- The age of the child who stutters. For instance, very young children (say 1.5-2 years old) could be assessed and tracked for up to six months to decide whether they will recover spontaneously. In contrast, an older child who stutters (say, 7–12 years old) should be a higher priority for referral to treatment.

- The severity of stuttering in the child who stutters is an important factor. It is our belief that clinicians should conduct comprehensive assessments on the severity of stuttering as well as the extent of the negative influence of the stutter on the child. If the stutter is severe or if it is creating a negative influence then treatment should be offered rather than waiting for a chance that the child may recover. In contrast, a child who stutters with a mild stutter may be left for a period of time to determine whether the stutter will decline and disappear.

- It goes without saying that that treatment should only occur if the parents of a child who stutters are in favour of this. If parents do not wish their child to have treatment, they should be extensively advised on the long-term potential risks of stuttering, and they should be encouraged to keep in regular contact with the clinician regarding the progress of their child.

- The decision to treat or not treat will also be influenced by any concurrent disabilities that the child may have. If a child who stutters has other disabilities then the potential impact of treatment on the other disability must be assessed. Clearly, the decision as to whether children who stutter should be treated or left to see whether they recover is a complex and difficult question to answer and not at all straightforward.

The increase in stuttering prevalence through early to middle adulthood may also be attributed to relapse issues (Craig, 1998a), or to other factors not yet understood. Perhaps it also reflects a potentially greater openness to discuss our problems and admit to them. The decrease in stuttering prevalence in older ages is consistent with current thought (Bloodstein, 1995) but cannot yet be explained. Given the above, a proportion of clinical resources should be channelled into services for adults, and especially into strategies (such as anxiety reduction techniques, cognitive therapy, self-esteem and self-confidence enhancement techniques, social skills training and so on) that are known to reduce risks of relapsing back to pre-treatment severity (Craig and Andrews, 1985; Andrews and Craig, 1988; Craig, 1998b; Craig, Hancock and Cobbin, 2002; Hancock and Craig, 2002).

Males, in comparison to females, have been shown to be at higher risk of stuttering. Evidence suggests that the male:female ratio is at least 2:1 in younger children, and that this ratio increases into adolescence where it peaks at 4:1 (Craig et al., 2002). Again, these epidemiological data can be explained by the high recovery rate that occurs as children grow older. Although males and females seem to have more equivalent risks at an early age, we know that males have less capacity in speech motor resources in the crucial developmental years, and so they remain at higher risk of stuttering than females as they grow older, and are thus less likely to recover from stuttering. As genetic influences contribute less input into susceptibility to stutter in older ages, and treatment/relapse/experience/personality factors become more influential, male predominance to stutter declines into mid-adulthood, to 2.2:1, and continues to decline into older adulthood (50+ years), to 1.4:1. The male vulnerability to stuttering argues for care when assessing the risks of stuttering in young boys. This is especially the case if a family history of stuttering exists. However, this does not mean that girls should be passed over for treatment opportunities. Both males and females have risks of stuttering into older ages.

The incidence or risk of stuttering is identified from prospective designs in which new cases of stuttering over a designated period of time are determined in a population that is initially free of stuttering. Studies (Andrews and Harris, 1964; Mansson, 2000) that have employed a prospective design suggest that the risk of stuttering in children ranges between 3% and 5% of the population at risk. As the cumulative risk of stuttering over the entire lifespan has not been investigated, other than in the retrospective study by Craig et al. (2002), data from this study can only provide weak estimates of the risk (more than likely underestimates). The study by Craig et al. (2002) found a risk of approximately 3%, with a 95% CI upper bound of 4–5%. The risk was higher in older children (3.4%) than in young children (2.8%), perhaps due to new cases emerging in this age group. Natural recovery seems to have influenced risk in adolescents (2.2%). As perhaps expected, the adult cumulative risk of stuttering was lower, at around 2%, almost 1% less than the risk in children.

In a population of 140 million adults (say, adults represent 70% of 200 million people), a potential 2.8 million people have a heightened risk of stuttering. Furthermore, there may be as many as 600 000 up to one million people stuttering at any one time, depending on the age of the person (obviously a higher prevalence in children). Given the potential for stuttering to negatively affect the psychosocial and employment prospects for those who stutter through their lifetime (Craig, 1990; Craig and Calver, 1991; Craig et al., 2003), these figures argue for substantial resources being allocated to treatment facilities for adults who stutter. This is especially the case as data do suggest that living with a chronic disorder such as stuttering does raise anxiety levels after living with the problem for some years. Initial symptoms seem to include raised concerns about communication, but symptoms can increase in intensity and become more severe and diverse. By adulthood the symptoms of many people who stutter can resemble those with social phobia or generalized anxiety disorder (American Psychiatric Association, 1994; Stein, Baird and Walker, 1996; Craig et al., 2003). Clearly, we need to employ epidemiological data to improve the future lives of children who stutter.

Acknowledgements

This research was funded by the University of Technology, Sydney, and a Commonwealth Department of Health Grant (NHMRC). Thanks also to the following funding bodies who also contributed financially to the research: the Big Brother Movement; the Australian Rotary Health Research Fund; the Sunshine Foundation; and the Inger Rice Foundation. Thanks also to Dr Karen Hancock, Ms Karen Peters, Ms Karen Siccardi, Mrs Magali Craig and Mr Charles Lo for their assistance in conducting this research.

Chapter 2
The assessment of children who stutter

ROBERTA LEES

Introduction

School-aged children who stutter are no longer beginning to stutter, but by this time have had some experience of stuttering and of reactions to stuttering. In response to this they may have developed avoidance behaviours, fears of speaking and a self-concept of being someone who stutters. Like all school children, they are developing independence from their parents and becoming increasingly influenced by their peer group, particularly in relation to their social and emotional functioning. They will be influenced by what is happening in the home, in school and with their peers, so that their behaviour, including speech behaviour, will show considerable variability. In addition to this Manning (2001) has commented that people who stutter are sometimes able to 'turn on fluency' when the situation seems to demand this.

It is against this background of constant variability that the clinician seeks to obtain a representative 'picture' of children who stutter. At any time when children are attending clinic for assessment purposes it is very difficult to know if they are experiencing a 'good/middling/bad' day. This is particularly true when assessing before the clinician has really got to know a child. Although assessment is a continuous process, in practice much of the assessment is carried out before initiating treatment. This allows the clinician to gain as good an understanding of a child as possible, and to ensure that the treatment given is related to the child's social, emotional and educational needs. Many clinicians will make multiple observations in as many situations as possible, and over as long a period of time as possible. However, 'assessment-only' sessions can not continue for too long otherwise parental co-operation might diminish. So, there is often an overlap between assessment being carried out and treatment beginning. In order to understand the child and the context in which he or she lives, assessment of the child along with information from parents and teachers can provide the clinician with a reasonable overview of the child. Throughout all assessment procedures the child must be placed at the centre. During treatment the clinician will continue to assess the child for indications of progress or indeed lack of progress, to help to ascertain if the treatment approach is appropriate.

Theoretical models

Sometimes assessment procedures are dictated by theoretical models. Manning (2001) cites the revised Component Model of Riley and Riley (2000), which takes as its basic premiss that the onset of stuttering is linked to a 'vulnerable system' in young children. It is the clinician's task to identify the components that could be contributing to this 'vulnerability' in the speech production system. Following this model the clinician would assess for physical attributes (attention span and speech motor co-ordination), temperamental features (sensitivity, expectations of self) and listener reactions (communication environment, secondary gains, teasing or bullying).

The Demands and Capacities Model (Starkweather, 1987) is based on the premiss that the demands placed on the child outweigh the child's ability to respond fluently. The clinician then tries to elicit the demands placed on the child (environmental or self-imposed) and the child's cognitive, linguistic and emotional capacity to respond. Starkweather and Gottwald (1990) give details of their assessment procedures in relation to this model. Siegel (2000), amongst others, has raised the problem that 'capacity' is impossible to measure and the clinician is really measuring the child's performance. Hence, he and others have suggested that the model be renamed the Demands and Performance Model. Whatever the model is called, the clinician is seeking to identify the child's inherent abilities and the stressors placed on that child. Other theoretical models will similarly dictate how clinicians go about assessing children who stutter.

Many clinicians will follow the assessment procedures laid down by the authors of specific treatment approaches, which they are following. However, the following comments are intended to be general features often assessed in children who stutter, and are not specifically related to any one model of stuttering or treatment approach.

Assessing behavioural characteristics of stuttering

Dysfluency

Speech samples are taken in order to gain some impression of the level of fluency or dysfluency and the child's ability to 'get a message across' to a listener. It is impossible to ensure that one sample of speech taken in a clinic is representative of that child's communication and for that reason a number of samples might be taken both inside and outside the clinic. Although multiple samples are likely to give a more representative picture of a child's speaking ability, there is always the problem of the child 'turning on' fluency if a recording device is seen in the vicinity. Recording a child's speech without the child's knowledge can have repercussions in the clinician's relationship with the child and not least in the ethical considerations of the therapeutic situation.

Yairi (1997) recommends that speech samples should be of at least 500 syllables, and that these should be taken over at least two separate days to take into account, to some extent, the variability of stuttering behaviour. Shapiro (1999) suggests that samples should be around 300 words in length or five minutes of the child talking, and he suggests taking samples with and without communicative pressure; pressure being created in clinic by the clinician speaking quickly, interrupting the child or abruptly changing topics. Another way of obtaining five minutes of the child talking is to record 15 minutes and analyse the middle five minutes, assuming that the child will by then have become accustomed to the recording device and not yet tired of it. The clinician would then assess the amount of stuttering, either directly from the recording or would make a transcript of the child's speech and mark the instances of stuttering. Making a transcript is certainly more time-consuming but could be a useful task for a trained assistant.

It is then necessary to decide what will be classified as stuttering. Ingham and Cordes (1992) describe inter-rater and inter-clinic differences in the identification of stuttering. Lack of an adequate definition of stuttering contributes to intra- and inter-rater reliability problems in its measurement. These are fundamental problems in research, but it can be useful for practising clinicians to provide a written definition of stuttering for themselves, to assist in obtaining some reliability. Although by no means perfect, this can help to provide some standards against which clinicians can make judgements of change.

Most clinic speech samples will include reading and conversation. If children are more fluent when reading, it is possible that they are being aided by not being required to formulate the language to express their ideas. On the other hand, if children are less fluent when reading it is possible that they are avoiding words on which they think they will stutter in conversational speech. Such avoidance is not possible in a reading task. The reading passage should be on a level that is well within the child's reading ability.

Picture description tasks are often used in addition to reading, or as a replacement in children who cannot yet read. Conversation with a young child can be very difficult as, in order to elicit some 'spontaneous' speech from the child; the clinician often asks a series of questions, so that 'conversation' effectively becomes a question and answer session. The clinician should attempt to ask very open questions or engage children in a discussion about something that would interest them, in order to obtain as much spontaneous speech as possible. These are fairly typical 'in clinic' assessments.

Perhaps surprisingly, there is very little normative data on how a fluent child would perform such tasks under similar conditions. Greig (1999) conducted a survey of the amount of dysfluency in a group of 30 children aged between 8 and 9 years, who were not regarded as having any problems with speech or fluency. The children carried out a picture description and reading task as well as conversing with the investigator and these tasks were carried out with the children in pairs. Each session was videotaped and this videotape was used for analysis with a clear description of dysfluency being given. A range of 0–13.8% dysfluency on picture description was found, 0–6.1% dysfluency on the reading task and 1.8–11.8% dysfluency in the conversation. However, no intra- or inter-rater reliability measures were used. It is clear that more normative data need to be collected, in particular using the same types of speaking situation as would be used with a child who stutters in clinic. It is also useful to obtain speech samples taken from the child's normal environment. Co-operative parents are usually very willing to bring a tape of the child speaking at home, usually when the speech is particularly dysfluent, so that the clinician can understand what is concerning the parents.

It can be difficult to compare the results of two clinicians, not only because of the problems of definition of what is stuttering, but also because of differences in the basic unit of assessment viz. syllables or words. Boberg and Kully (1985), and Guitar (1998), prefer to use the syllable as they consider this to be the basic unit of speech. Hayhow (1983) also favours the syllable as the basic unit of assessment, arguing that words vary in length, the rhythm of speech is built around the syllable and that the problem of more than one instance of stuttering occurring in a polysyllabic word is avoided.

The calculation of the percentage of stuttered syllables (%SS) is carried out thus:

$$\frac{\text{Total dysfluency} \times 100}{\text{Total number of syllables 1}}$$

Some authors do calculate the percentage of stuttered words (%SW), and Andrews and Ingham (1971) suggest that this can be converted to %SS by multiplying the %SW by 1.5.

Following the calculation of %SS or, in some cases, %SW, clinicians often find it useful to comment on the severity of the stuttering. However, this can be meaningless unless the clinician uses a standardized procedure or at the very least describes what is meant by 'severe', etc. One often-used assessment is the Stuttering Severity Instrument (Riley, 1994), which is based on two 200-syllable speech samples: one of oral reading and one of conversation. The overall score is based on three sub-components: frequency, duration and physical concomitants. The %SS is calculated in each task and added together to give a frequency score which is then converted to a task score. The duration score is based on calculating the mean duration of the three longest blocks and, again, this is converted to a task score. The physical concomitants score is based on the clinician's subjective judgement of how noticeable or distracting the physical concomitant movements are, and this is converted to a task score. From the sum of these three task scores a severity rating is derived. This has the benefit of having a standard procedure; however, McCauley (1996) has criticized the validity and reliability of this method, but it remains a widely used assessment of stuttering severity. Other rating scales are based on 5-, 7- or 9-point scaling systems, some with well-defined points for each score. However, Cullinan, Prather and Williams (1963) suggested that scales using non-defined points or defined points have provided roughly the same ratings.

In addition to quantitative measures of the amount of dysfluency, it is useful to gain some information on the quality of dysfluency. Bernstein Ratner, in Chapter 9, elaborates on the necessity to analyse the quality of the dysfluency, particularly for children who stutter who have a language problem. She argues that this is a necessary prerequisite for differential diagnosis between those children for whom stuttering is the primary problem and those who have some dysfluency stemming from a language formulation problem. To assist with this the clinician should record the types of dysfluency and frequency of these types.

Speech rate

One measure of the effectiveness of a child's communication is that of speech rate. This measure, according to Bloodstein (1995, p. 8), 'is not so highly correlated with any other measure of severity as to be considered merely its equivalent and yet is sufficiently related to other measures as to suggest that it may be reflecting an aspect of severity that they do not adequately take into account'. Certainly, this measure can give some idea of how severely restricted a child is in getting a message across to listeners. Normative data on speech rate do exist, and the reader is referred to Guitar (1998) for more information on this. It should be borne in mind that many symptom treatments do initially have the effect of slowing speech rate, but, ultimately, the aim is to help children to reach more normal rates in relation to their peers.

Calculation of speech rate is carried out by means of the following formula:

$$\frac{\text{Total number of syllables spoken} \times 60}{\text{Total time taken (in seconds)}}$$

When calculating speech rate the clinician should count only the syllables or words that the child would have said, had he or she not stuttered. The reader is referred to Guitar (1998) for more information on this.

Length of stutter-free utterances

Costello and Ingham (1985) commented on the usefulness of this measure to show change pre- and post-therapy. It is a simple matter to revisit the speech sample used to collect the information on the amount of dysfluency the child has and to calculate the mean of the three longest stutter-free utterances. This takes very little time and may prove to be a useful guide to change. This is a promising measure, although more research is required to establish its value in practice.

Naturalness ratings

Naturalness ratings tend to be carried out only after treatment has started, and most studies of the naturalness of speech after therapy have been conducted with adult clients. Lees (1994) commented that many studies on naturalness have involved listeners rating the speech of the client, but there is very little information on clients' assessment of the quality of their own speech, particularly when these clients are children. If children perceive their speech to sound unnatural when using specific taught techniques, it is unlikely that they would then be motivated to apply these techniques. The perception of naturalness of the speech by the child is particularly important for a child's motivation to transfer what has been learnt in therapy to situations outside the clinic. This could be a useful area to assess and it might serve as a good predictor of success.

Associated behaviours

Many authors have referred to associated behaviours, such as concomitant movements, as 'secondary' behaviours, but as Zebrowski (1995) has noted that these behaviours are present within a few months of onset, the use of the term 'secondary' must be questioned. Clinicians should keep a careful note of all observable concomitant behaviours as a reduction in these post-therapy could be seen as a relevant variable when assessing the efficacy of a given treatment technique.

Many children, even as young as 7 years of age, are very aware of their stuttering and some are very anxious to hide it. Sometimes their efforts to hide the stuttering are obvious, for example the child puts his or her hand over the mouth in the mistaken belief that this somehow disguises the stuttering. Other children, in particular the slightly older school-aged child, will use devices such as sound or word avoidance, and the apparent 'success' of this strategy depends on the breadth of the child's vocabulary and ability to predict 'difficult' sounds or words and change them around quickly. These devices have been carefully explained by Van Riper (1971). Ingham (1984) remarked on the difficulties involved in measuring these, and to date no satisfactory technique has been found. Much depends on the observational skills and understanding of the clinician. Nevertheless, it is useful for clinicians to note any such behaviours, with subjective impressions of any notable change in their frequency.

Non-behavioural aspects of stuttering

The attitudes held by a child towards speaking will affect the choice of treatment, and the child's prognosis. Healey, Scott and Ellis (1995) describe the use of fluency-shaping techniques for children who have a relatively good attitude about themselves and their stuttering. Stuttering modification techniques are more likely to be used with children who are more sensitive about stuttering. Thus, it is important to gauge this at a first assessment.

Use of questionnaires

This is a relatively quick way of obtaining information about a child's feelings and attitudes, but is usually more effectively used after the clinician and the child have got to know each other. Guitar (1998) describes the use of two questionnaires to elicit information on the attitudes held by the child towards speaking. The A19 scale (Guitar and Grims, 1977) has 19 closed questions to which the child responds with 'yes' or 'no' and the Communication Attitude Test (Brutten and Dunham, 1989) has 28 questions requiring the child to respond using a 'true or false' dichotomy. As Guitar (1998) pointed out, these questionnaires are probably ineffective if given before a trusting relationship between child and clinician has been built up. There is also the danger that children might respond in the way in which they believe the clinician wishes.

Interviewing the child

The clinician, particularly one experienced in working with dysfluent children, can often make a subjective judgement of a child's feelings and attitudes, based on the child's verbal and non-verbal responses. However, in order to gain information from a child, a trusting relationship must be developed so that the child feels free to speak to the clinician. The clinician can explore the child's views on stuttering, on speaking fears and on how the child copes with a feared situation.

The amount of information gained depends on the child's insight into stuttering and willingness, and ability to communicate this to the clinician. Rustin, Botterill and Kelman (1996) discuss interviewing the very young dysfluent child, beginning with very general issues and moving to speech. They use open-ended questions to encourage a child to talk, and they ask the child if it is sometimes difficult to talk, eliciting situations which are difficult and how the child deals with these. They finish with an intriguing question: 'Let's pretend I can do magic and can change something about you, what would you like me to change?' (Rustin, Botterill and Kelman, 1996, p. 39). Although these questions were designed for a younger child, the basic ideas would apply to the 7- to 12-year-old age group, although some modification would be required, particularly for the older children in this age range.

Written information from a child

Some children, especially those in the upper age range, might be willing to write a story about themselves, particularly if they can do this on a computer. Such stories can be very revealing about a child's feelings and attitudes in general, and about speaking in particular. One idea taken from personal construct psychology is to ask children to write a self-characterization sketch in which children write about themselves in the third person, as if written by someone who knows them well. Hayhow and Levy (1989) discuss ways of analysing this self-characterization, such as identification of themes and words or phrases which are repeated. This can provide a useful insight into how a child perceives the world, though again this also depends on the skills of the clinician in interpreting this.

Use of drawings

Drawings have been used with adults who stutter to gain some insight into how they perceive their stuttering. Stewart and Brosh (1997, p. 49) describe drawings done by adults who stutter as a 'useful adjunct to other self rating scales'. The author observed a clinician in Germany asking a child to draw his family members as if they were animals and the clinician interpreted this as indicating how a child perceived his or her position in the animal pack. This author then asked one of her clients (a boy of 10 years) to draw his family as if they were animals. Pre-therapy the child drew himself as a little bird, but post-therapy he drew himself as a lion. The other members of his family were either sheep, pigs or eagles, relating differently on both occasions to his mother, father and sister. He seemed to have a limited repertoire of which animals he could draw, but it can be argued that he seemed to change from a small insignificant bird to a more powerful animal. This type of assessment can be useful, depending on the child's imagination and the clinician's interpretation of these drawings. It could also serve as an adjunct to other assessment procedures.

Interviewing parents or carers

Throughout this section the term 'parents' will be used, though it is recognized that this might not be the case and some will be carers, etc. The single term 'parents' is used to facilitate a less clumsy linguistic style.

It is important to recognize that parents are often very stressed when they come to clinic, and they can harbour feelings of guilt, believing that in some way they might have caused their child to stutter. At the start it should be made clear to them that they can be very helpful in their child's treatment and that they did not cause the stuttering.

From the outset the clinician must gain the trust and co-operation of the parents as they will be working jointly to help the child. Manning (2001) comments that the initial meeting with the parents is the first opportunity for clinicians to demonstrate their understanding of stuttering in general, and the impact of this on the child and the family. The clinician might then attempt to gain a fuller understanding of the child and the context in which he or she lives, but this is achieved in a spirit of trust and co-operation. A useful starting point, as recommended by Guitar (1998), is to ask an open-ended question, such as 'Tell me about your child's speech'. This can lead to a discussion, rather than a question and answer session. Clinicians will have a number of questions which they wish to ask, but it is more productive to have a discussion with the parents, gaining as much information as possible, and then 'fill in the gaps' at a later session. Typical information that might be sought would include the child's history of stuttering, reactions to it, the parents' reactions to stuttering and their perceptions on the child's temperament. The clinician would also wish to know about family history of stuttering, family history of recovery from stuttering (Yairi et al., 1996), how the child copes at school and socially with friends. For fuller details on this the reader is referred to Guitar (1998).

Interviewing teachers

It is useful to gain some information from the teacher on how a child is coping, both educationally and socially, in the classroom. The teacher might report difficulties in reading, or specifically in reading aloud, or might have some information on the child's ability to form friendships with peers in the class. Answers to questions such as 'Does X volunteer answers in class?' can give some insight into how stuttering might have affected the child. It is difficult to measure this in any systematic way, but the teacher's perceptions are still of value to the clinician, as they indicate how someone who sees the child for a good proportion of time views the child's willingness to speak and ability to form social relationships.

So many pressures are now on teachers to complete schedules of work in a given period of time that clinicians must beware of asking teachers to complete a long, detailed questionnaire or even a long report on a child, though this would be helpful. If time allows it is sometimes easier for both to meet briefly and discuss these issues. This would also give the teacher the opportunity to ask the clinician about stuttering in general and the best way to respond to the child who stutters in the classroom. Some authors (Guitar, 1998; Manning, 2001) also take this opportunity to give teachers an overview of the therapy programme. Ideally, the clinician would also visit the classroom to gain some information on the general atmosphere, how much talking is permitted or expected and how much the child participates in classroom activities. Information from the teacher adds to the growing profile on the child, which gives the clinician a better view of the child in context and can also be useful for evaluating changes in the child post-treatment.

Assessment of other aspects of a child's speech or language ability

The number of children who stutter who also have a concomitant phonological disorder is uncertain as estimates vary quite considerably. Louko, Conture and Edwards (1999) summarize these differences in estimated prevalence in relation to the co-occurrence of stuttering and disordered phonology as varying from 16% (Blood and Seider, 1981) to 67–96% (St Louis and Hinzman, 1988), whereas Conture (1990) concludes that approximately one-third of children who stutter will have disordered phonology. Arndt and Healey (2001) explain the differences in these estimates of prevalence in terms of methodological differences in the various studies. Bernstein Ratner, in Chapter 9, elaborates further on the problems of defining this population. However, it is useful to carry out a screening test of phonology on all children who stutter, with a more detailed norm-referenced assessment being given if a child has a phonological problem. Many such assessments exist, but may have a cultural bias, so it is important for clinicians to use an assessment that relates to the cultural group of the child. It is also possible that a child has had a phonological disorder in the past but this has now resolved either naturally or as a result of treatment. If the latter, the clinician should attempt to obtain details of past therapy; it is possible that the child might now have the idea that speaking is difficult.

The role of language skills in the development of stuttering is unclear. Andrews and Harris (1964, p. 102) found that children who stutter had some form of 'language disability', and this generated much research into the language skills of children who stutter. Bernstein Ratner, in Chapter 9, discusses the role of language and dysfluency, and it is strongly recommended that children referred for stuttering should undergo language assessments. Again, norm-referenced assessments are the preferrred choice. Bernstein Ratner assesses the use of these assessments and the analysis of narrative language samples and the reader is referred to her chapter for more information on this.

Assessment of temperament

There has been much controversy about the role of temperament in the development of stuttering. Guitar (2002) presented an interesting hypothesis that emotions related to fear, escape and avoidance are in the right cerebral hemisphere and that there is evidence of high levels of right hemisphere processing in stuttering. Guitar (2003) expanded on this by carrying out a physiological measure of temperament using acoustic startle response, based on the view that sensitive individuals have a greater magnitude of response. He compared 14 adults who stuttered with 14 adults who did not stutter and found a significantly greater response in the stuttering group, though no correlation was found between the extent of the startle response and the severity of stuttering. Guitar (2003) also used a paper and pencil test of temperament, the Taylor Johnson Temperament Analysis (Taylor and Morrison, 1996) and found differences on the 'nervous' dimension between the two groups. This type of assessment has not been carried out with children, but Guitar has hypothesized that emotionally reactive temperaments might interfere with recovery from early stuttering. If this were correct we would expect to see a more reactive temperament in the older school child, who is less likely to recover spontaneously. The role of temperament in the prognosis for the school-aged child who stutters requires further investigation before clear guidance can be provided for the practising clinician.

General comments

As stuttering is a multidimensional problem, its assessment is complex. In order to understand children and their behaviour, assessment will be an ongoing process with many informal observations made along the way, although there will be an initial burst of assessment activity. It is important to build as full a picture of a child as is possible, and, although much can be obtained by the use of standardized assessments, the value of a skilled clinician's observation should not be underestimated. One area where there is no formal means of assessment is that of gauging a child's willingness to speak, a point raised by Conture and Guitar (1993). If children do not speak very much or say very little when they do speak, is this due to the stuttering, the child's temperament or some other factor? Obviously, subjective impressions of a child's willingness to speak can be gained from teachers, parents and even from the child's friends, but it can be difficult to interpret these impressions.

The child must be central to the process of assessment. Much of our assessment has been linked to what clinicians and sometimes parents or teachers think about the child who stutters but the child's view should be at the centre of therapy. Sometimes children are referred for treatment against their wishes: it is the parents who wish the child to be treated. If the views of the child are discussed with the clinician and the clinician acknowledges and respects these, treatment is more likely to be successful.

Feeding back information

Clinicians should feed back information to children at a level that they will understand and in a way which will encourage them to participate in a collaborative effort. Sometimes this can be encouraged by using analogies which a child can relate to. Examples include Sheehan's iceberg, with the explanation that what we feel is often hidden and in this case is under the water, or Conture's hosepipe, which uses the analogy of a knot appearing in a hosepipe, stopping the water from flowing freely. Clinicians can then take this opportunity to clarify their role in the treatment of the child and of the commitment required by the child. The concept of being equal partners in a joint quest should be clear.

The clinician should also provide the parents with some information on stuttering and on details of their child's assessment. The clinician's decision about whether or not a child should be present at this point would depend on the maturity and sensitivity of the child. All positive aspects of what the parents have already done to help the child should be emphasized. An outline and explanation of the proposed treatment would also help parents to understand what to expect from treatment and give them an indication of how they will be able to assist the clinician and, very importantly, how much time they might need to spend on this. The parents' reaction to this is also a good way of gauging their level of commitment. Throughout, the clinician should be accepting of the parents and their views while fostering an atmosphere of trust.

Teachers also require some information on the nature of the child's problem, although care must be taken to avoid contravening relevant legislation on data sharing. However, with the child's and the parents' agreement, information about the child or about stuttering in general can be given to the teacher, along with suggestions on how the teacher and the clinician can work together in the suggested treatment programme. It is important to consider a child within his or her social environment and to feed back any permissible useful information to others in that environment. Enlisting the co-operation of relevant others could be helpful to a child who stutters and assist progress in treatment.

Assessment depends on taking a structured, disciplined approach, which provides child, clinician and parents with a good understanding of the problems being experienced. Good baseline measurements provide a way of monitoring change, and can be combined with the child and parental views to build a rich picture of progress. Involvement of teachers, where possible, can help to reinforce relevant messages and approaches. Stuttering presents particular challenges to the clinician, and careful assessment is a key component of therapy.

Chapter 3
Does it work?

CAMERON STARK AND ROBERTA LEES

Introduction

Clinicians want to help their clients. In the absence of clear-cut evidence – a common situation in any branch of healthcare – it often feels better to offer a treatment that seems plausible, rather than no intervention at all. At the very least, it seems reasonable to offer interventions that appear unlikely to do any harm. This may not be as satisfactory an approach as it first appears. Alderson and Groves (2004) list a range of interventions in various areas of health and social care that seem likely to work, ranging from mentoring for children with anti-social behaviour (Roberts et al., 2004) to adenoidectomy for children with recurrent middle ear infections (Koivunen et al., 2004). In practice, these interventions have not been found to deliver on their theoretical promise. In other cases, an interim outcome measure suggests the treatment works, but this does not translate into an improved outcome for the patient. Doust and Del Mar (2004) give two examples. A treatment for a cardiac arrythmia was thought to work because it made the ECG look normal, but later studies found that it increased the number of deaths. Similarly, fluoride increases bone density but increases fracture rates. It is necessary to be clear that the outcomes being evaluated are those that are likely to be important to the client.

Clinicians have to help interpret the available evidence for clients. In the client group considered in this text, discussion with responsible adults will also be required. Being clear about the evidence base to treatments, and how to deal with conditions of uncertainty, are important for clinicians in this situation. Clinicians of all disciplines often feel that their clinical experience is a good guide for what works. There are several reasons why clinical experience, as well as being helpful, can be misleading. Some conditions may improve spontaneously, as with stuttering in very young children. Other conditions fluctuate over time. This is of particular importance in stuttering. A related issue is regression to the mean: conditions often present when they are particularly severe, either because this is when they are noticed, or because their severity encourages parents or children to seek treatment. For this reason researchers often take multiple baseline measures before initiating treatment, for example Mathews, Williams and Pring (1997). This could usefully be done if there is a waiting list for treatment, although clinicians might wish to spend their time treating children rather than assessing those on the waiting list on numerous occasions. Other potential problems include clients who want to please the therapist, and place a positive interpretation on their symptoms. Clinicians may also overestimate the impact of a treatment when making later assessments. For all these reasons clinical experience, whilst invaluable in forging relationships with clients, may provide a limited guide to the effectiveness of individual treatments.

Assessing the value of therapies

When deciding on the likely value of a clinical treatment, there are several areas to be considered by the practitioner. Archie Cochrane, the British epidemiologist, suggested that relevant questions included the following (Haynes, 1999):

• Can it work?
• Does it work in practice?
• Is it worth it?

These are considered in turn below.

Can it work?

Much research asks this question. Evaluation studies are often undertaken in specialist units, using staff employed for the purpose. In many cases protocols will be followed rigorously, sometimes with methods of checking adherence. Establishing whether something works in this situation is referred to as 'efficacy'. Brook and Lohr (1985, p. 711) defined this as 'the probability of benefits to an individual in a defined population under ideal conditions of use'.

This is likely to be the best chance for a treatment to have an effect. If a treatment cannot be shown to work in such a situation, it seems unlikely that it can be expected to be effective in routine practice. In stuttering this refers to treatment being shown to be effective in clinical conditions but would not include speech measures taken outside clinic. The main type of trial used to demonstrate efficacy is the randomized controlled trial. Some treatments that have encouraging results in non-controlled trials prove disappointing in randomized controlled trials.

The quality of a randomized controlled trial has to be assessed before concluding that a result is likely to be valid. In deciding this, it is useful to consider the key components of a randomized controlled trial. The two main requirements for a randomized controlled trial are genuine uncertainty, and informed consent from participants. It is unethical to conduct a trial in which it is already known that one treatment option is more effective in the circumstance in which it is being trialled, as this would deny access to a better treatment to people in the other treatment arm. Randomized controlled trials also need to be large enough to have a reasonable chance of identifying a worthwhile difference in outcome between the groups. Studies that are too small often lead to inconclusive results. It is often unclear if a result showing no benefit is an indication that a treatment does not work, or if the study is simply too small to have detected a difference. Studies often report confidence intervals that are compatible with either no benefit, disadvantage for the treatment groups or a reasonably effective treatment. This is little help to the clinician. Trials that are too small to have a good chance of identifying a real difference are usually regarded as unethical, as they expose clients to an uncertain treatment, but with no real prospect of answering the research question. The two main ways of getting round this are to conduct trials of adequate size in the first place, and to combine the results of smaller studies (discussed further below). One of the reasons why there are so few randomized controlled trials in stuttering therapy is possibly because this is a low incidence disorder and therefore it is difficult to conduct studies with large enough numbers to demonstrate the efficacy of a treatment approach.

A randomized controlled trial is structured to reduce bias, or at least to account for possible biases. Possible participants are identified. They are then usually screened against entry criteria (for example, age, diagnosis, severity of stuttering, presence of co-morbidity) before entry to the trial. Informed consent has to be obtained, and some people will decline to be entered in the trial. A good-quality randomized controlled trial will include details on the number of people screened for inclusion, the number refusing entry, etc. Entrants will then be randomized, usually to two treatment arms (one for the current gold standard treatment, or 'treatment as usual', and one for the active treatment). Some trials have more complex designs, but all tend to be variants on a theme.

Allocation to the treatment arms is by random allocation, hence the name of the trial as a whole. There are various means of randomization, but the essence of the process is that it should be genuinely random. Other means of randomization, such as alternate allocation, are usually regarded as 'pseudo-random' and would usually exclude the trial from incorporation in systematic reviews (discussed further below). Studies sometimes stratify allocation to groups to take into account factors known to affect treatment outcomes.

Assessments are then undertaken at pre-specified points, and the outcomes compared for the different groups. Allocation to groups is often blind in drug trials, in the sense that the person treating does not know if the individual has been allocated to the treatment group or not. This is far more difficult in trials of complex interventions, such as those in speech and language therapy, as the clinician will almost invariably know to which group a person is allocated, as otherwise treatment cannot be offered. In some cases the assessment of outcome is undertaken by a person who does not know what treatment was provided: a double-blind trial.

Analysis of trials can then be on a pragmatic, or an intention to treat basis. A pragmatic analysis takes the view that, if the treatment is not administered, it is not possible to benefit from it. This therefore usually calculates benefit excluding people who dropped out from the trial, or were excluded for some other reason. An intention to treat analysis asks a slightly different question. It assumes that a clinician will not know in advance who will drop out of treatment, and asks what proportion of a group allocated to a particular treatment is likely to benefit from it. This can be a useful distinction in studies where adverse effects can be important, such as drug trials, or in treatments where adherence to the therapy might be a problem. The latter would be more likely in the case of stuttering treatment.

In therapy trials, the clinicians will often deliver the treatment to a strict protocol. In some cases, the therapy will be video- or tape-recorded and a sample checked for compliance with the protocol. This is different from the situation in routine practice, and this is discussed further below, and in the concluding chapter. As discussed earlier in the book, measurement of symptoms can be very difficult in stuttering. Trials will often measure speech in different situations in order to attempt to provide a rounded assessment. Client and parent views (if relevant) are often collected, and studies will often take account of inter- and intra-rater variation in measurement. Although strict in measurement, this type of trial tries to deliver a defined treatment to a defined population in a reproducible manner.

Does it work in practice?

The next stage is often the cause of conflict between different research groups. Having established that a treatment can work, the next question is whether it works in routine practice. This is known as 'effectiveness'. There are various strands to this, including:

- Can the same results be obtained by a different group of researchers?
- Does it work with a different mix of clients?
- Can a 'second generation' of therapists produce the same effects, when not directly associated with the originators of the therapy?
- Can it produce useful effects in a normal clinical setting?
- Can it produce effects outside the clinical setting?

It might be argued that the first question is still confirming efficacy, but it is assumed here that a treatment has been demonstrated to be effective. Repeating a drug trial is far easier than repeating a complex speech and language therapy intervention. Trial reports try to provide enough information to allow replication, but this is difficult. Research groups capable of replicating clinical trials are often associated with competing approaches. If they fail to produce similar results to the original research group and initial site, this can lead to views that they have somehow failed to replicate the precise method used in the original study. While doubtless true on some occasions, it is also the case that a method has to be clearly enough described, or good enough teaching materials available, to allow it to be delivered by others.

The mix of clients is also often an issue. Exclusion criteria are often applied in studies. This produces a clear trial, but can be unrepresentative of routine practice. Practising clinicians may not be able to exclude anyone with a concomitant speech and language disorder, or who have received previous treatment, for example. In some trials, age group, cultural surroundings or ethnic background may be important. Failures of treatment may not be because the method itself is not efficacious, but rather because it does not suit the new range of people. Again, there are often arguments between research groups about this type of issue, which can make it difficult for clinicians to obtain the information they need to make their own treatment decisions.

The training of clinicians can also be contentious. For a treatment to be delivered across the world, it has to be able to be taught to others. If it fails in practice, however, it can be difficult to tease out whether this is because it has been taught incorrectly, for example because others have failed to grasp the nuances of the technique. In a clinical setting, in addition, it is likely that clinicians will incorporate a new technique into their own clinical practice. This will often involve having less time available than in the trial programmes, and with less intensive training and support. Issues of skill mix and level of experience also often factor in to this. This all results in a large step between efficacy and effectiveness.

Is it worth it?

Clinicians are often uncomfortable about discussions of cost effectiveness. Many practitioners working in services that are free at the point of delivery feel that cost should not be an important consideration. In all healthcare systems, however, there are likely to be greater demands on services than can be met with the resource available. It is possible to feel that more should be invested in healthcare overall, or to believe that the distribution of resource within healthcare is inequitable, while still accepting that difficult decisions may need to be made about the use of departmental budgets.

To the extent that there is greater demand than resource, decisions need to be made about investment choices. If clinicians leave them to others because they feel it is unethical to engage in such debates, then the quality of the decision-making is likely to suffer by their absence. The key concept in resource allocation, apart from resource scarcity, is opportunity cost.

Opportunity cost refers to the next best use of the resource, that is, it is the opportunity given up in order to pay for the chosen initiative. For example, if a unit invests time and effort in the earlier treatment of stuttering, then this may be a resource which could otherwise be invested in the development of, for example, services for children with autistic spectrum disorder. On a small scale, this is the same decision as health authorities in their various forms have to take on, for example, investment in speech and language therapy as opposed to additional paediatric intensive care or more availability of renal dialysis.

Given that every decision has an opportunity cost, it is reasonable to expect that the value of different interventions is considered. When looking at a speech and language therapy intervention, the choice may be between a treatment producing a 20% increase in fluency over the best other treatment, for example, but costing 50% more in staff time. Most decisions are of this nature, with a trade-off between costs and benefits, often with no clearly correct answer. There are similar issues on matters such as early interventions for stuttering. Most young children who stutter will improve spontaneously. If early referral is encouraged, the literature suggests that fewer children will develop persistent stuttering, but at the cost of treating many children who accrue limited benefit from the treatment, as they would have improved in any case. As before, there is no clearly 'right' answer, and the choice will vary depending on what other demands exist and how much emphasis is placed on the problems of the children who do develop persistent stuttering. The problems of allocation of limited health resources in Australia, Europe and the USA are discussed by Reilly (2004, p. 5), who argues that with more policy makers seeking evidence of effectiveness and efficiency there must be a move away 'from basing treatment decisions on opinion, past practice and past teaching towards clinical decision-making that is guided by science and research – in other words, the evidence'. This evidence will come from clinicians and researchers working collaboratively, so that clinicians have a reliable basis on which to make clinical judgements. As Block (2004, p. 83) says, 'Clinicians need to focus on evidence to ensure a close and responsible relationship between research and clinical practice'.

Defining the evidence

Numerous attempts have been made to define or describe treatment effectiveness for stuttering (Conture and Wolk, 1990; Bloodstein, 1995; Conture, 1996; Cordes, 1998; Zebrowski and Conture, 1998), and most authors discuss the importance of obtaining 'objective' measures of speech behaviour. The speech measures should be representative samples of a child's speech and should be repeated a number of times. The treated speech should sound natural and should be transferred to the child's everyday environment. Although some authors (Cordes, 1998; Yaruss, 1998a) argue that changes in the observable characteristics of stuttering post-treatment are the most important treatment outcomes, other aspects of the child might usefully be assessed to indicate a change after treatment. Indeed, Starkweather (1993) and Bernstein Ratner (1997a) *inter alia* have commented that counting stuttering alone is not a sufficient indicator of either the severity of the problem or of therapeutic success. In addition to such 'objective' speech measures, aspects of the child are also considered. Summarizing these aspects from descriptions of treatment effectiveness previously mentioned, the child should have no need to monitor speech constantly, and fears about speaking should be diminished, so that the child should be able to speak to anyone at any time. In addition, Zebrowski and Conture (1998) consider that any indices of improvement should include the parents' perception about the amount of stuttering and the emotional well-being of the child, the reduction of parental anxiety about the child's stuttering and some subjective impressions from the class teacher about the child's emotional state in the classroom as well as his or her educational achievement. Mowrer (1998) has also argued against assessments of treatment effectiveness being made only by the clinician. He logically comments that parents are in a position to repeatedly observe their children interacting in normal communication environments and are useful informants in determining whether the skills taught in treatment are used on a daily basis.

Each of these indices for measuring changes in the child who stutters will now be discussed.

Changes in speech behaviour

It seems obvious that measures should be taken of changes in the child's overt stuttering behaviour, but this in itself raises a number of issues. If the treatment aims included changes in the way the child spoke, for example increased fluency or modification of stuttering, then speech samples would be required to show that these changes had taken place. In order to demonstrate that these changes have occurred outside the clinical environment samples would be required from a number of speaking situations, preferably ones that are typical for that child. Samples would also be taken in clinic, or wherever the child is treated, but it would be useful to obtain speech samples in a different room from the one in which the child is treated. Boberg (1981) discusses the reasoning behind this, viz. it is possible that the client will come to associate increased fluency with the treatment room. However, the circumstances under which the clinician works will determine the feasibility of this. The length of the speech sample is also a relevant factor. If a clinician, or an assistant, were to transcribe these samples then they can not be particularly long for the reason of time required for transcription. Many authors use samples of one minute, or some use 300–500 words, but it is difficult to argue that such short samples of a child's speech are representative of that child's normal speaking behaviour. The timing of these assessments would also be important, and there is general agreement that these should occur before and during treatment and at varying intervals after treatment, but long enough to assess the long-term effects of treatment. Observer-based estimates of stuttering frequency counts are the most popular method of judging the outcomes of therapeutic intervention, although there are concerns about the validity of such measures. Clinicians and researchers do not always agree on what they are recording as stuttering. Arguably, each clinician can define stuttering in his or her own way and take measures of each child based on their own definition. On a very small scale this allows clinicians to have some way of showing change in the speech behaviour of their clients, but it does not resolve this fundamental problem for stuttering research.

Speech rate can also be a useful measure of outcome but, as Ingham and Cordes (1997) point out, the small speech samples that are taken cannot reflect the variation in rate that pragmatic factors demand in normal speaking situations. In Chapter 2 Lees has also argued for more information on normative data for children carrying out similar tasks to those given to the child who stutters when enrolled for treatment. Ingham and Cordes (1997) cite Backer, Brutten and McQuain (1995), who have tried to measure speech rate automatically using acoustic recognition systems. These authors comment that these systems recognize syllable structure relatively well, but when the integrity of the syllable boundary diminishes, for example in treatment techniques such as prolonged speech, their usefulness becomes limited. Ingham and Cordes (1997) also cite Tiffany (1980), who concluded that individual speakers probably have their own ideal speech rates, leading to Perkins' (1973) conclusion that the speaker should be asked if the rate is comfortable. Along with measures of speech rate, a measure of the degree of comfort of the child with the rate could also be a useful outcome. It remains to be seen if the child who is more comfortable with the speech rate as suggested by the clinician is then less likely to experience relapse.

Conture and Guitar (1993) commented on the lack of studies on speech naturalness ratings on the treated speech of children who stuttered. For the practising clinician it can be very difficult and time-consuming to ask a number of raters to judge the naturalness of the speech of a client. This type of activity can also lead to problems of inter-rater and possibly intra-rater reliability. One solution to the problem, as suggested by Ingham and Cordes (1997), is to ask the client. Children as young as 7 or 8 years will have some ideas about how 'normal' their speech is sounding to them and such measures would therefore be of clinical significance.

Measures of the percentage of stuttered syllables (%SS) and of speech rate provide quantitative data on the success of stuttering treatments.

Aspects of the child

The question concerning the amount of monitoring of speech that children feel they are required to do to maintain fluency can only be answered by the individual child. Initially, the clinician will encourage a child to self-monitor in order to achieve changes in fluency, but ultimately it is hoped that the child will be able to maintain fluency without constantly monitoring speech output. It is a sterile therapeutic goal to help a child to gain fluency if that fluency can be maintained only by constant self-monitoring of speech. Thus, it is important to ask a child how much monitoring he or she feels is required, and this could be indicated on a numerical rating scale. Although this method lacks objectivity, it does give the clinician some measure of this, as perceived by the child. Related to this, Ingham and Cordes (1997) recommend asking the client about the amount of self-perceived effort that is required to produce fluent speech. Children could be asked about how hard it is to speak fluently and how much they have to think about this.

Questionnaires are available for assessing children's attitudes towards speaking (for a discussion of these, the reader is referred to Chapter 2), but questionnaires are not without their problems. They have the advantage of being convenient for the clinician and they can be administered to a number of children who stutter. However, they do depend on the maturity and honesty of the child. Guitar (1998) describes scales such as the A-19 and the Communication Attitude Test, but these do demand a dichotomous response: a problem with many questionnaires. Sometimes children wish to reply 'sometimes' or 'in certain circumstances', but this is not possible in any questionnaire which has a yes/no or true/false response format. Nevertheless, it is important to assess how a child feels about speaking in different situations, and again an obvious solution is to ask the child. Block (2004) commented on the need to take into account the views of the client. For some children the greatest problem is the stuttering, for others it is the difficulty in initiating or responding to verbal interaction, whilst for others it is the perceptions and reactions of listeners (Zebrowski and Conture, 1998).

Alternatively, reports from parents could be used concerning their views on the child's confidence in speaking or amount of stuttering. This is further discussed by Cook and Botterill in Chapter 6. Similarly, reports from teachers on a child's speech behaviour, and their interpretation of this, could be useful; for example, a teacher might report that the child is more fluent and is speaking more in the classroom, or indeed that the child is stuttering more but contributing more in the classroom. This can provide qualitative data, which form part of the outcome measures for stuttering treatment.

It is clear that there is no single measure of treatment efficacy for children, and both quantitative and qualitative data will be required to adequately show change in the child who stutters.

Long-term outcomes

There is a woeful paucity of long-term outcome studies for treatment of stuttering in general, not specifically for a given age group. In the case of children it is therefore difficult for clinicians to choose a therapeutic technique and be able to discuss with any confidence the expected outcomes with parents, teachers and relevant others in the child's environment. The need for long-term outcome data is paramount. There are often methodological problems in obtaining long-term follow-up results; for example, children move away from the district or are now fluent and their parents no longer have the time or inclination to remain in touch with the clinician. Whatever the causes, the problem remains that there are insufficient long-term reports on stuttering treatments. This was amply demonstrated by Cordes (1998), who found that of 81 reports of treatment effects in 64 research articles only 40 included any follow-up or maintenance data. Cordes (1998) used a reduction in the frequency of overt, observer-judged stuttering as her basic outcome criterion. Long-term results give an indication of the effectiveness of maintenance strategies or, the other side of the coin, the frequency of relapse. It is also important to the practising clinician to have some information on predictors of relapse. An additional problem is raised by Conture and Guitar (1993): there is often a lack of focus on the process of recovery rather than simply the amount of recovery. Does a rapid change in stuttering behaviour give a poorer prognosis for long-term recovery than a slower change over time?

Relapse

Maintaining change of any behaviour can be difficult, and this is best demonstrated with adults attempting to stop smoking, lose weight, etc. It might be assumed in children that the behaviour to be changed is less ingrained, but as the way we speak is very much part of our identity the problem might not be so straightforward. However, Manning (2001) comments that relapse is much less likely with children than it is with adolescents and adults. Very little is known about relapse rates in children, and comments in the literature on very low relapse rates sometimes refer to very young children who have a higher probability of spontaneous recovery. (For further information on this the reader is referred to Chapter 1.) The second author has anecdotal evidence of a few children treated by her who seemed to have adequate levels of maintenance of fluency at approximately two years post-treatment. However, some of these children have been re-referred approximately 8–10 years later, when they were undertaking important school examinations. There is little known about the number of clients treated as children who then return for treatment as young adults at important times in their lives. When assessing the effectiveness of treatment, measures are not taken 8–10 years after treatment. However, it is important to measure relapse rates even up to two years post-treatment. Relapse is not an 'all or none' phenomenon, but, rather, some change in the child, which is regarded as a deterioration since the end of the treatment process. Craig (1998b, p. 3) defined relapse as 'the recurrence of stuttering symptoms that were perceived as personally unacceptable after a time of improvement'. Researchers who use stuttering frequency measures as the primary outcomes usually define acceptable results as between 2%SS (Craig, Feyer and Andrews, 1987) and 4%SS (Boberg, 1981). Craig et al. (1996), using a criterion of 2%SS to reflect relapse, estimated this to occur in approximately 30% of children aged 9–14 years treated for stuttering. It is useful to have a measurable criterion against which to assess the amount of relapse that has occurred, but it could be argued that relapse has occurred when the child or another in the child's environment has become anxious about the child's fluency. This, again, raises the issue of the relative importance of qualitative as well as quantitative data. Manning (2001), citing Egan (1998), makes an important distinction between 'lapse' (a small slip) and 'relapse', which would suggest that a time element should be built into any definition of relapse. Referring to adults who stutter, Craig and Calver (1991, p. 283) defined relapse as 'stuttering to a degree which was not acceptable to yourself for at least a period of one week'. This definition puts the client at the centre of any decision concerning the occurrence of relapse.

Predictors of treatment outcome

Delineating predictors of outcomes in general, or predictors of outcomes in specific treatment programmes (if these are different), would add to the database on outcomes that could be used by clinicians. In the study by Hancock and Craig (1998), with children who stuttered aged 9–14 years the authors found that the older group (12–14 years) tended to have a higher pre-treatment stuttering frequency score, possibly because they had been stuttering for longer. This group also had higher post-treatment stuttering frequency scores, demonstrating a relationship between pre-treatment severity and post-treatment outcomes. The authors commented that these children required more treatment to reach a satisfactory outcome. Starkweather and Gottwald (1993) also found that younger children (aged 2.3–5.6 years) who were more dysfluent also required more treatment. It seems likely that, regardless of the age of the child, the more severe the stuttering, the more treatment the child will require. Another important variable in the study by Hancock and Craig (1998) was the level of anxiety in the children, as measured by the State–Trait Anxiety Inventory for Children (STAIC) (Spielberger et al., 1972). Children showing higher post-treatment anxiety were less likely to relapse, and the authors suggest this might have been caused by these children practising their fluency skills more. Craig further expands on this information in Chapter 1. Zebrowski and Conture (1998) commented that the presence of additional phonological problems might be a relevant factor in determining the effectiveness of therapy. They cite studies by Conture, Louko and Edwards (1993) and by Bernstein Ratner (1995a) which have indicated that children who stutter and have concomitant phonological disorders often make little or no progress in therapy. Zebrowski and Conture (1998) also hypothesize on the role of family history of stuttering, oral motor ability, temperament, language and language processing status on treatment success. It seems likely that many more factors are involved in relapse but these have either not been delineated or they have been difficult to measure, for example children's ability to cope with listeners' reactions to their new fluency or the effects of changes in the family structure, although the latter is possibly linked to a child's temperament.

Study designs

In research on treatment of stuttering much emphasis has traditionally been placed on quantitative data, for example %SS, speech rate. More recently, there has been a growing awareness of the importance of qualitative data, for example child's/parents'/teachers' reports. Tetnowski and Damico (2001) have argued for greater use of qualitative data in stuttering research.

In studies to assess the effects of treatment single case studies are used, which have the advantage of providing details over time. Each subject is studied in depth and each serves as his or her own control. The design in such studies is often ABA. However, although these studies are useful, their results cannot be generalized and must be treated with caution. Multiple single case studies still have the advantages of studying each case in depth but do have increased numbers. Often, reports are on groups of children who stutter, who have undergone a specific treatment, and before and after treatment measures are given. As Ingham and Riley (1998) point out, this type of design needs an extended pre-treatment baseline and multiple measures over time within and outwith clinic. Stability is usually measured in a 3- to 4-month no-treatment period. Again, subjects serve as their own controls and differences recorded between pre- and post-treatment indicate the extent of the changes. Occasionally, different treatment techniques are compared, so that group data for each technique are aggregated and compared. Sometimes exclusion criteria for these groups are not given, thus making replication of the study impossible. Some studies ignore the children who drop out of the treatment, but studies of these children can give very useful information on the treatment *per se* or on predictors of outcome. In some studies 'success' is claimed, with no definition of this. It is also possible that in some well-designed studies the effects are attributed to only certain components of the programme, and further study is required to delineate these components. Lastly, the long-term effects of the programme are frequently missing. However, many clinicians are collecting data in their clinics and, although these data may not reach the highest standards of evidence-based practice, they should not be discarded, a point made by Block (2004).

Conclusions

In an age of evidence-based practice clinicians are being required to read and evaluate more research literature than ever before. It is important that undergraduate clinicians develop the necessary skills to achieve this, and most undergraduate programmes have substantial courses on research design and methodology. It is also vital that practising clinicians continue to engage with research findings, and this is currently being achieved through various forms of continuing professional development, for example by membership of special interest groups, attending conferences or seminars. When working with children, clinicians are meeting parents who are now better informed about stuttering through access to Web-based information and through increased attention to this problem from the media. Clinicians require good evidence of treatment outcomes and these are likely to be based on quantitative and qualitative data in the future. Mowrer (1998) argued for an even balance among experimental, applied and observational research. Block (2004) commented that evidence-based practice requires a flexible service delivery, variety of treatment options and open discussion with the stakeholders. Although many problems exist in the definition and measurement of treatment outcomes, the process cannot be ignored for the sake of the child and significant others in the child's life, and for the sake of future clinicians who will be seeking evidence of the effectiveness of treatment programmes.

Chapter 4
Considerations and overview of treatment approaches

ROBERTA LEES

The context of stuttering and its intervention

Stuttering typically begins in the pre-school years and the critical period during which it becomes habituated is between five and seven years of age (Manning, 2001). This means that 7-year-old children already have a habit factor to confront as well as some possible negative responses to their dysfluency from others in their environment. At a time when a child is learning to cope with the educational and social demands of school this can be an added burden, and the problem of stuttering becomes much more than the 'simple' behavioural characteristics of the disorder. When a child first attends for treatment of stuttering, it is important to understand the child and his or her context. Stuttering does not occur in a vacuum but, rather, in a social situation, and it can vary in severity, sometimes quite unpredictably. It is important for the clinician to try to understand the child and to apply treatment techniques best suited to that child. This implies that the clinician will acquire a deep and accurate understanding of the child and that, having done so, will then know which treatment technique to apply. Unfortunately, reality does not always match this ideal situation and often clinicians use their 'favourite' treatments. There have been various comments in the literature that sometimes the most popular techniques are not the best evaluated and the best-evaluated techniques are not the most popular (Cordes, 1998; Costello Ingham, 2003). However, clinicians do need an understanding of a number of therapeutic techniques suitable for this age group and they can then evaluate these techniques and build up a body of literature to serve future clinicians in this field.

Before initiating treatment a full assessment of the child will be made and the following variables will be considered by the clinician: the age and severity of the stuttering and the child's readiness and motivation for treatment. Conture (1982) commented that the age of the stuttering is more meaningful than the age of the child. It could be assumed that there is likely to be a relationship between the length of time the child has been stuttering and the amount of treatment required (Lincoln and Onslow, 1997). The severity of the stuttering has also been shown to be related to relapse rates. Craig (1998b) has shown that the more severe the child's stuttering, the more likely it is that the treated speech behaviours will relapse within 12 months of treatment. The child's readiness and motivation for treatment are largely based on the clinician's judgement. The increasing independence of school-aged children, and the need to be part of a social group with its own pressures to conform, will have an effect on how children perceive themselves and others. In one experiment Franck et al. (2003) examined how children aged 9–11 years perceived an adult who stuttered. A 47-year-old adult was videotaped after treatment for stuttering. Fluent segments of the tape were shown to one group of children, whilst dysfluent segments were shown to a different group of children. A semantic differential bipolar adjective pair scale was used to assess the perceptions of the children. The children who viewed the 'dysfluent' tape ascribed significantly more negative traits to the speaker than those who had viewed the 'fluent' tape. Although the speaker in this case was an adult, it does show some preference by this age group for more fluent speech. The authors suggest that children need some education about stuttering. This negative perception of those who stutter would have an effect on children who stutter, who may by this time have internalized their stuttering so that it is now part of them and they see the world through the eyes of someone who stutters. Children's perception of themselves will affect the motivation or desire for treatment. The clinician must be sensitive to the feelings and needs of the child, and much has been written about the qualities of the clinician. Qualities of empathy, caring, sensitivity, flexibility and honesty are viewed as necessary (St Louis and Lass, 1981; Ramig and Bennett, 1997). It is important that the clinician is caring and shows interest in the child and a willingness and competence to help the child. Manning (2001, p. 3) comments that 'the professional and personal attributes of the clinician will interact with the characteristics of the client, resulting in a unique and dynamic combination during each therapeutic relationship'. The effect of the personal qualities of clinicians on their success in treating children who stutter is difficult to gauge, but it seems likely that this is a factor in determining outcomes.

Just as stuttering does not occur in a vacuum, treatment must also take account of the child, others in the child's environment and the facilities available to the clinician. Sometimes treatment of the child will take place in the school where the clinician has relatively easy access to the teacher but not always easy access to the parent. Alternatively, treatment might be delivered in a clinic and the clinician might be able to meet with the parents, especially if they have brought the child to the clinic, or sometimes treatment is delivered in the home. In the UK both generalist and specialist clinicians work with children who stutter. The specialist clinicians often work in a specialist clinic, or are part of a specialist team which visits schools and clinics. It is important that the clinician has some contact with parents and teachers, and, if face-to-face contact is not possible, then at least communication by telephone can be achieved in most instances. In rural areas, which are sometimes sparsely populated, consideration must be given to the most effective form of service provision, given that it is unlikely that there will be specialist stuttering clinicians in this setting. Kully (2002) described the use of telecommunication for the effective delivery of treatment. She uses telecommunications to deliver specialist treatment to children a very considerable distance away from her clinic, but these children also visit clinicans in their local clinics. Kully (2002) comments that clients and their families preferred the telehealth sessions to travelling a considerable distance for specialist treatment, although they did indicate that these were not the same as face-to-face interactions. Kully has found this a useful mode of treatment, though she does caution about technical, legal and cost issues. Thus, the facilities available to clinicians often affect their ability to work with others in the child's management but inventive use of modern technology has considerably aided this process. In addition, the clinician may be in a position to deliver treatment to children in a group; alternatively, the caseload or the problems of a child might dictate one-to-one treatment. (For further information on group therapy the reader is referred to Chapter 8.) Thus, the assessment results, the ability to involve others in a child's treatment and the resources required will affect the clinician's decision on a treatment approach.

In this chapter a brief overview of treatment and related aspects will be given, but there will be no attempt to highlight any one particular treatment approach. Specific approaches are presented in Chapters 5–8. In much of the literature on stuttering a distinction is often made between fluency-shaping and stuttering-modification techniques. Fluency-shaping techniques place emphasis on teaching the child to speak fluently, and there is often an assumption that a child's attitude towards speaking will improve when he or she can speak fluently. On the other hand, stuttering-modification techniques focus more on the child's attitudes and feelings about speaking while the child is taught to stutter in a relaxed way. Some clinicians, for example Guitar (1998) or Healey, Reid and Donaher (Chapter 10 in this volume), discuss combining both approaches. Another way of looking at treatments for stuttering is that used by many authors who explicitly or implicitly acknowledge three aspects of stuttering, often referred to as the ABCs (Conture, 1990; Cooper and Cooper, 1995; Zebrowski and Kelly, 2002). These are the affective (emotional), behavioural and cognitive (attitudinal) aspects, and each of them can proportionately assume greater or lesser significance in any one child who stutters. Treatment techniques vary in the extent to which these three aspects are targeted, and Zebrowski and Kelly (2002) comment that speech behaviour is the easiest of the three to change.

Some clinicians target only the speech behaviours in the belief that when the child is able to speak fluently, fears of speaking and negative communication attitudes will disappear. Others target the affective and cognitive aspects whilst trying to help the child to modify the stuttering behaviour. Involving the child in selecting the treatment approach might help to motivate him or her, and certainly puts the child at the centre of the treatment process. This could be a useful strategy to try to prevent relapse, which will be discussed later in the section on transfer and maintenance strategies in this chapter.

Dealing with affective aspects

It is important that children are able to talk about their emotions to a clinician whom they perceive as non-judgemental and accepting of what they say. In the first instance, the clinician must gain the child's trust, and it is often useful to talk about the child's interests, gaining his or her confidence, before broaching the topic of stuttering. In order to elicit the child's emotions Cooper and Cooper (1985) have an interesting drawing to which children can relate. They use a picture of a person bent over with monkeys on his back and the child has to identify his or her own monkeys. This visual aid helps children to understand and relate to the concept of bringing a discussion of emotions into the open. It is also possible to use Sheehan's (1975) analogy with an iceberg, and to discuss the part of the iceberg under the water. Zebrowski and Kelly (2002) talk about different emotions and engage the child in discussion of his or her experiences of these emotions. They describe how this might engage children in emotional reminiscences in which they recall times when they were happy, sad, etc., and they praise the child for good memory or good insight. During discussions with the child about emotions the topic of teasing and bullying might arise. Mooney and Smith (1995) carried out a postal questionnaire survey of adult members of the British Stammering Association and obtained a 30% return rate. From the returns 82% reported being bullied at some time in their lives, with 93% of this group perceiving the bullying to be related to their stuttering. The ages of most prevalent bullying were 11–13 years, followed by 8–10 years. The true prevalence of bullying of children who stutter is difficult to gauge, but the clinician should be aware of the possibility of this.

In order to help a child to cope with the negative emotions often associated with stuttering, Van Riper (1973, p. 435) discussed the clinician talking about stuttering to the child 'in a context of rewarding warmth'. He tried to take the mystery and the accompanying unpleasantness out of stuttering by making an analogy with learning a difficult motor skill, and, in the process, experiencing difficulties. Williams (1971) used similar types of analogies and taught the children new motor skills whilst discussing the difficulty in doing this and the fact that we all make errors. Zebrowski and Kelly (2002) discuss the use of self-disclosure, role play and utilizing a hierarchy of speaking situations. Increasing a child's confidence and self-esteem have often anecdotally been linked to changes in the child's stuttering behaviour. High anxiety generates low self-esteem and, although the relationship of anxiety to stuttering is unclear (*see* Craig, 1990 for a discussion of this), there is some suggestion that adults who stutter have higher levels of state anxiety in a demanding speech situation. In Chapter 1 Craig and Tran discussed trait anxiety in the older child who stutters and concludes that, although no differences were found, there are differences in communication fears between children who stutter and children who do not stutter, in the 9–14 age group. Blood et al. (2001) compared adolescents who stutter with adolescents who do not stutter on measures of communication apprehension and self-perceived communication competence. They found that twice as many of those who stutter had high communication apprehension as those who did not stutter, and three times as many of those who stutter perceived themselves as having poor communication competence as those who did not stutter. Although information on this is lacking in the pre-adolescent child, the use of techniques to increase perceived communication competence and decrease communication apprehension could usefully be evaluated. Using personal construct theory (Kelly, 1955), Hayhow and Levy (1989) focus on how children construe themselves and how they construe others. They utilize a life history book incorporating photos, mementoes and a family tree to explore similarities and differences between family members which, they maintain, may help the child to develop a stronger sense of self. They also ask children to comment on important aspects of other people then describe how they think others view them. They use this exercise to point out that children who stutter often imagine that others think only of their shortcomings, but of the strengths of others. They then test this out with the child in an attempt to invalidate the child's hypothesis, and to show that others do think about the strengths of the child who stutters.

If a child has reported teasing or bullying, a useful pack to be used in schools, *Bullying and the Dysfluent Child*, has been produced by the British Stammering Association (1995). The focus of this pack is the classroom climate, and a series of classroom activities suitable for children aged 7–11 years is discussed. These activities encourage children to talk to each other, negotiate, confront difficult issues and experience pressure. This pack is useful for children who do not stutter as well as for the child who stutters.

Targeting the behavioural aspects of stuttering

Van Riper (1973) asked the child to identify his stuttering behaviour in a non-detailed way. Cooper (1965) used the stuttering apple to allow a child to describe what happened when he or she stuttered using the apple as a concrete means of describing this. The idea was that the core problem is 'getting stuck on words', and the child delineated what he or she did when stuttering. From these descriptions clinicians can then describe to the child what is happening in the vocal tract when stuttering occurs. Conture (1990) uses the analogy of a garden hose with a knot in it, which is a simple concept and most children could relate to this. The explanations must be related to the age, interests, linguistic comprehension and intellectual ability of the child. Ramig (1999) describes the use of the 'speech helpers' using diagrams, models and tactile cues. From such descriptions some children can evolve ways of helping themselves to increase fluency, often by slowing speech rate. When children believe that they have evolved a method of controlling fluency they are more motivated to use this than when the clinician presents a method of fluency control to them. Cook and Botterill, in Chapter 6, discuss how the child is presented with a number of techniques and then selects a 'user-friendly' one.

Many approaches to the treatment of the stuttering symptom involve a decrease in speech rate. Numerous authors describe the child slowing speech rate, for example Runyan and Runyan (1999), Shapiro (1999). Slowing speech rate can be interpreted in a number of different ways, such as using longer pauses at the end of utterances, prolonging sounds which can be lengthened (vowels, for example), and some descriptions include continuous voicing. Logan discusses different techniques in Chapter 7. It is helpful to the child if the clinician also slows down initially and models the required speech pattern. Some authors, for example Zebrowski and Kelly (2002), advocate the clinician then increasing speech rate to teach the child to resist time pressure. Other techniques, such as easy voice onset, pre-aspiration (for example /^{h}a/), and light articulatory contacts, placing the articulators in a light manner (particularly useful in the articulation of plosives) are often used. Attention is also given to some other aspects of speech production, for example breathing, where the child is encouraged to attend to managing airflow. Runyan and Runyan (1999) describe the use of visual aids to assist with the presentation of these techniques. Behavioural approaches using positive feedback for fluent speech and negative feedback for stuttered speech have also been used. These techniques are essentially changing the way the child speaks and focusing the child's attention on speech, although this can be done in a fun way. Some authors, for example Williams (1971) and Conture (1990), stress the concept of forward movement so that the child does not focus on a word on which he or she becomes stuck. In order to assist the child to learn this new way of speaking, material is often presented in a very programmed way following on the basic tenets of Ryan's (1974) Gradual Increase in Length and Complexity of Utterance (GILCU) or Costello's (1983) Extended Length of Utterance (ELU) programmes. Numerous programmes exist which incorporate a number of these features, for example:

- Systematic Fluency Training for Young Children (Shine, 1988).
- Easy Relaxed Approach – Smooth Movement (Gregory, 1991).
- Fluency Rules Programme (Runyan and Runyan, 1999).

With so many forms of treatment available it is important to gauge how effective these are. Costello Ingham (2003) summarized that, from the published reviews on treatment approaches, the aspects of treatment deemed to be beneficial are:

- Negative feedback contingencies for moments of overt stuttering.
- Beginning treatment with a reduced length of utterance.
- Beginning treatment with slow, prolonged speech which is later shaped to natural sounding stutter-free speech.
- Facilitating the client's changes in the use of the phonatory and respiratory systems.

The child must feel comfortable using such techniques, and this includes feeling prepared to use them when not in the clinician's presence. Prosodic features of speech must be retained as far as possible so that the naturalness of the ensuing result is not compromised. If children think that their speech sounds very 'different' from that of the peer group, motivation to practise these fluency-enhancing techniques will be reduced. For further information on naturalness ratings in the treated speech of those who stutter, the reader is referred to Lees (1994) and Schiavetti and Metz (1997). It is therefore important that the new-found fluent speech must be shaped towards normal sounding speech as soon as possible.

Sometimes children have difficulty understanding concepts of slowing rate, using easy voice onset, etc., and a number of adjuncts are often used. Children are now growing up in a society which places so much emphasis on the use of computers, mobile phones and other electronic devices that it could seem natural for the child to have a device to assist with fluency. Relaxation-based devices, such as biofeedback, have been used for many years and the reader is referred to Craig (in Chapter 5) for more information on this. Machines that alter auditory feedback also have a long history, with waxing and waning popularity. These include devices to delay auditory feedback, mask auditory feedback or shift the frequency of auditory feedback. Many of these devices also have the effect of reducing speech rate and they do give the person who stutters the experience of increased fluency. However, much of the research in this area has been carried out with adults.

As well as, or instead of, teaching fluency-enhancing behaviours, some clinicians teach stuttering-modification techniques. Guitar (1998) describes this as teaching the child to modify his stutters from 'hard' to 'easy'. Van Riper (1982) modelled this 'easy' stuttering, then stuttered in unison with the child in this 'easy' way. He then used cancellation, though said it was not popular with this age group. Cancellation involves the child stuttering in the 'old', 'hard' way then going back and saying the word again in the 'new', 'easy' way. Van Riper then used 'pull outs' which involved the child starting to stutter in the 'old' way then 'pulling out' in the 'new' way. He did not use preparatory sets with children, as he was afraid that this would encourage them to scan ahead and increase sound or word fears. Preparatory sets involve the child predicting on which word he or she is likely to stutter, and changing to the new form of stuttering. Dell (1989) describes using all three stages, and involving the child in goal setting, such as how often the child will modify his or her stuttering in a five-minute period.

Dealing with cognitive aspects of stuttering

The thoughts and attitudes of children are often focused on their beliefs on what they can or cannot do (self-efficacy). Langevin and Kully (2003) discuss obtaining information on this from children aged 8 and over, using the Self Rating of Effects of Stuttering – Children (Langevin and Kully, 1997). If children believe that certain speaking situations are difficult then it is almost certain that they will experience problems in them. It is therefore necessary to identify these attitudes and beliefs before attempting to change them. Zebrowski and Kelly (2002) explore these using 'I think' statements, for example there could be a discussion on similarities and differences between family members, friends and so forth. Children can be encouraged to think about what they do well and what they do not do quite so well. Although the clinician would try to give a child as much confidence as possible, realism should not be sacrificed. The clinician could use counselling techniques, such as reflecting back their thoughts to the children. This helps to show them that the clinician is interested in what they are saying and helps them to clarify their thoughts. Such discussions can begin with non-contentious topics, gradually moving to discussions of stuttering.

The clinician is aiming to reinforce positive attitudes and minimize or change negative attitudes towards speaking. Just as in changing affective aspects of stuttering, it can be useful to begin by discussing attitudes in general, then discussing stuttering in particular. Zebrowski and Kelly (2002) point out that the clinician might need to challenge statements and draw the child's attention to inconsistencies between thought and action. They also comment that there might need to be some focus on changing the attitudes of others, for example peers, relatives and so forth. For children who are mature enough, Zebrowski and Kelly (2002) recommend actively involving the child in discussion of attitudes to expect, who might hold these, how to elicit them and how to respond to them. They believe that it is empowering to a child to be actively involved in trying to change attitudes, and it allows the child to talk openly about the topic of stuttering. Guitar (1998) discusses eliminating avoidance behaviour by the use of analogies to demonstrate the relationship between avoidance and development of fear, leading to more avoidance. It is obviously more meaningful if analogies can be used that relate to the child, such as fear of spiders or fear of the dark, but if this is not possible Guitar (1998) describes fear of the high diving board at the swimming pool and the value of using lower boards first. The rewards of facing and conquering fears are discussed in order to motivate the child. He also gives the child practice of speaking in as many 'real' situations as possible, though with some modifications, such as reduction in number of listeners. He encourages children to talk openly about stuttering in the belief that this empowers them in a situation in which they previously felt helpless or at least disadvantaged. Stewart and Turnbull (1995) also encourage children to talk about stuttering and the fact that they are receiving treatment with those with whom they feel safest. They report that children are often surprised at how interested the listener is in this information. These authors apply personal construct theory to help children to reconstrue themselves, others, stuttering and speaking situations in a more positive way.

Transfer and maintenance strategies

However the child is treated, the clinician works towards the transfer and maintenance of changes gained in treatment. Finn (2003) commented on the need for a greater understanding of the process of change and the identification of variables critical to promoting durable change. He cites Bandura's (1977a) comments that self-efficacy is an important concept underpinning human behaviour change. Self-efficacy is a child's belief in his or her ability to effect this change. The child's preparedness for change must also be a relevant factor. Prochaska, DiClemente and Norcross (1992) describe different stages of change from the pre-contemplation stage, where the client is either unaware of the problem or has no intention to change, to the preparation stage, where the client is ready to change, and to the action stage, where the client begins to make some changes. If children are in the pre-contemplation stage when referred for treatment it would be very difficult to motivate them to co-operate with the therapeutic process. This relates to Finn's (2003) comments that self-managed change is often the most enduring, involving a child in collaborative goal setting, self-monitoring and using self-reward or self-punishment. It is important that a child is an active participant rather than a passive recipient of treatment. Much of this depends on the maturity of the child as well as on his or her readiness to change. However, Conture (1990) has pointed out that for many children the skills learnt in treatment do transfer relatively easily.

Much of the literature on transfer and maintenance activities refers specifically to transferring fluency to situations outside the treatment location. Finn (2003) advocates incorporating elements of a child's real life into the treatment setting, for example including parents and teachers in the clinical location, and probing for changes in desired settings such as the playground in school or the classroom. These probes could consist of audiotaped samples or could consist of the child's self-report or collateral reports from teachers, parents or therapy assistants. Runyan and Runyan (1999) place a discriminative stimulus at home or in school to act as a reminder to the child to use fluency-enhancing techniques. These could be small, unobtrusive items which convey meaning only to the teacher and the child or to a parent and the child. When the listener looks at or touches the item the child is reminded to use the fluency-enhancing techniques. Westbrook (1994) also describes the use of 'Jacob's secret speech bracelet', in which each bead represents a particular strategy to be implemented and the child wears this bracelet as a reminder to use the fluency techniques. Ramig and Bennett (1997) use a speech folder which is sent between home and the clinic to ensure that parents are in a position to help the child transfer speech activities from the clinic to the home. Hierarchies of speaking situations are often used in which the child transfers the newly learnt fluency techniques from clinic to the 'easiest' speaking situation first, then gradually practises in increasingly difficult situations. This involves children in deciding which situations are 'easy' and which are 'difficult' from their point of view and it shows them a natural progression in treatment, allowing children to gauge when they are progressing, even in small steps. Logan provides further information on this in Chapter 7.

It seems common sense that if a child's feelings and attitudes about speaking have been targeted in treatment then transfer and maintenance of increased fluency will be more likely. However, at present there is surprisingly little hard evidence of this in the treatment of children. In one study with adults who stutter, Evesham and Fransella (1987) found that adults taught fluency-enhancing techniques were more likely to retain their fluency if they had also been given some additional help using personal construct psychology concepts.

Once regular treatment stops it is likely that a child will continue to visit the clinician with decreasing regularity over a period of some months or years. Shapiro (1999) and Manning (2001) maintain contact with children over a period of two years, whereas Lincoln and Onslow (1997) recommend a period of five years. It seems likely that this relatively long period of contact is necessary in order to ensure that a child has been able to maintain the gains achieved during therapy during periods of growth with increasing emotional and social maturity.

Involving others in the child's treatment

Rustin (1987) described stuttering as a context-sensitive problem, so that involving others in a child's environment in the treatment process should take some account of this. Parents of children who stutter often give varying degrees of commitment to assist their child during treatment. The amount of help they are willing or able to give depends on their other commitments and their attitudes towards stuttering. The author has met parents who think their child is stuttering to gain attention, and this is a source of annoyance to them. On the other hand, many parents are totally committed to helping their child. It should be stressed to parents that they have not caused the problem: their importance, in terms of helping the child with the problem, can be emphasized. Bernstein Ratner (1993) provides the analogy of childhood diabetes, in which the parents have not caused the problem but where they can help their child to control his or her diet to help with this condition. Parents do need some positive feedback, and Conture (1990) commented on how they need to be rewarded for their insight and courage when they seek help. Rustin, Botterill and Kelman (1996) lay much stress on the involvement of parents and they believe that it is not possible to help a child beyond the confines of the clinic room without the help of the parents. Craig (in Chapter 5) and Cook and Botterill (in Chapter 6) expand on the role of the parents in the treatment of a child.

It is helpful to give parents information about stuttering, and about the treatment being proposed for their child. Information should be given slowly to parents, as too much information too quickly can be overwhelming (Manning, 2001). Guitar (1998, pp. 304–305) discusses five aims when working with parents:

- Explaining the treatment programme and the parents' role in it.
- Explaining the possible causes of stuttering.
- Identifying and reducing fluency disrupters.
- Identifying and increasing fluency-enhancing situations.
- Eliminating teasing.

Again, the qualities of the clinician must be raised, as a sensitive and competent clinician who is a good communicator is more likely to be successful in gaining the parents' co-operation. Indeed, the clinician needs to understand the theoretical rationale as well as the basic steps of the treatment programme being recommended for a child, so that parents' questions can be answered clearly and with confidence. This author uses the Demands/Capacities model as a framework for explaining the possible factors underlying stuttering, but the level of explanation offered varies according to the needs and wishes of the parents. With guidance from the clinician, parents do often take an interest in identifying situations where their child is more fluent or more dysfluent. This helps to make some sense of what seemed to them to be illogical variability in the child's fluency levels and helps them to focus on their child's fluency as well as dysfluency. When parents become aware of 'patterns', for example the child is usually more dysfluent when competing with siblings, parents feel empowered to help as this is something they can understand and deal with. Parents are often in a good position to deal with teasing, either from siblings or from friends. The use of parent groups can also help to give parents a feeling of support not only from the clinician but also from others in the same positions as themselves.

It can also be useful to involve other members of the child's family in treatment so that they have a greater understanding of stuttering and what they can do to help. Sometimes myths about stuttering can be passed down through families, and parents can be put in a position where the clinician gives advice that is contrary to that given by the child's grandparents. If necessary, the clinician can meet the parents and the grandparents, and with sensitive handling the situation can be resolved amicably. Involvement of others in this positive way helps to prevent teasing and allows a child to feel supported. Manning (2001) also raises the possibility of encouraging children who stutter to have a 'speech buddy' who will support them when neither the clinician nor parents are there. The speech buddy is a child who is likely to be with the child who stutters when that child enters new, demanding speech situations. The speech buddy should attend some treatment sessions to find out how best to help.

As children spend approximately 30 hours per week in school, the involvement of teachers in the child's treatment is often advocated. Much has been written about the teacher's role in helping the child who stutters in class (Gottwald, Goldbach and Isack, 1985; Stewart and Turnbull, 1995; Guitar, 1998; Lees, 1999; Manning, 2001), and much of this relates to giving teachers general information about stuttering, plus specific information about a child's treatment programme and dealing with children who stutter in the classroom. The general advice often includes recommending that the child who stutters is called on early to read aloud or to answer questions in class but should generally not be exempted from such activities. If a child does stutter when speaking in class, the teacher can paraphrase what the child has said, giving it extra import. Teachers can also be given information on fluency-enhancing situations, such as role play, and Manning (2001) describes a child being encouraged to take at least a non-speaking part in the school play or a part of producing mechanical or animal noises. However, it is salutary to note Stewart and Turnbull's (1995) comments from a teacher that the clinician's advice is often related to the child as an individual and not as a member of a social group. Bearing this caution in mind, clinicians can gain useful information from teachers about how children cope in the classroom, for example 'Does the child volunteer information, ask questions or only answer questions?', and in the playground, for example 'Does the child play with others or alone?'. Some clinicians work in the school and have easy access to teachers, whereas others visit schools occasionally to give this information and to find out about how a child is coping. Stewart and Turnbull (1995) recommend that clinicians visit the classroom to find out more about the atmosphere in the class, how much talking is permitted or expected and to meet the friends of the child who stutters. The clinician should discuss visiting the classroom with the child so that the child is prepared for this and is not embarrassed by it.

In an ideal world, teachers would be given good information about stuttering during their undergraduate programmes, but, as teachers have an increasingly busy undergraduate programme, this can not be guaranteed. Stewart and Turnbull (1995) have organized half-day groups for teachers, parents and children who stutter, and in these groups information about stuttering is provided along with discussion on reacting to the child who stutters and how children who stutter would like others to react to them. This is a short experiential course which the authors have evaluated informally. The responses from parents and teachers suggested that some felt the knowledge they gained to be the most important factor, for some it was the insight they felt they now had, while others mostly valued the practical ideas. In sessions with teachers, videotapes such as 'A Chance to Speak', produced by the British Stammering Association (1996), plus numerous tapes from the Stuttering Foundation of America, can give very useful information quickly and easily. If teachers feel that they have a reasonable understanding of stuttering, they are more likely to show willingness to discuss this with the child. In this way teachers can then show children that they are willing to help and support them in the school environment, and act as an advocate for the child who stutters in this situation. Manning (2001) realistically points out that teachers should be alerted to situations in which a child might have been considered to be a good, that is, quiet, pupil in class before treatment, but after successful treatment he or she might be speaking more and be more noisy in class.

When does therapy stop?

This is a difficult question for clinicians, and much depends on the aims of treatment and how the clinician evaluates outcomes. If the clinician's aim were to increase fluency then treatment might cease when a child has reached a criterion level of fluency. However, in order to assess if transfer activities had been effective, this criterion level would be based on the child's fluency in everyday speaking situations. This could then involve the child carrying a recording device or it could depend on the child's report on his or her fluency level, giving the child responsibility for maintaining fluency. Alternatively, a report on the child's fluency from the parents or the teacher could suffice. Gottwald and Starkweather (1995) cease treatment when parents and teachers feel confident about their ability to manage a child's fluency. If they have been centrally involved throughout the child's treatment they will be able to make decisions about fluency disrupters and managing the environment to minimize these.

If the aims of therapy included dealing with either the affective or cognitive aspects of stuttering, then some kind of report on this would be expected to show that the child's speaking fears or avoidance behaviour had diminished or that the child had increased confidence in the speaking situation. The question then remains of how much the avoidance behaviour has diminished before treatment can stop. At present there are no fixed criteria for this, and the decision rests on clinicians' judgement. This can be a difficult area in which to 'prove' that change has taken place. It is possible to show a change of score on an attitude test, or it is possible to have a report from parents or a teacher saying that the child is now more willing to volunteer speech. Currently, clinicians must rely on such reports to influence their decision to stop providing treatment.

Often, a child reports feeling ready to cope with speaking in everyday situations without regular visits to the clinician. If the child gives such a positive report, and this is accompanied by a report either from parents or teacher that the child is speaking more freely in everyday situations, it might be a useful time to stop treatment. If the child indicates that he or she is ready to stop treatment but there is no corroborative evidence of any improvement either in fluency levels or in attitudes towards speaking, then the clinician would have to pursue this with the child. The child might have lost motivation to continue treatment or might genuinely feel more confident about speaking. Some clinicians have remarked anecdotally to the author that they consider that some children need a break from treatment if they lose motivation. However, there seems to be no 'hard' evidence that this is useful.

Concluding remarks

It is clear that numerous approaches exist to the treatment of this age group, many of which need sound evaluation over a period of time to gauge their effects. The role of significant others in children's treatment also needs sound evaluation, although it seems logical to involve others with whom the child is interacting on a regular basis in order to transfer the treatment gains into everyday situations. It is difficult at present to exclude the effects of the personal qualities of clinicians when considering the results of differing treatment techniques. A challenge lies ahead for clinicians to assess the effectiveness of different programmes and to look for factors in a child's history that would point to one treatment being more effective than another with each child.

Chapter 5
Combination treatment for the older child: fluency shaping and speech muscle feedback therapy within a behavioural regimen

ASHLEY CRAIG

Introduction

The American Speech and Hearing Association report entitled *Research Needs of Stuttering: Roadblocks and Future Directions* (Cooper, 1990) identified a number of problems in the treatment and research into child stuttering, especially the older child who stutters. Problems included poor and biased measurement of stuttering, a lack of measurement of stuttering in the long term following treatment, and a lack of measuring stuttering in the home, school and social environments. The report concluded that sample sizes used to verify efficacy have usually been small, limiting our knowledge about how effective it will be for all children (generalization). Very few studies have employed matched control groups to test whether the treatment rather than other factors (such as time) had led to an improvement in stuttering. The report also suggested that the neglect of researching treatment effectiveness in older children is caused by the perception that they can be more difficult to treat. As a result an urgent need existed for well-controlled clinical trial research aimed at developing and investigating the success of stuttering treatment for older children and young adolescents. This chapter discusses and presents a treatment rationale, including principles and treatment effectiveness for older children. The chapter will also examine the potential for delivering a combination of treatments.

Evidence shows that as children who stutter grow older, their stuttering can disrupt social and psychological growth, and possibly cause substantial anxiety problems (Cantwell and Baker, 1977; Baker and Cantwell, 1987; American Psychiatric Association, 1994; Beitchman et al., 1996, 2001; Craig et al., 2003). The reader is referred to Chapter 1 for a fuller discussion of this. As can be imagined, stuttering also has the potential to limit the choice of vocation open to people who stutter. Although stuttering is found at all age levels, most children begin to stutter before adolescence, more commonly between two and five years of age, with the highest peak at around four years of age (Bloodstein, 1995).

Other than acquired stuttering, which has a sudden onset caused by trauma of some nature, stuttering is believed to be a neurological disorder that mostly affects the systems involved in the motor aspects of speech (Andrews et al., 1983; Hulstijn, Peters and van Lieshout, 1997; Craig, 2000). As already stated, coping with a problem like stuttering over many years can raise risks of the development of problems such as abnormal levels of anxiety and distress, lowered employment opportunities and lower than desired quality of life (Craig, 1990; Craig and Calver, 1991; Menzies, Onslow and Packman, 1999; Craig et al., 2003). Furthermore, people who stutter also have higher external locus of control scores than people who do not stutter (Craig, Franklin and Andrews, 1984; Andrews and Craig, 1988), suggesting that they perceive their life to be less likely to be controlled by their own efforts and ability, and more by luck, chance or powerful others. A high external locus of control is known to be associated with feelings of helplessness (Craig, Franklin and Andrews, 1984).

Given the above dynamics, it is crucial that efficacious treatments be developed for children, especially as they reach adolescence when many important lifetime decisions begin to be made. The best evidence does suggest that psychological damage is more a risk for adolescents who stutter in comparison with younger children, hence the urgency for effective treatment (Craig and Hancock, 1996; Craig et al., 2003). This chapter will describe and discuss treatment rationales and regimens for the older child (say, aged 8–14 years) which have been scientifically trialled and shown to be effective in reducing stuttering down to acceptable levels in both the short and long term, as well as reducing levels of anxiety and concerns about communicating verbally. Before treatment rationale and protocols are described, the definition and nature of stuttering will be discussed.

Definition and nature of stuttering

Stuttering has been defined as 'interruptions to the fluency and flow of speech, where the person knows what he or she wishes to say, but is unable to because they are experiencing either: (a) involuntary repetitions of syllables, especially when starting words, (b) involuntary prolonging of sounds and (c) unintentional blocking of their speech' (Craig et al., 1996, p. 811). It may also involve unnatural hesitations, interjections, restarted or incomplete phrases, and unfinished or broken words can also be part of the problem. Associated symptoms can include eye blinks, facial grimacing, jerking of the head, arm waving and so on. As the child grows older there is a risk that these behaviours will become more pronounced. These behaviours are thought to be mostly learnt and unconsciously acted, and appear to have been adopted by people who stutter in an attempt to minimize the severity of the stutter (Bloodstein, 1995). Unfortunately, the concomitant behaviour (such as eye blinks) loses its distraction power to reduce stuttering, and often the person who stutters can be left with the overt behaviour. Therefore, as the person grows older the stutter develops in complexity and severity. As a consequence, people who stutter can become increasingly embarrassed at the moment of the stutter, and eventually they may come to fear a social setting where they have to speak (such as talking to someone using the telephone). Avoidance becomes a more common strategy as a child develops and ages (Bloodstein, 1960). Avoidance is the long-term danger for a child who stutters, as it can potentially limit social and personal growth.

Rationale of treatment for stuttering

It is important that treatments for stuttering address the underlying problems associated with the disorder. For example, if a disorder has a biological cause then optimal treatment should ideally address the biological cause. It has now become accepted that stuttering has a physical or biological basis which is most likely multifactorial in origin (Smith and Kelly, 1997). Stuttering is likely to involve a number of physical dimensions, including perceptual, acoustic, kinematic, electromyographic, respiratory, linguistic and autonomic or central nervous system factors (Smith and Kelly, 1997). For instance, stuttering consists of disruption to speech muscle activity (for example, rapid repetition of a syllable or a block on a sound); adults who stutter show greater activity in the non-dominant hemisphere while speaking than non-stuttering control subjects (Fox et al., 1996). They tend to have slower reaction times when speaking (Andrews et al., 1983), they often have irregularities in breathing (Bloodstein, 1995) and they show higher levels of muscle activity and stiffness in the speech muscles (facial and laryngeal) before and during speaking (Craig and Cleary, 1982; Bloodstein, 1995).

Further evidence continues to support a physical cause of stuttering. It usually begins at an early age of two to six years when the speech-motor cortex is developing. For example, the mean age of onset of stuttering in children has been shown to be around two to five years (Bloodstein, 1995; Craig et al., 1996). Stuttering is unlikely to occur after maturation of the speech-motor cortex, except in cases where an injury results in damage to the brain (such as in stroke or traumatic brain injury). People who stutter have been shown to have delayed speech acquisition and they are more likely to have articulatory problems and reduced capacity to manage motor tasks involved in speech (Andrews et al., 1983; Bloodstein, 1995). Research also suggests that stuttering has genetic origins (Andrews et al., 1983; Yairi et al., 1996). Males are more likely to stutter and to have a family history of stuttering (Craig et al., 1996). If an identical twin stutters, there is a substantially higher chance that both twins will stutter compared with non-identical twins (about 60% to 20%, respectively). Stuttering is possibly inherited by the transmission of a single major gene or a major gene plus multiple genes (Yairi et al., 1996). Furthermore, the evidence available (Andrews et al., 1991) strongly suggests that inheriting stuttering is an interaction between a genetic predisposition (70%) and the influence of the environment (30%). The epidemiology of stuttering is discussed in more detail in Chapter 1.

As suggested above, stuttering may also involve environmental factors. It is suspected that social, psychological and behavioural dimensions can influence its development and severity (Craig et al., 2003). It stands to reason that the continued experience of stuttering would have psychological consequences. For example, the severity of stuttering usually increases when someone who stutters becomes fatigued or anxious, and particular social contexts and words can be linked to more severe stuttering (Bloodstein, 1995; Craig et al., 2003). Because of societal demands and pressures, stuttering is generally associated with higher levels of trait and state anxiety (Craig et al., 2003). Furthermore, anxiety associated with stuttering often reduces to normal levels after treatment that successfully reduces stuttering severity (Craig, 1990).

Given all the above, what is a reasonable rationale for treating the problem? First of all, it is important to say that treatment should ideally be tailored to meet the individual circumstances of the client. However, based on the available evidence, I suggest that a reasonable rationale to treating stuttering would involve primarily addressing the biological basis of the problem. Having said this, the clinician should plan for the possibility of treating secondary symptoms such as anxiety and shyness.

Let us assume that stuttering is a biological disorder involving neural deficits in speech processing and that this deficit results in physical symptoms. A primary goal of treatment should therefore be to address these physical symptoms. For instance, treatment should enhance the brain's capacity to process speech (for example, improve co-ordination of respiratory, supralaryngeal and laryngeal systems using increased airflow and reduced speech rate as taught in fluency-shaping techniques), reduce the demands associated with speech (such as reduce speech rate, reduce fears associated with speaking) and reduce motor dysfunction (for example, improve control over muscle tension levels before and during speech as taught in electromyography (EMG) feedback therapies). Additional possible components that are known to enhance neural capacity devoted to speech include encouraging a healthy lifestyle, increasing positive and confident feelings, and training the person who stutters to take regular pauses between phrases. In addition, components may need to be added to the treatment regimen to assist the older child or adolescent to cope with potentially difficult environmental contexts, which may raise their severity of stuttering.

For instance, social skills and anxiety management components could be introduced to train someone who stutters to speak fluently when people are speaking very quickly around them, or when they are speaking in complex and demanding social situations, such as using a telephone, talking to strangers or when speaking in front of an audience.

Treatment protocol

An appropriate rationale for treatment of older children might then be to: optimize factors that enhance speech motor neural capacity, minimize factors that reduce speech neural capacity and use strategies that help them cope with environmental contexts that pose high demands. In a recently completed clinical trial (Craig et al., 1996; Hancock et al., 1998), two treatments (namely a fluency-shaping technique called 'Smooth Speech' and EMG feedback) designed to address these three requirements were shown to be effective in the short term for substantially reducing stuttering in at least 90% of children aged 8–14 years, and in more than 75% of the children in the long term. It is believed these two treatments were successful because they addressed the biological problem by enhancing a child's speech motor resources, thereby lowering the risk of the speech software from corrupting when speaking (as evidenced by the stutter). Step-by-step details of the protocol for the Smooth Speech and EMG feedback treatments investigated in the above controlled trial have been presented elsewhere (Craig, 1998a). The protocol for these two treatments will now be briefly described, as will other issues important to developing a successful stuttering treatment protocol.

Smooth Speech

Smooth Speech is designed to help people who stutter to control their stuttering by teaching them to:

- stabilize their breathing by teaching them to increase levels of airflow before and during speech
- stabilize muscle activity by decreasing the amount of muscle tension associated with speech (for example, by using gentle onsets before a phrase)
- regulate breathing and speech muscle activity by teaching regular pausing while speaking
- improve fluency skills by intensive practice of speech
- maintain speech naturalness
- increase their feeling of control over their speech and raise their levels of self-esteem.

Smooth Speech is a simplified form of speech that allows the person who stutters to speak fluently. It is a derivative of prolonged speech, except there is no emphasis on continuous vocalization. Prolonged speech attempts to reduce stuttering by, initially, slowing speech rate, prolonging syllables and vocalizing continuously. Eventually, speech rate is increased up to normal levels, although the emphasis upon continuous vocalization remains. However, continuous vocalization is a characteristic that results in a distinctly unnatural speech style. Smooth Speech was developed in order to remove this unnatural quality. Instead, it retains the speech rate control but emphasizes continuous airflow, with unvoiced sounds remaining unvoiced. In the clinical trial, children received instruction on respiratory control, where easy, relaxed diaphragmatic breathing during speech is demonstrated.

Another fundamental characteristic of Smooth Speech is the use of gentle onsets and offsets. This involves beginning phrases with airflow and using soft articulatory contacts. In addition, a phrase/pause speech pattern is taught. Pauses at the end of the phrase serve to minimize difficulties in finding words to express an idea. Pausing also helps a child to restore neural capacity and develop a controlled breathing pattern. The emphasis with Smooth Speech is on the end-product being natural-sounding speech at a normal speech rate.

In the clinical trial referred to above (Craig et al., 1996; Hancock et al., 1998), two Smooth Speech formats were developed and tested. One consisted of an intensive one-week programme in which children were trained to use Smooth Speech over one week with clinicians. A group of as many as five children received instruction in Smooth Speech in formal sessions from 9.30 am to 4 pm, involving group conversations during which they practised their fluency at gradually increasing speeds. The children began speaking with Smooth Speech at very slow speeds (around 50 syllables per minute; SPM) and they increased this speed in jumps of 5–10 SPM as they progressed throughout the week. By the end of the week the children were speaking at speeds of at least 180 SPM. Each participant underwent practice sessions (of approximately 5 hours) before the one-week intensive programme to ensure that they were familiar with the skill. Follow-up occurred on a monthly basis for 3 months, then 3-monthly up to one year. It is highly recommended that regular follow-up is undertaken after this type of treatment.

The other form of Smooth Speech involved a less intensive format in which parents took a more dominant role along with the clinician. Treatment was conducted once a week over 4 weeks, from 9.30 am to 4 pm, with follow-up monthly for 3 months then 3-monthly up to one year. A clinician led the group. However, once the clinician was confident that parents had successfully learnt the technique, the parents took over the role of therapist for their children, with the clinician supervising. After working initially as parent–child teams, group conversations and games took place as well as transfer assignments outside the clinic. The rationale for this therapy was to teach parents to be therapists so that the majority of therapy would take place at home. Standard protocols for the two Smooth Speech treatments were developed, and the clinicians involved in the treatment were experienced with the protocols. To control for inter-clinician variations in delivery of the treatment, all the clinicians involved were trained to adhere to the protocol.

EMG feedback

EMG feedback (Craig and Cleary, 1982; Bloodstein, 1995) is designed to help people who stutter to control speech muscle dysfunction by teaching them to:

- reduce muscle tension to low levels before beginning to speak, by use of computer-driven speech muscle activity feedback
- lower overall levels of muscle tension while speaking
- learn to control their speech muscle tension, called 'EMG mastery', in the absence of the computer feedback
- help people who stutter to raise their levels of confidence, increase their feeling of control over their speech and raise their levels of self-esteem.

Full details of the EMG feedback protocol are available (Craig, 1998a).

This therapy attempts to train children to become aware of, and control, tension of the speech muscles. A dual EMG channel biomonitoring system, optically isolated for safety, was used in the clinical trial (Craig et al., 1996); this consisted of a computer interfaced with electrodes attached to the speech muscles, allowing immediate and direct feedback of muscle activity in microvolts. The interface comprised an analogue-to-digital conversion. Disposable silver–silver chloride electrodes, with a universal connector, were initially attached to the child's face and designed to pick up activity in the zygomaticus, levator anguli and superior obicularis oris muscles, and a grounding electrode was placed approximately 4 cm above the active site. A second site (inferior orbicularis and depressor anguli oris muscle site) was also used to transfer subjects' skills once they had learnt control in the first muscle site. A group of as many as four children received EMG feedback therapy in formal sessions from 9.30 am to 4 pm over one week.

Initially, the children were taught to raise and lower their muscle tension without speaking. Once this was achieved, a hierarchy system was followed, commencing with simple words and progressing eventually to conversation level. Once the children achieved muscle control and they were showing almost no stuttering with and without computer feedback, they progressed to the next stage. These fluency skills were then transferred by reminding the children to be fluent while playing board games, during group conversations and outside the clinic as well as during shop assignments and telephone calls. EMG-based games were also played throughout the week, and these served to maintain interest of the children as well as to reinforce their EMG mastery. Follow-up occurred on a monthly basis for 3 months, then 3-monthly up to one year. It is highly recommended that regular follow-up is undertaken after this type of treatment.

Behavioural therapy regimen

Best evidence suggests that stuttering treatments such as Smooth Speech and EMG feedback, which are designed to address directly the symptoms of stuttering, should be delivered in a cognitive–behavioural therapy context (Craig and Cleary, 1982; Craig, Feyer and Andrews, 1987; Craig et al., 1996). This means that strategies to increase airflow or reduce speech muscle tension while speaking should be delivered in a regimen that sets achievable behavioural goals, assesses behavioural outcomes, rewards outcomes, involves transfer and maintenance procedures, and employs behavioural assignments to reinforce skills. The advantage is that secondary symptoms, such as anxiety and psychological upset, can also be addressed by use of cognitive–behavioural therapy approaches.

Combination treatment

Unlike clinical trial research, in which there is little freedom to vary treatment components, therapy can be individually tailored to meet children's needs. This raises the possibility of combining known treatments that have been shown to be efficacious. It is my belief that a very positive strategic approach would be to combine a Smooth Speech approach with an EMG feedback approach as they complement each other very well. Some examples will illustrate the benefits.

- Smooth Speech requires children to relax their speech musculature before speaking (that is, reduce speech muscle tension). EMG feedback provides excellent feedback on this as well as providing a specific outcome (that is, by how much have children relaxed their muscles).
- EMG feedback does not alter speech patterns, as a fluency-shaping technique does, and so has the potential to lessen any tendency for the post-treatment speech product to sound unnatural.
- Smooth Speech requires the child to increase airflow before speaking, which will generally have the effect of reducing speech muscle tension.
- EMG feedback therapy has more potential to be enjoyed by older children because it involves the child interacting with computer technology. EMG-based games can be used to reinforce therapy goals, and this variety of strategies relieves the possible boredom that can come with sitting through intensive Smooth Speech programmes.

As further evidence of the efficacy of combining these two treatments, Hancock and Craig (2002) investigated the effectiveness of treating stuttering in older children who had experienced some difficulties in maintaining treatment success. The programme involved teaching Smooth Speech and EMG feedback techniques in a self-management cognitive behavioural programme. Groups consisted of up to four children and parents (that is, at least eight individuals per group). Treatment was conducted twice a week, over 2 weeks, from 9.30 am to 4.00 pm, with a fifth day option in the third week if treatment skills had not been adequately transferred and generalized outside the clinic environment. An experienced clinician led the group. However, once the parents were trained and skilled in the techniques, and provided appropriate feedback to the children, parents assumed the role of therapist for their child.

The first day consisted of speech retraining, with education and exercises in Smooth Speech and EMG feedback. Once the children mastered the skills taught in the Smooth Speech and the EMG feedback skills, with and without computer feedback, they progressed to more complex speech tasks. Transfer skills, such as playing board games, group conversations outside the clinic and shopping assignments and telephone calls, then took place on days 2–5. The format for groups varied according to the age of the children, as some were older adolescents (aged 12–14 years), whereas others were younger (aged 8–11 years). For example, younger children used games predominantly as a means of therapy and conversation, whereas older children engaged in group conversations more frequently.

From day two, in addition to the Smooth Speech and EMG feedback techniques, self-management skills were taught, and these emphasized the importance of self-responsibility, self-evaluation, self-effort and motivation in the achievement of self-set goals. The programme was structured so that the emphasis was shifted away from external control and placed on self-control. Specific self-management skills included training in appropriate self-evaluation and self-monitoring of stuttering. This consisted of the children recording in a speech diary their speech performance after assignments. Completing the speech diary required the children to record stutters and to evaluate correct use of the Smooth Speech and EMG feedback techniques. The children were required to correct stutters as they occurred during therapy in order to increase self-monitoring.

At home during the evenings of the programme, the children were asked to complete a self-monitoring form every 2 hours. This involved recording on a Likert-type scale how well they had spoken in the previous 5 minutes. The children were also trained to employ self-reward for fluency and for achieving practice goals. In order to reinforce self-responsibility, discussions were held from day one on the importance of helping oneself rather than pleasing parents or therapists. In addition, the importance of being motivated to achieve and maintain treatment gains was reinforced. Specific suggestions were given on how to improve motivation levels and how to maintain fluent speech despite lifestyle demands. The importance of daily practice (an analogy with sporting skills) and of varying its format in order to remain motivated and maintain treatment gains was reinforced.

Links between thoughts, feelings and behaviour were also discussed. Cognitive techniques were then applied to overcome any attitudinal barriers to success. Examples were given of appropriate self-talk before and during a difficult speaking situation in order to enhance fluency (for example, 'I will think about my fluency skills rather than worrying about stuttering'). Self-talk was also used during treatment to help subjects cope with the experience of dysfluency. Part of the nature of control is the expectation of all possibilities, including failure. The children were taught skills for dealing with failure when it occurred. For example, they were trained to recognize high-risk situations, such as fatigue, negative moods and threatening environments, and they were taught methods of coping with these situations (such as to view stuttering as a sign that they need to focus on fluency skills rather than pushing through stutters and adopting a sense of hopelessness). In addition, the children were taught simple relaxation techniques (breath awareness, isometrics, for example) to enhance their control of muscle tension and anxiety. Discussions were held about the need to use physical relaxation in order to think clearly, and to use positive thoughts to help cope with difficult speaking situations. The children practised simple relaxation exercises that could be used just before, during or after an anxiety-provoking speaking situation. The results of the combined programme will be discussed later; however, it did result in significantly reduced stuttering as measured by the percentage of stuttered syllables (%SS) and increased speech rates, measured by SPM, 2 years post-treatment.

Maintenance and anti-relapse procedures

Relapse (that is, a return of stuttering after successful treatment) and maintaining treatment gains continues to be a significant clinical problem (Craig, 1998b). From adult research, it is estimated that approximately one-third of treated adults experience difficulties in maintaining fluency in the long term (Craig, Feyer and Andrews, 1987; Craig, 1998b). Self-report studies suggest that most subjects experience cycles of relapse and fluency (Craig and Calver, 1991; Craig and Hancock, 1995). In these studies, almost all subjects who believed their fluency had decayed also believed that they had recovered their fluency through various strategies such as practising fluency skills, participation in self-help groups and seeking additional professional help (Craig and Calver, 1991; Craig and Hancock, 1995). Even less research has been conducted on maintenance and relapse in children and adolescents. However, Craig et al. (2002) and Hancock and Craig (2002) have now reported data on maintaining treatment skills and possible anti-relapse strategies in older children. These two studies suggest that it is essential that structured maintenance strategies be incorporated into the treatment protocol. For example, in the clinical trial, follow-up that involved assessment of homework (such as speech assignments) and troubleshooting occurred on a monthly basis for 3 months then 3-monthly up to one year. It is highly recommended that regular follow-up is undertaken after stuttering treatments.

Principles of treatment

There are general principles of treatment that should always be employed by clinicians to ensure that stuttering treatment effectiveness is optimized. These include the following.

A comprehensive diagnosis

A comprehensive diagnosis must always be made before treatment is initiated. Initial assessment must determine whether a child *does* stutter, as well as the nature and severity of the stutter. For example, diagnosis should determine whether a child stutters or whether the dysfluency is normal in nature. Stuttering is different from normal dysfluency, as it occurs frequently, and signs of struggle or tension often result as the child attempts to speak. Commonly, a child who stutters will repeat syllables rather than the whole word (unless, of course, it is only a one-syllable word, such as *I, me, to* and so forth).

The diagnosis should determine individual characteristics of the child so that therapy can be tailored to address these characteristics. For example, are there any predisposing factors likely to impede treatment outcome? It is also important to determine whether the stutter may be attributed to genetic factors or another cause, such as head injury, as a traumatic injury cause may influence the type and course of treatment. Any evaluation should elicit information on the onset of stuttering (the age at which the child began to stutter), any family history of stuttering, the natural course of the stutter over the child's lifetime and any prior treatment.

The severity and nature of stuttering must also be determined, and therefore a speech and language diagnosis should be conducted in order to ensure that the child *does* stutter, as well as to isolate any complicating factors which may limit treatment efficacy (for instance, coexisting articulation or learning disorder). The reader is referred to Bernstein Ratner (Chapter 9) and Healey, Reid and Donaher (Chapter 10) for further information on this. Usually, the severity of stuttering is best measured by use of a behavioural assessment that involves estimating from speech samples (Craig et al., 1996) the frequency of the stuttering (%SS) and the speech rate (SPM). A high %SS (>10%SS) and a low SPM (<100 SPM) (most adults will speak at approximately 200–250 SPM) usually result in very severe stuttering (frequent stutters and low speech rate).

Evaluation of concomitant behaviours is also needed, and these behaviours may also be targeted in therapy; however, they usually disappear if the stuttering is eliminated. An assessment could also include trait anxiety (measured in a comfortable and relaxed setting) as well as state anxiety linked to various speech tasks (for instance, directly before and after a telephone call). Social anxiety can also be measured, as well as using scales that measure communication fears and perception of control (for example, locus of control or self-efficacy expectations). Although there is no evidence to suggest that those who stutter are vulnerable to depression (Craig, 2000), a comprehensive mood and personality assessment would be useful for clinical purposes.

Professional approach

It is imperative that clinicians conduct therapy in a professional, caring and accepting manner. For example, clinicians should work on developing a positive relationship with older children and their families. Clinicians should also work on not showing favouritism when conducting therapy with a group of children. It is equally important to realize that it is neither the parents' nor the child's fault if a child stutters. Rarely will stuttering be caused by the way parents discipline or raise their children.

Conscription of family and friends

As when treating a young child who stutters, it is very important that family and friends are conscripted into treatment to help an older child to achieve treatment goals. There are many strategies that clinicians could use to enhance the support of family and friends in order to assist the older child. However, to maximize treatment outcome, it is strongly suggested that clinicians provide some training for family and friends in the use of the strategies listed below.

Rewarding fluent speech rather than punishing stuttering

Parents and family can praise a child who stutters when he or she speaks fluently. For example, verbal praise ('Well done' or 'That's great talking') and non-verbal appreciation such as smiling and hugging. Using praise will help to relax children who stutter and will help to raise their confidence. Praise is a very powerful motivator. However, the type of praise should be negotiated with older children, as frustration or embarrassment can result if they are not comfortable with the type of praise given. Parents or family must also ensure they do not punish children who stutter. They may not believe that they punish stuttering, but it is not difficult to do this as they are understandably emotionally involved. For example, parents or family members can become angry or frustrated when their child stutters, which can cause the stuttering to become worse. Punishment can also occur if the parent simply ignores the child who stutters. Although such punishment may reduce stuttering, the effects are usually minimal and only temporary. In contrast, rewarding fluent speech is likely to result in a sustained increase in fluency.

Highlight stuttering by referring to it gently

Having said that punishment is not desirable, mild admonishments can be used in conjunction with rewarding statements. For example, 'That was a stutter, how about repeating it'. It is essential that parents or family make such statements in a non-threatening and positive manner.

Slow down your speech

It is important for the long-term maintenance of fluency skills that the family become a model for the child who stutters by regularly using slower speech. Parents must encourage the child to slow down his or her speech and relax the facial, neck and chest muscles.

Take regular time out to help

Time slots of up to 10–15 minutes each day can be used to concentrate on treatment skills where reward can be used for fluent speech, and the parent can monitor and give feedback on any stuttered words that occur. This time slot, and the content and tasks employed, should be negotiated with the older child. Rewards can be used to encourage this practice.

Create a relaxing environment

Stuttering tends to become worse when a child is nervous or upset. General relaxation prompts, such as 'Calm down,' 'Take it easy,' 'Slowly' and 'It's OK', can be used to calm children who stutter and encourage them to use treatment skills. Use rewards and prompts that are encouraging. Prompts are powerful behavioural reinforcers and can be either verbal or non-verbal in form. Again, it is imperative that the tone of voice of the parent or family member is not punishing but encouraging. Do not overuse these prompts, using them too frequently could become a punishment!

Allow them time to speak

Encourage (and perhaps train if necessary) parents and family to interact socially and verbally with the child who stutters, in a manner that encourages fluency and social growth. For instance, it is important that they give the child sufficient time to speak and express his or her feelings or needs. Also, parents and family should try not to interrupt, talk over or complete the sentence for the child.

Use appropriate rewards

It is difficult for older children to control their stuttering, and appropriate rewards contingent with successful achievements have the potential to make the task easier and more enjoyable. Rewards need to be sophisticated and motivating (for example, short- and long-term rewards), and need to be tailored to the desires of the individual. Take time out to discover what rewards a particular child. Do not overuse a reward, as it may soon lose its reinforcing power. Use natural rewards as often as possible (smiles, hugs, praise and so forth).

Encourage relaxation

Parents can encourage their child to practise relaxation at home. There are many ways a child who stutters can learn to relax, such as:

* deep and slow breathing
* isometrics – tensing up muscles, holding the tension briefly (say 5 seconds) and then letting the tension go while saying 'Relax'
* learning imagery or contemplation methods
* receiving massage
* aerobic exercise
* stretch exercises (Craig, 1998a).

Encourage self-responsibility

Parents must encourage their children to be responsible for their own talking, and it is important that they do not to talk for them. Talking on a child's behalf (when he or she is present) will only belittle the child and reduce self-esteem. Parents should remind children who stutter that they are in control of their lives, and that they can control their stuttering if they put treatment strategies into practice. Failure will occur now and then, and teaching children to learn from these experiences will help them to succeed more often.

Efficacy of treatment for stuttering for older children

There have been numerous unsubstantiated theories about stuttering propagated over the decades and many different approaches to its treatment arising from those theories (Bloodstein, 1995). However, very few of these treatments have been shown to be efficacious using rigorous scientific research (Craig, Feyer and Andrews, 1987; Craig, Chang and Hancock, 1992; Moscicki, 1993). For various reasons, clinicians and researchers have been unwilling, or perhaps unable, to test stuttering treatments rigorously and fewer still have been willing to replicate. One result of this state of affairs is the difficulty for clinicians to treat with confidence people who stutter. If we do not base treatment decisions on the best scientific evidence, then the selection of what is believed to be an effective treatment is likely to be based on any of: what the clinician believes has been successful in the past, clinical expertise and intuition, and adherence to some authoritative therapeutic tradition. If this situation occurs, the treatment selected may be less likely to be the best possible choice for the child who stutters. The measurement of effectiveness and efficacy is discussed further in Chapter 3.

Clinicians have an obligation to provide stuttering treatment services that have been shown to be effective in achieving therapeutic goals. This emphasis on demonstrating treatment efficacy in a scientific and rigorous manner is the major goal of 'evidence-based healthcare' (Sackett et al., 1996). Evidence-based healthcare argues that the role of intuition, clinical experience and pathophysiological reasoning are not sufficient grounds for making clinical decisions. In contrast, evidence-based healthcare emphasizes the crucial role that knowledge from clinical research should play in clinical decision making.

An evidence-based approach assumes that health professionals are able to conduct a literature search of research materials and are able to reach an appropriate decision about the validity of the research reported in the literature. For example, the outcomes of clinical trials are sometimes questionable, and clinicians need to be able to discriminate between valid and poor research. Results can be flawed by low subject numbers, poor design, invalid measures, low reliability, and too much emphasis on statistical rather than clinical significance (Craig et al., 1996). Therefore it is an imperative that health professionals know how to distinguish a high scientific standard in clinical studies from studies with low scientific standards.

In an editorial of the *British Medical Journal*, evidence-based healthcare has been defined as the 'conscientious, explicit and judicious use of current best evidence in making decisions about the care of individual patients' (Sackett et al., 1996, p. 71). Sackett et al. (1996) suggest that clinical experience should be integrated with the best available clinical evidence from systematic and rigorous research. Neither is sufficient by itself, and both are absolutely necessary when treating people who stutter. These authors go on to discuss how clinical evidence should invalidate, and therefore replace, previously accepted diagnostic techniques and treatments with more powerful and efficacious treatment strategies. In this way, the health professional becomes more effective in clinical care (Sackett et al., 1996). The influence of evidence-based healthcare means that substantial change is occurring in areas such as medicine, dentistry, nursing and psychology. However, evidence-based healthcare is also beginning to affect the quality of evidence for the treatment of fluency disorders. Good evidence has now been provided on the efficacy of treatments for stuttering in older children and adults (Craig, Feyer and Andrews, 1987; Boberg and Kully, 1994; Craig et al., 1996; Lincoln et al., 1996; Hancock et al., 1998; Ingham and Riley, 1998; Harrison and Onslow, 1999).

In a critical review of treatment success for children who stutter (Craig, Chang and Hancock, 1992), Smooth Speech and EMG feedback were believed to hold great promise as potential treatments. However, at that time their efficacy had not been rigorously scientifically tested. These two treatments were therefore investigated to determine their efficacy in reducing stuttering and enhancing the mood of older children who stutter. The emphasis of the clinical trial was to evaluate the effectiveness of stuttering programmes that were thought promising, and that could be applied in the community. Altogether there were 97 children who participated in the study: 27 in an intensive Smooth Speech programme; 25 in a less intensive home-based Smooth Speech programme; and 25 in an EMG feedback treatment programme. Twenty stuttering children were conscripted into a no-treatment control group.

The children were of a similar age (mean age was approximately 10–11 years) and the ratio of males to females in each group was approximately 4:1. Severity of stuttering was assessed by %SS when the children were talking in a conversation and by their rate of speech in the conversation (SPM). The children were assessed in three contexts: in a clinic conversation talking to the clinician, on the clinic telephone talking to a family member or friend and talking to a family member or friend in the home environment. To control for language ability, only those children who were progressing normally in their speech for their age were included in the programme. Most children began stuttering early (average age 4.7 years; range 2–11 years) and they had been stuttering for most of their life (average 6 years). About two-thirds of the children had received therapy prior to the study, although in most cases the intervention had been carried out several years earlier. No children had received therapy in the 3 months before pre-treatment assessment. For ethical reasons, the no-treatment control children were offered therapy after waiting for 3 months. It would be unlikely that substantial improvement would occur after this period in the absence of structured treatment.

The results of the clinical trial showed that all three treatments were successful in reducing stuttering and enhancing psychological status for the majority of stuttering children aged 9–14 years who participated in the study. There were no significant differences between the group means in treatment efficacy, as measured by stuttering severity across time. Figure 5.1 shows the substantial reduction in stuttering frequency that occurred in all children regardless of which treatment they received. The contrast to the lack of improvement in the no-treatment control subjects is quite obvious. Stuttering severity levels during a conversation at home, in the clinic or during a telephone call were reduced by at least 85% immediately after treatment.

Although stuttering severity scores increased slightly at 3 months, 1 year and a mean of 5 years after treatment, these increases were not significant. In contrast, the stuttering severity for the stuttering age-matched control children actually remained elevated for the 3 months in which they participated in the study.

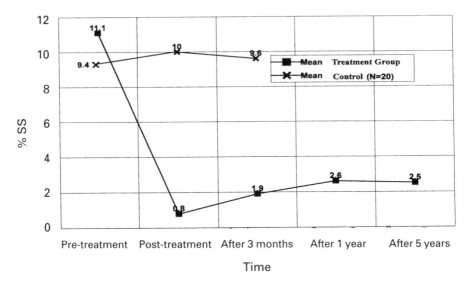

Figure 5.1 Mean frequency of stuttering (%SS) for clinic conversation in all subjects (three treatment groups merged) up to a mean of 5 years, and for the control group up to 3 months after treatment (after 3 months all control children were withdrawn from the study and offered best treatment).

Table 5.1 shows that, after a mean of 5 years, the majority of children improved their fluency by approximately 75% as a result of treatment. These results are very encouraging. Most subjects maintained the speech gains they had made immediately after treatment, up to an average of 5 years after treatment. The children maintained an improvement of at least 75–80% after 5 years, with approximately half of them having either very low or no stuttering in the long term across the three assessment contexts (clinic, home and telephone). The majority of children were speaking more quickly (ranging from 180 SPM to 200 SPM) and were considered to be speaking acceptably and naturally by themselves, the clinician and their parents. Another positive aspect of this study is not only that treatment for older children works but that different types of treatment were shown to be efficacious.

Based upon these results, clinicians have a range of treatments from which they can choose in order to tailor treatment to older children who stutter. This is particularly advantageous when considering individual differences in client preferences for particular treatment styles. Not receiving the preferred treatment may negatively influence motivation and thereby

Table 5.1 Mean percentage improvement scores for frequency of stuttering (%SS) 1 year and an average of 5 years after treatment*

Variable	All children in the three groups (n = 62)	EMG feedback therapy (n = 19)	Intensive Smooth Speech treatment (n = 21)	Home Smooth Speech treatment (n = 22)
Pre-treatment to 1 year after treatment:				
Improvement in stuttering during a clinic conversation (%)	74	73	72	76
Improvement during a telephone conversation (%)	70	78	72	61
Improvement during a conversation at home (%)	73	74	–	72
Pre-treatment to a mean of 5 years after treatment:				
Improvement in stuttering during a clinic conversation (%)	79	80	76	80
Improvement during a telephone conversation (%)	75	79	76	71
Improvement during a conversation at home (%)	79	79	–	79

*Three treatments combined and for the individual treatments.
Only 62 of the 97 subjects were contactable after a mean of 5 years.

outcome. There was also a trend for children to become less anxious after the 5 years. These findings are similar to others who have found psychologically beneficial results after similar treatment (Blood, 1995; Blood et al., 2001). The results of this clinical trial strongly suggest that the anxiety levels of older children and young adolescents who receive effective treatment will remain lower than the norms for their age. The results for the communication fears (assessed by Communication Attitudes Test – Revised [CAT-R] scores) also suggest that the children were more willing to communicate in situations requiring speech, providing further evidence of their enhanced psychological well-being. Overall, the results of this controlled trial are very pleasing.

Relapse management after treatment for stuttering

The results from the clinical trial suggest that relapse, or failure to maintain fluency gains, occurs in about 25–30% of children. For example, parental feedback suggested that as many as 25% of the treated children were not acceptably fluent in the long term. The results from the objective measures, such as %SS and SPM, across the three speech contexts also suggest that approximately 25–30% of children had regressed to unacceptable levels of stuttering after an average of 5 years after treatment (Hancock et al., 1998).

Relapse is a crucial area needing further research in stuttering (Craig, 1998b). However, we do know about a number of factors that predispose people who stutter to relapse. For instance, those with a greater severity of stuttering (higher levels of %SS and low SPM) have a raised chance of relapse (return of stuttering after improvement) in the long term (Craig, 1998b). Relapse management programmes or booster programmes have now been shown to improve fluency in those who relapse severely or slightly in the long term after their initial treatment (Craig et al., 2002; Hancock and Craig, 2002). We conducted a further study that was designed to investigate the effectiveness of offering a booster treatment for 12 older children or adolescents who had participated in the above-mentioned controlled trial, and who were experiencing difficulties maintaining the fluency gains resulting from the initial treatment. In addition to strategies such as Smooth Speech and EMG feedback, this booster programme included strategies known to be effective in reducing risks of relapse (Craig, 1998b). Components included:

- Smooth Speech skills
- EMG feedback skills
- self-management skills that emphasized the importance of self-responsibility, self-evaluation, self-effort and motivation in the achievement of self-set goals
- cognitive techniques that included positive self-talk aimed at enhancing

levels of perceived control over their stuttering (for example, 'I am the master of my speech'); perceived control or self-mastery has been found to be related to long-term outcome in a number of areas as well as stuttering (Craig, 1998b)

- relaxation exercises that involved simple muscle and thematic relaxation techniques (for example, breath awareness, isometric exercise, imaging a peaceful scene) designed to enhance their control of muscle tension and anxiety.

The need to use the relaxation exercises in order to think clearly and focus on fluency skills was discussed. It was also pointed out that relaxation could be used in combination with thought-control techniques in order to cope with difficult speaking situations.

The results of the booster study demonstrate the power of combining Smooth Speech strategies with EMG feedback therapy delivered in a behavioural therapy regimen. It was successful in producing significant reductions in %SS, increases in SPM and speech naturalness after 2 years. The outcomes for the 12 subjects after the booster treatment were compared with their outcomes from the initial treatment programme completed about five years previously. Although outcomes were similar up to 12 months after initial treatment, the booster treatment was associated with significantly reduced %SS and increased SPM 2 years after the booster programme compared with the results after the initial treatment. The efficacy of the booster programme is shown in Figure 5.2, in which changes in frequency of stuttering resulting from initial treatment are compared with changes resulting from the booster treatment.

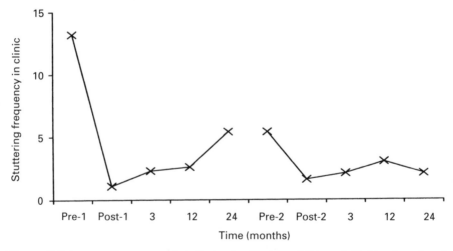

Figure 5.2 Average frequency of stuttering in 12 older children: initial treatment and booster treatment.

Conclusions

There is now substantial, scientifically reliable information available from clinical trial research with older children which demonstrates that stuttering can be treated effectively by use of fluency-shaping and EMG feedback techniques (Boberg and Kully, 1994; Craig et al., 1996; Hancock et al., 1998; Craig et al., 2002; Hancock and Craig, 2002). Adult treatments based upon treatment strategies similar to those used for adolescents have also been shown to be effective (Craig, Feyer and Andrews, 1987). Efficacy was demonstrated by the following changes in the children:

- stuttering reduced to acceptable levels
- substantially improved fluency
- natural speech at normal speech rate levels
- decreased anxiety and communication-related fears
- improved feelings of self-control.

Furthermore, this improvement was in evidence in the home, on the telephone and in the clinic. These gains were maintained into the long term (after at least 2–6 years). Given this evidence, there is no doubt that cognitive–behavioural treatment that contains fluency-enhancing strategies (such as Smooth Speech and EMG feedback therapies) is effective at reducing stuttering for the majority of older children who stutter.

In addition to this, our research suggests that a combination of these treatments has added advantages for older children who stutter (Craig et al., 2002; Hancock and Craig, 2002). The evidence strongly suggests that efficacy will be enhanced over either treatment (Smooth Speech or EMG feedback) offered alone in a behavioural regimen. A combination approach could be used especially for children who experience difficulties in maintaining their fluency after their initial treatment (as in the study by Hancock and Craig, 2002) or for those children who are expected to be a challenge for standard treatments, for instance those who have relapsed badly (as in the study by Craig et al., 2002). This combination of Smooth Speech and EMG feedback presented within a cognitive–behavioural regimen was shown to be effective in lowering relapse rates in children who had serious difficulties maintaining their fluency skills after their initial treatment. Given the neuronal plasticity of the developing brain in older children, we see here an opportunity for clinicians to become involved in the management of stuttering using pedigree treatments. Based upon research results, the vast majority of children receiving Smooth Speech and EMG feedback treatments delivered in a behaviour therapy regimen should improve their stuttering in the long term by at least 70–80%. For these children, stuttering may never again be a significant problem.

Acknowledgements

This chapter was written with the support from the National Health and Medical Research Council in Australia, from the Big Brother Movement of Australia, an Australian Rotary Health Research Grant, the Australian Research Council and from the University of Technology, Sydney. Thanks also to Dr Karen Hancock, other co-researchers and, of course, to the many children whom we have been able to treat for stuttering over the years.

Chapter 6
Family-based approach to therapy with primary school children: 'throwing the ball back'

FRANCES COOK AND WILLIE BOTTERILL

Introduction

Although many therapists are confident in their ability to help the younger child who stutters, this may not be the case when providing therapy for children in primary or elementary school. These children are likely to have been stuttering for several years, the problem is becoming more complex, more firmly established and is less likely to resolve without help.

The psychosocial and environmental aspects of the stuttering become significant as the child's experience of his difficulty becomes more ingrained. He becomes increasingly self-conscious and sensitive to the reactions of other people and, as he grows older, acceptance by peers becomes more important, with teasing or bullying emerging as a potential problem for all who appear or feel 'different'. At this age there are increasing academic challenges, with oral communication being highly valued as an educational target throughout the curriculum (Rustin et al., 2001).

At this stage, in an attempt to reduce the perceived penalties of stuttering, the child may begin to predict and avoid feared situations, develop strategies to disguise or minimize the problem and begin to limit some types of social interaction. These cognitive, affective and behavioural responses are as important to consider in therapy as the overt stuttering behaviours.

This is also a distressing time for parents as they realize that the early reassurances of natural recovery were misguided for their child. They become increasingly aware of the consequences of their child's stutter and concerned about his or her ability to cope socially and academically, and, in the longer term, about future career prospects. Many parents feel quite powerless to help and anxious that they may be perpetuating the problem unknowingly. However, as we shall describe, parents and other carers are central to the effectiveness of therapy and become partners in the process.

This chapter will endeavour to make this multidimensional problem manageable and to encapsulate an approach to therapy that is adapted for each client and family circumstance. Therapy is a creative process and the breadth and specific content needs to be customized as it happens.

The overall goal is to build a child's confidence and competence in communicating and to use the resources of the family and others to support this endeavour. The process of achieving these aims is an intricate interaction between the therapist's professional skills, the individual family, the therapeutic relationship and the content and context of therapy.

Following a brief review of the multifactorial nature of stuttering, this chapter describes the central principles of the approach taken at the Michael Palin Centre for Stammering Children, London. This includes the components and goals of therapy, the techniques and resources which are necessary and the research currently being undertaken at the Centre, highlighting problematical issues related to research into stuttering and therapy.

A multifactorial disorder

The theoretical rationale underpinning all therapy conducted at the Centre is based on the perspective of stuttering as a 'multifactorial disorder' (Riley and Riley, 1984; Starkweather, 1987; Wall and Myers, 1995; Rustin, Botterill and Kelman, 1996; Shapiro, 1999; Conture, 2001; Manning, 2001). For the young child who stutters, there is evidence to suggest that predisposing physiological and linguistic factors may be significant in the onset and development of stuttering, and that it is the interaction of these with psychological and environmental aspects that contributes to its persistence. As the child matures, these factors, to a greater or lesser degree, may continue to have an impact on the overt features of stuttering and consequent cognitive, affective and behavioural responses.

Support for the role of underlying physiological factors in stuttering has come from studies investigating speech motor control (Ingham, 1998; Caruso, Max and McClowry, 1999; Peters, Hulstijn and Van Lieshout, 2000), brain structure and functioning (De Nil et al., 2000; Fox et al., 2000; De Nil, Kroll and Houle, 2001; Ingham, 2001; De Nil et al., 2003; Ingham et al., 2003) and genetics (Ambrose, Cox and Yairi, 1997; Felsenfeld, 1997). There is now a large body of research suggesting that speech motor control is disrupted in people who stutter (Ingham, 1998; Caruso, Max and McClowry, 1999; Peters, Hulstijn and Van Lieshout, 2000), and the notion that the predisposition to stutter may be inherited is widely accepted. Studies of family history, twins, and patterns of affected relatives have repeatedly illustrated genetic effects (Yairi, Ambrose and Cox, 1996). Interestingly, it has been shown that the tendency for children to recover spontaneously or to develop persistent stuttering is genetically transmitted (Ambrose, Cox and Yairi, 1997).

Numerous studies have been published investigating the relationship between linguistic factors and stuttering. Bernstein Ratner elaborates on this in Chapter 9. From a developmental perspective, stuttering generally emerges at a time when a child's linguistic system is undergoing a period of rapid development, and it has been suggested that stuttering may begin at a time when children 'make the transitions between lexically and grammatically governed strategies for producing utterances' (Bernstein Ratner, 1997a, p. 116). Stuttering is more likely to occur on utterance-initial and clause-initial words (Bernstein Ratner, 1981; Wall, Starkweather and Cairns, 1981) and on utterances that are longer (Gaines, Runyan and Meyers, 1991; Weiss and Zebrowski, 1992; Logan and Conture, 1997; Conture 2001) and more complex (Bernstein Ratner and Sih, 1987; Kadi-Hanifi and Howell, 1992; Weiss and Zebrowski, 1992). In addition, it has been found that subgroups of children within the stuttering population present with additional speech and/or language problems (Bernstein Ratner, 1997a, Louko, Conture and Edwards, 1999). A child's linguistic profile has also been found to play a role in recovery and persistence (Paden, Yairi and Ambrose, 1999; Watkins and Yairi, 1999; Rommel, 2000).

The association between stuttering and emotional factors has been demonstrated over many years. Cognitive, affective, somatic and behavioural responses to persistent stuttering are commonly discussed in the literature. Feelings of fear, anxiety, shame, embarrassment, guilt and self-consciousness are frequently reported by individuals who stutter (Sheehan, 1970; Prins, 1993; Bloodstein, 1995; Murphy, 1999; Manning, 2001). Repeated communication failures and the fluctuations and variability in stuttering contribute to feelings of helplessness and ineptitude for many individuals. Negative predictions and beliefs about speaking can have a detrimental effect on social behaviour and therefore on overall communication skills (Rustin and Kuhr, 1999), whereas strategies to cope with the problem by avoiding the feared consequences can become a significant part of the problem.

Finally, the influence of the environment on stuttering has been debated at length. Conture (2001, p. 60) describes stuttering as a 'complex interaction between the environment of the person who stutters and the skills and abilities the person who stutters brings to that environment'. Shapiro (1999, p. 125) stresses that 'stuttering, and other communication disorders exist and must be addressed within a family context'. A child's perception of the environment and of his functioning within it is important for understanding the dimensions of interpersonal behaviour. Argyle (1982, as cited by Rustin and Kuhr, 1999) describes the importance of 'meta-perception' in relation to social skills. This refers to the fact that during social interaction individuals not only judge others, but are also concerned with how they are being judged and that this can have a significant effect on behaviour.

The communication environment is therefore as important as the individual who presents for therapy, and the family dynamics are an essential ingredient in the therapy process (Starkweather, Gottwald and Halfond, 1990; Kelly and Conture, 1992; Wall and Myers, 1995; Manning, 1996; Zebrowski, 1997; Conture and Melnick, 1999; Gottwald, 1999).

The principles that guide therapy

Comprehensive therapy

This multifactorial perspective of stuttering proposes that each child has a different profile of factors contributing to the development and persistence of their stuttering. Therapy programmes should be similarly comprehensive and designed not only to help children make changes in the way that they communicate, but also to explore and address the developing attitudes and beliefs which affect their confidence in their ability to communicate. Personal change is a challenge for anyone but particularly hard for a child, however strong his or her incentive. All children who stutter need a high level of family or carer involvement to support the process of change. Parents are key role models in their child's environment. They have a significant influence on the child's developing beliefs and attitudes, developing self-esteem and confidence, and problem-solving abilities and social communication skills. The abilities that the family brings to therapy influence the therapeutic process, whereas previous experience of therapy, negative or positive, shapes their hopes and fears about the future.

Sharing the responsibility for change between the child, the therapist and the family has become the hallmark of the work carried out at the Centre for this age group.

The therapeutic relationship

The foundation of effective therapy is the development of a role relationship between the clinician, the child and the family. The importance of this partnership in the assessment process is discussed in Chapter 2. A successful alliance is built on a shared perception of the problem and an equal partnership in the therapeutic endeavour, with clear goals including self-advocacy and empowerment. If clinicians are to play their part in exploring and facilitating change, there must be trust, empathic understanding and genuine respect between client, the family and clinician.

The nature and importance of this relationship is discussed widely in the counselling literature. Spinelli (1994) reviews the research and concludes that it is 'the bond' formed between the therapist and the client that is the crucial factor in successful therapy and that this seems to be independent of the theoretical model or the therapy approach. He suggests it is the quality of listening and a sense of 'being with and for' the client that is central to the relationship. Wampold (2001) suggests that specific treatments or techniques account for less than one per cent of the variance in improvement among psychotherapy patients, but that it is the therapist that counts, not the therapy *per se*.

The expertise of the clinician

Speech and language therapists have a wide range of skills that make them uniquely qualified to carry out detailed assessments and implement structured speech management and communication skills programmes. However, as the stuttering problem becomes more complex, clinicians need to develop their understanding of the breadth and depth of the disorder, the historical perspective, current research issues, theoretical explanations of onset and development as well as the concordance and debate around different therapy approaches and their application. In addition counselling skills, now considered core components of the speech and language therapists' education, are fundamental to understanding and managing a problem which can be significantly affected by psychological factors.

Speech and language therapists use many core counselling skills, irrespective of client group, and continuing professional development is gained through further reading, training, supervision, reflective practice and experience. The counselling skills that are discussed in the literature include active listening, empathy, reflecting, clarifying, summarizing, questioning, accepting, encouraging and supporting among many others. Corey and Corey (2002) add warmth, flexibility and sense of humour to this list. Manning (2001, p. 33) also highlights humour as an essential ingredient in facilitating change: 'Humor seems to be a factor worthy of consideration in the treatment process, for many features of change are indicated by humor as people achieve mastery, distance, and a conceptual shift concerning their situation'.

It has been interesting to note the increase in the number of recent texts and chapters devoted to counselling skills in relation to therapy for stuttering (Crowe, 1997; Bloom and Cooperman, 1999; Shapiro, 1999; Manning, 2001).The aim of counselling could be described as guiding individuals to a personal understanding of the difficulties they face and the changes they wish to make, in ways that respect their values, personal resources and capacity for self-determination. Van Riper (1973) clearly demonstrated the need for a counselling style when he described the desirable attributes of a clinician as empathy, genuineness, charisma and optimism in the client's own potential for self-healing.

Major influences

It is important to be able to draw on theoretical models to support and develop these counselling skills and to explain the challenges and 'roadblocks' that occur in the process of therapy. The therapeutic approach described in this chapter is guided by a range of theoretical perspectives, including learning theory (Skinner, 1953), family systems theory (Minuchin, 1974), personal construct theory (Kelly, 1955), cognitive theory (Beck, 1995) and solution-focused brief therapy (De Shazer, 1996). Although it is beyond the scope of this chapter to describe these in detail, key concepts are described below.

Behaviour therapy

Behaviour modification therapy (Ryan, 1974; Shames and Florance, 1980) was an exciting and positive influence in the early 1970s and 1980s. Highly structured regimes of fluency-shaping, using prolonged speech in graded activities, demonstrated rapid control over stuttering, whereas contingent reinforcement for fluent utterances of single words through to conversational exchanges showed many examples of excellent results within the clinical setting. The treatment goals were explicit and fluent speech was charted, cultivated and extended (Ryan and Van Kirk, 1978; Shine, 1988; Webster and Wohlberg,1992).

Although these programmes were very successful at modifying speech behaviours, they did not address the cognitive and affective dimensions of the problem. Advocates of the theory maintained that as fluency came under voluntary control, there would be a consequent positive effect on the associated negative beliefs and feelings. For some clients this appeared to be the case; however, for many others, although the clinical gains were impressive, they did not address the underlying issues that are essential for transfer and long-term maintenance of fluency skills.

Behavioural methodology continues to influence many aspects of our work. Key principles, such as setting clear and achievable goals and structuring therapy into small manageable steps with built-in schedules of reinforcement, continue to influence the way skills acquisition is approached.

Family systems approach

The study and development of family systems therapy has provided a theoretical rationale for involving the family in all aspects of assessment and treatment. The child is seen in the context of the family system, where one part of the family cannot be understood in isolation from the other members of the system. The parts of a family system are interrelated, so that change in one has an influence on the other members of that system (Andrews and Andrews, 1990, pp. 16–21).

Shapiro (1999, p. 128) highlighted these views from the literature on family systems and therapy:

- The behaviour of each member of the family is understood more completely when the beliefs, patterns and customs of the entire family are understood and taken into account.

- A fluency disorder is frequently embedded in the pattern of family interactions.
- Every family adopts certain roles over time, an understanding of which is critical to involving the family in treatment.

Families play a key role in building and supporting children's confidence and autonomy, as well as providing a safe environment for experimenting with new skills and innovative ways of tackling difficulties. A successful family is one that feels empowered: the child who stutters and his family need to feel that they have developed their own strategies and that it is what *they* do that makes a positive difference.

Personal construct psychology

Personal construct theory and therapy (Kelly, 1955) has had a significant impact on the methods adopted by clinicians in the UK (Botterill and Cook, 1987; Dalton, 1987, 1994; Evesham, 1987; Hayhow and Levy, 1989; Fransella and Dalton, 1990; Stewart and Turnbull, 1995; Williams, 1995). Interestingly, recent textbooks from the USA also include personal construct psychology as a central counselling approach for stuttering (Shapiro, 1999; Manning, 2001). Personal construct psychology looks for explanations of behaviour, feelings, motivation, learning and experience, *within* each person (Fransella and Dalton, 1990). The theory is optimistic and has at its core the assumption that movement and change are continuously occurring and inevitable.

Fransella (1972) proposed that, over time, being a person who stutters becomes a familiar and predictable role for many individuals, whereas being fluent is unfamiliar territory. She proposed that people who stutter develop a highly elaborated system of 'constructs' related to speaking and the 'self' as a dysfluent speaker. Fransella (1972) argued that it is this elaborate construct system that offers the safety of predictability and meaning. From this perspective, it is possible to see how rapidly acquired fluency skills could throw the client into psychological 'chaos' and, when faced with unfamiliar and unpredictable experiences, 'relapse' into familiar patterns of behaviour: a safe option from the client's point of view.

Making the psychological transition from a person who stutters to a person who does not, is considerably more difficult than controlling the overt speech behaviours, as it involves change on different levels. Change, particularly as a result of therapy, requires a person to develop alternative constructs – to reconstrue events, a process that is difficult because it means attempting new ways of thinking and behaving. The task of the therapist is to learn more about the family's construct system, to build up a detailed understanding of the way the child sees himself and his current situation, to see the world 'through the client's eyes' (Botterill and Cook, 1987, p. 149).

In addition, the therapist's role is then to help children to consider and experiment with alternative views (constructions) of themselves, their stuttering, their responsibility for their situation, and the effect of speech modification techniques. This approach fundamentally alters the way we approach therapy. It helps us to reconstrue 'motivation' and 'relapse', and explains the challenges that each child faces as he or she experiments with managing the stuttering.

Cognitive theory

There are two key ideas derived from cognitive theory that are particularly relevant to stuttering. First, cognitive theory states that thoughts, feelings, physical responses and behaviour are linked. In other words, what people think affects how they feel emotionally and physically, and also affects how they behave.

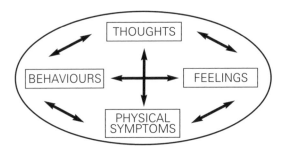

Figure 6.1 A cognitive model.

Applied to stuttering children, negative thoughts or predictions are typically focused on an expectation that stuttering will occur, for example 'I'll get stuck', and, importantly, that there will be some undesirable consequence of this. Children who are able to identify negative thoughts typically report that they are related to:

• how they will come across, for example 'I'll look stupid', 'I'll sound weird'
• how others will react, for example 'They'll laugh', 'They'll make fun of me'
• what others might think of them, for example 'They'll think I am stupid'.

Given these negative predictions, it is natural for uncomfortable feelings such as anxiety or embarrassment to be triggered and for physical responses such as increased heart rate or having 'butterflies' to be noticed. Behavioural responses, such as deciding to change a word to one that seems safer, deciding not to speak at all or struggling harder to 'force' a word out, can be understood as part of a chain reaction. They can be regarded as a way of coping, albeit unhelpfully, with the predictions being made and the feelings being experienced.

Second, Beck proposed that coping strategies or behaviours resulting from negative predictions tend to reinforce rather than reduce fears, and thus ultimately reinforce the problem. Applied to stuttering, an example of this vicious circle is found in the way that choosing to avoid a feared word, on the one hand a way of coping, actually intensifies fear of that word because the individual loses the opportunity to find out that they can say it successfully, or that the worst doesn't happen should they stutter. In our experience, this idea of the vicious circle of stuttering is one that parents and children readily relate to, and one that sets the scene for considering alternative ways of managing moments of stuttering.

We have found that parents find the concept of the cognitive cycle valuable in understanding their own cognitive, behavioural and affective reactions to their child's stuttering, and why desensitization strategies are essential for the whole family. Cognitive theory gives us a model and methods to explore the way a client's and family's beliefs, assumptions and experiences affect the day-to-day reality of stuttering, and to give systematic guidance to clients in discovering more helpful ways of viewing, interpreting and judging events.

Solution-focused brief therapy

This technique emerged in response to a growing need for 'time limited' therapy. It focuses on finding solutions to difficulties that are already in the individual's repertoire and do not therefore require the acquisition of new skills. There are a number of underlying assumptions to solution-focused brief therapy, many of which echo what has already been described above. Key to these is that making a *small change* will set in motion a solution to the problem, as a change in one part of the system leads to changes in another part (Selekman, 1993; Burns, 2005).

The therapeutic process can be condensed into two main activities – first, finding out in some detail what the client's goals are, and then finding out what the client is already doing that is likely to help. Establishing clear, detailed goals is an essential part of solution-focused brief therapy, both as a yardstick for measuring progress, and as a way of eliciting and elaborating the small steps towards these goals. This is often a more difficult task than it first appears; for example, children and parents state clearly that their goal is increased fluency but have not considered the details of 'what' and 'how' life will be different when they are more fluent.

Directing the family's attention to the times when they are managing well; that is, the times the child is more fluent or when they are less worried about it, the therapist helps shift the focus of enquiry away from the problem and towards possible solutions.

This fundamentally optimistic view of a person's capacity to change, places the individual in control of both the outcome and the means by which it can be achieved. It emphasizes that individuals already have the skills and resources to reach their goals and that it is the role of the clinician to elicit, highlight and reinforce these skills during therapy.

Summary

The models and methods outlined above influence the style and content of the clinical practice at the Michael Palin Centre for Stammering Children, whether these are directed at the individual client or focused on the family group. Behavioural methodology allows therapy goals to be structured into small and achievable steps. A systems approach ensures that significant others, who interact and support the child who stutters, are included. Personal construct therapy shows the importance of understanding the client's view of the world, the personal meaning of stuttering and the challenge of changing well-established beliefs. Cognitive theory explains the power of the self-fulfilling prophecy and the role of negative thoughts, images and appraisals in reinforcing the cognitive, affective and behavioural components of stuttering, whereas solution-focused brief therapy ensures that we consider the strengths and skills that the client and family bring to therapy and identify potential solutions that are already within their repertoire.

The themes which are common across these approaches include the following.

- A sense of optimism that change is possible and that there are alternative ways of viewing events and making choices.
- The importance of developing knowledge and skills to explore the options, experiment with change, reflect on the process, select new goals and challenge unhelpful beliefs and assumptions.
- The assumption from the beginning that therapy is time-limited and that the client's developing knowledge and skills will generate an explicit action plan for dealing with later setbacks.
- The importance of enabling clients to answer their own questions, to find their own solutions and to develop robust self-help strategies through guided discovery.

The previous section has given a brief overview of the principles and the theoretical models and methods that shape this approach to therapy. The next section will briefly consider the importance of assessment, and explore the core goals and components of therapy, clinical pathways and the thorny issue of evidence-based practice.

The assessment protocol

The multifactorial framework proposes that each child who presents in the clinic will have a different profile of physiological, linguistic, environmental and emotional factors that have contributed to the onset and persistence of the stuttering problem. The detailed assessment protocol is divided into two separate parts: a child assessment and a consultation with the parents. It is an important opportunity for the therapist to demonstrate empathy and perceptiveness in understanding the child's history and unique experience of the problem. The family, before investing in therapy, will want to discern how much knowledge the clinician has about stuttering in general, and how much skill in understanding their unique perspective.

The child's point of view

The informal interview is an important opportunity to find out more about the child's awareness of and insight into the stuttering as well as any coping strategies that the child may be using. Children of all ages are frequently knowledgeable and perceptive about their stuttering, and it is important to discuss it openly and easily. The level of concern that a child expresses is highly variable; some children appear relatively unconcerned, whereas for others the stutter is a source of great frustration and distress.

The following topics are covered.

The child assessment

As with any speech and language therapy assessment, formal procedures are complemented by thoughtful questions and accurate observations about the child's overall communication skills and needs.

The assessment procedures include an informal interview to understand the child's perspective, observations about his or her social communication skills, formal receptive and expressive language measures, and a fluency assessment.

Description of the stutter

The ability to describe, or to demonstrate, the characteristic of the stutter gives valuable information about the child's 'ownership' of the problem. Clinical experience has shown that the child who demonstrates an understanding of what he or she does physically when stuttering (rather than 'It just happens') often responds well to making changes with his or her speech.

Coping strategies

It is useful to consider the following:

- What is the child already doing that is helpful?
- What strategies has the child developed to minimize or disguise the problem?

Although some of these efforts may seem to compound the stuttering, it is also important to remember that developing *any* strategies demonstrates a willingness to experiment with making changes rather than just feeling 'helpless'.

Previous therapy

If the child has had previous therapy it is important to ascertain his or her opinion of the benefits (or not) of this in real life. There are instances when a child reports and demonstrates 'fluent speech' skills using a variety of techniques, but he or she may also disclose the difficulties in transferring these into the social environment. This experience could have led to a loss of confidence in therapy, and may influence the child's decision about further therapy.

Others' reactions

Many children in this age group become increasingly sensitive to others' negative reactions to the stutter, which then has an effect on their confidence in speaking.

Advice

Children are often in receipt of well-meaning advice from a variety of sources. It is helpful to determine what the child finds most helpful and what he or she would like people to do 'more of' or 'less of'. This information contributes to the recommendations.

Impact of the problem

Rating scales are a useful and concrete tool for helping children to signify how 'big' the problem is for them, and how 'confident' they feel in managing it on a day-to-day basis. In addition, open-ended questions about school, teachers, friends, home life, lifestyle and hobbies will indicate the role that stuttering may play in everyday life. Direct questions about teasing and bullying, and how the child copes, provide information about areas that may need to be tackled during therapy (for example, problem-solving, liaising with the school).

Readiness for therapy

The timing of therapy is important; attempting to conduct therapy with an unwilling child is rarely recommended – however motivated the parents may be. In some cases it may be helpful to hand the responsibility for 'opting into' therapy over to the child. Choices can be offered for the timing of the next review session to check progress (for example, 6 weeks, 3 months or 6 months). Offering some 'time-limited' trial therapy sessions can also be useful.

Social communication skills

Stuttering can interfere with all aspects of communication, and can be frustrating for the child who stutters and for the conversational partner. During the assessment, observations are made about the child's use of eye contact, listening and attention, turn-taking and conversational skills. The child's general presentation, level of confidence and ability to engage in the assessment process will also inform recommendations.

Language assessment

As discussed above, the research literature suggests that some children who stutter have skill deficits that may be underlying or contributing to their dysfluency. Bernstein Ratner elaborates on this in Chapter 9. Clinical experience shows that some children have quite subtle linguistic difficulties. There may be word-retrieval problems, or an uneven profile of skills – with good ability in one area, such as vocabulary, but deficits in another, for example syntax. Some children have superior language skills with the ability to formulate complex language structures, but perhaps without the underlying speech motor skills required to manage these fluently (Peters and Starkweather, 1990).

Assessing a child's linguistic skills will provide important information regarding any impact these may have on the fluency problems, as well as providing other areas which may need to be targeted in therapy. Formal measures routinely include the *British Picture Vocabulary Scales* (BPVS) (Dunn et al., 1982) and the *Renfrew Action Picture Test* (Renfrew, 1988). For a fuller investigation of linguistic functioning the *Clinical Evaluation of Language Fundamentals* (Semel et al., 2003) or the *German Test of Word Finding* (German, 1986) may be used as necessary.

Fluency assessment

Stuttering is notoriously variable, and whatever measures are taken within a clinic should be considered as a 'snapshot' of the presenting speech symptoms on that occasion.

Where possible, speech samples are taken within the home environment of the child as well as within the clinic to offer objective data about the frequency of stuttered syllables (%SS) and rate of speech in terms of syllables per minute. In order to expand the value of %SS scores, we consider overt severity and the individual's perception of the moments of stuttering. The overt severity of the stuttering is evaluated using the *Clinician Stuttering Severity Ratings* (Yairi and Ambrose, 1999). In this instrument, the therapist rates severity in terms of the frequency of stuttering, the duration of the longest blocks (or greatest number of reiterations), the amount of tension and extent of secondary behaviours. This results in a score between 0 and 7. Children and parents are invited to rate the 'representativeness' of the speech, the severity of the stuttering during the sample, the use of avoidance, the amount of effort or struggle involved and the child's confidence in managing the moments of stuttering.

The Communication Attitude Test (Brutten and Dunham, 1989) and the Locus of Control Scale for Children (Nowicki-Strickland, 1973) are also used alongside self-report rating scales for both children and parents, which are currently under development at the Centre.

Collectively, these provide more information about each child's perception of the:

- degree to which their speech is disrupted in a range of everyday situations
- level to which they feel apprehensive about speaking in these situations
- attitude about themselves as speakers
- behavioural concomitants (if any)
- ability to take personal responsibility.

Summary

Children are an important source of information regarding the difficulties they face, as well as the skills they have already developed for dealing with their stutter. They are more likely to engage in therapy when the therapist can demonstrate that their views have been listened to carefully, and with empathy, and when they are sure they will be included in any decisions. A child's opinion may be not the same as that of his or her parents, and this will need to be borne in mind when therapy options are being considered.

Parent consultation

This part of the assessment protocol offers parents the opportunity to give their account of their child's stutter. Therapists need to reassure parents that they have not caused the stuttering but that they will, with support, be the key individuals in helping their child to develop the confidence to manage the speech more effectively. Open questions guide parents through the range of factors that may have been and continue to be influential. The inclusion of both parents enhances the breadth and depth of the information gathered and establishes the principle of partnership from the outset.

Questions cover the onset and development of the stutter; the parents' opinions about possible causes (e.g. family history), the variability and frequency, the overt and covert characteristics as well as its current manifestation. Parental observations about the coping strategies that their child has developed and the ways in which they try to help are pertinent. Parents often report that they 'know we're not supposed to do x or y, but it seems to help'. By the end of the consultation, when both the parents' and the child's points of view are understood, prompts to help the child on a daily basis can be agreed by all parties. Rating scales, similar to those used with the child, offer a way of recording parents' current anxiety about the stuttering, their view of its impact and their confidence in knowing how to help.

It is also valuable to ask parents to consider their expectations of therapy. Many parents are realistic and while still 'wishing for a cure' they are likely to talk about their overall desire to help their child to regain confidence in communicating. Other parents may present a view of therapy as somehow 'administered' to the child, similar to the traditional medical model, and this would need to be taken into account when discussing therapy recommendations.

In addition to specific questions about the stuttering, more general questions about the child's lifestyle within and beyond the family setting, behaviour management, friendships and relationships, temperament and personality, as well as the family structure, will help the therapist to understand the child and the dynamics within the family. The early history and developmental milestones are covered in as much detail as necessary and there should be time for parents to elaborate on any particular issues that concern them.

Formulation

This is a summary of the consultation process, when the results and findings are fed back to the parents. The key facts, pertinent research and an explanation of the issues that appear relevant in terms of physiological, linguistic, psychological and environmental influences are summarized and therapy recommendations are presented for discussion.

Case example

Harry, aged 8.9 years, has been stuttering since he started to put words together at the age of three-and-a-half. A tape-recorded speech sample demonstrates 10.6% stuttered syllables (%SS) and a rate of 220 syllables per minute (SPM). His slower speech development had been attributed to a complicated birth, with a residual slight hemiparesis; however, his language assessment demonstrated advanced scores.

Harry's paternal grandfather and uncle both stutter, although neither have had therapy. Harry's parents describe him as a perfectionist, both in his schoolwork and when playing with his toys and enjoying his hobbies. He hates making mistakes. Harry has three siblings — one older sister and two younger brothers. Harry's parents were very concerned that their hectic lifestyle and chaotic home might be contributing to the problem, and they were working hard on establishing a routine in the morning 'rush hour' before school. There are clear physiological, linguistic, emotional and environmental components to Harry's stuttering.

Core components of therapy

As stated above, the overall goal is to increase the child's and family's confidence in managing the communication problem more effectively. In order to do this, the family needs greater knowledge about the psychological aspects of stuttering, about communication skills in general and about the options for managing the actual moments of stuttering. Although it is beyond the scope of this chapter to give a step-by-step description of the therapy programme, the following is intended to give an overview of the components which are individually tailored for each child and family.

Figure 6.2 illustrates the relationship between the three components of therapy that underpin all the Michael Palin Centre therapy programmes. It demonstrates that the cognitive aspects are as important as the communication and speech management skills. Each component of the model is introduced in terms of increasing knowledge and acquiring new skills: the *why*, *what* and *how* of therapy.

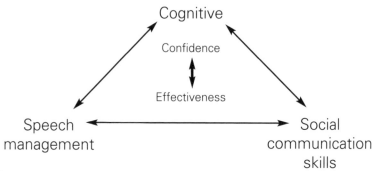

Figure 6.2 The core components of therapy.

Cognitive

This component is concerned with helping the child and his parents to explore and understand the cognitive, emotional and behavioural responses to stuttering. It is important to remember that the severity of the stuttering does not necessarily reflect the underlying psychological and emotional impact of the problem for the child or the parents. Many children who stutter explain that 'thinking about' their speech and anticipating difficulties makes the problem worse. As we have suggested earlier, it is the negative quality of the thoughts that leads to the feeling of helplessness. Pessimistic beliefs and predictions, together with tricks and strategies to hide or avoid the stuttering, usually reinforce the fears.

Many parents come to therapy anxious about their child's ability to cope with a problem that is baffling and over which they feel they have no influence. They have repeatedly witnessed their child's struggle to communicate in different situations and, despite their best endeavours, still feel powerless to help.

Acknowledging the stutter

The first issue to be addressed in therapy may be the conspiracy of silence about stuttering that so often exists. Parents have usually been advised in a variety of ways, and from many different sources, to ignore the stutter and not to bring it to the child's attention. This advice is based on the idea that young children will recover naturally, and that by focusing on the stutter, they will make it worse. However, children are often highly aware and are able to describe their difficulties, and talking about the experience of stuttering is often a relief. Learning to talk about the stutter calmly and objectively, and acknowledge it readily outside the clinical setting, with friends, family and strangers, takes courage and effort. Nevertheless, the reward of understanding and confronting the fear is a powerful tool in therapy.

Clinicians help parents to consider the advantages of being able to discuss the stutter naturally, just as they would any other matter causing concern, for example, maths, spelling, exams, making friends, going on school trips. Parents often say that once they have found a way of talking about the speech that feels natural and easy, their anxiety as well as their child's seems to reduce and become more manageable.

Thoughts and feelings

Many parents and children have developed a repertoire of negative cognitive, affective and behavioural responses to stuttering. Exploring and understanding the role that these have in maintaining the vicious circle of stuttering is clearly important.

This component of therapy helps children to understand the links between how they think, feel, speak and behave. Exercises help them to identify the overt and covert aspects of stuttering that undermine fluency in certain situations, and to contrast these negative thoughts, feelings and behaviours with those that operate when they are more fluent. This psychological component is a recurring theme as children and parents experiment with new techniques and activities. Identifying, checking and challenging negative thinking patterns in a variety of settings, whilst considering alternatives and reinforcing more positive thoughts and behaviours, becomes a routine part of therapy.

Parents, too, need to explore and understand the role their negative thoughts have in determining how they respond to their child's moments of stuttering. Thoughts such as 'He'll stutter', 'They won't understand him' or 'I can't bear it', go hand in hand with feelings of worry, fear or panic, which may lead to physical symptoms such as muscle tension, 'knots' in the stomach, flushing and a range of behavioural responses. For example, parents recall times when they have 'spoken' for their child, finished sentences, repeated what he or she said, or 'willed' the child to get the words out and then 'relaxed with relief' when it was over.

Case example

George, aged 10 years, decided to talk to his Mum about her 'reassuring' facial expression when he was talking to her. She was trying hard to look relaxed and encouraging, but he found it annoying because he felt it drew attention to his difficulties and put him under pressure.

Although it can take considerable courage, the rewards of confronting, understanding and acknowledging the stutter are a powerful way to reduce the fear and undermine its negative effect for both children and their parents.

Experiencing fluency

It is not only necessary to elaborate stuttering but also the experience of being more fluent. Most children are fluent much more often than they stutter, and they are able to describe the difference, for example 'I don't think about it – it's easy', 'I'm not in such a hurry', 'I know it doesn't matter if I do stutter'. Furthermore, they often have ideas about what they can do that helps them to be more fluent. Using this knowledge is an important part of therapy. Parents are often surprised by the level of understanding and awareness that their child demonstrates, and they find it helpful to notice the fluency and consider the resources they already have to tackle the problem.

Confidence and independence

Parents and children are also aware of the important link between their child's confidence and level of fluency. For many parents, increased confidence is the most important goal for their child in therapy. Children who experience negative reactions to stuttering become increasingly worried about speaking, and are less confident in their ability to communicate effectively. The decline in self-esteem and associated negative thought patterns is usually reflected in an increase in children's stuttering and a reduction in their oral contributions.

For this reason, the therapy has a strong emphasis on building children's self-confidence and self-esteem. This is achieved in a variety of ways, indirectly by increasing their knowledge about stuttering and developing their skills in managing it, and more directly by specific praise and self-affirmation techniques. Parents have many ways of enhancing their child's confidence; identifying what they are already doing, as well as generating new ideas, expands their repertoire. They are also introduced to a model of 'specific praise' for children (Faber and Mazlish, 1980). This model requires parents to notice a daily instance of good behaviour, to comment on what the child did and add an appropriate attribute, for example 'I *noticed* that you put your shoes away; that was really *helpful*. Well done!' This helps children to become aware of what they are doing well, and the verbal label builds and reinforces positive constructs about themselves.

An important part of developing self-confidence is encouraging more autonomy, particularly for children who may have become dependent on others to talk for them, such as when telephoning, buying tickets, shopping and asking for things. Parents often struggle to get the balance between being supportive and helpful, on the one hand, and 'letting go', on the other. Discussions, problem-solving and negotiation exercises all help parents experiment with ways of striking that balance.

Social communication skills

Effectiveness in social communication is much more than the ability to speak. Indeed, it has been suggested that as much as 70% of a message is conveyed non-verbally (Birdwhistell, 1970). Non-verbal signals are thought by some authors to be more important than verbal behaviour in expressing feelings and attitudes, as they indicate how a message should be interpreted (Argyle, Furnham and Graham, 1981). An improvement in the non-verbal interaction skills of those with communication impairment increases the effectiveness of their communication and, in turn, maximizes the social reinforcement they receive from others. The consequent rise in self-esteem and confidence levels also encourages an increase in their ability to initiate and maintain a conversational topic – skills which are vital to successful communication (Rustin and Kuhr, 1998).

Even young children who have recently started to stutter may reduce their eye contact during moments of difficulty in speaking. Some children have been so engulfed by their efforts to speak that the usual conventions of listening, observing and turn-taking within conversations are less well-practised or understood. Communication is a two-way process and it is important to convey the intended message appropriately not only as a speaker, but also as a listener. An increased awareness of the effect that deficiencies in social communication skills can have on a listener's interpretation of events is an important component of therapy. Parents are key role models in the child's environment, and family interaction styles are a highly productive channel through which fluency can be enhanced. Parents quickly tune into the fluctuations and variations in their child's stuttering in different speaking situations and begin to notice that their child is often more fluent when:

- the child has time to plan and organize what he or she wants to say
- the child is feeling confident about what he or she is saying or doing
- listeners give the child time to finish
- the child is not thinking or worrying about it
- the child is not under pressure to compete for speaking space.

During therapy, parents and their child focus on the family interaction styles using video to provide feedback and, with positive guidance from the therapist, begin to notice the styles that support and encourage their child's naturally occurring or 'managed' fluency. Older children and families also gain awareness of the value of developing social skills that reflect confidence and assertiveness in communicative settings.

A hierarchy of social communication skills is introduced through discussions, brainstorms, and videotaped activities that offer opportunities for identifying positive targets for change. The foundation skills usually include looking and eye contact, listening and turn-taking. More complex skills, such as problem-solving and negotiation, are then presented to explore new perspectives and more effective ways of interacting. Each skill is considered in terms of its importance and its effect on communication, particularly in terms of promoting confidence and self-determination for both the speaker and the listener. These are then practised in a variety of structured clinical exercises, again using video for immediate feedback and reinforcement.

Techniques

Brainstorms

This technique (Priestly et al., 1978) is a highly effective method of eliciting the family's and the child's own ideas about a given topic. Therapy that is based on ideas generated by the family is more likely to be taken on board than therapy in which ideas have been provided. The rules of a brainstorm are explained: having decided the topic, everyone is encouraged to take turns in offering suggestions, and all ideas are accepted and written down, no matter how impractical or 'off centre' they seem at first. Contributing to brainstorming encourages the creativity of the family to provide new ideas and perspectives that will carry the discussion forward.

Problem-solving

This technique provides children and families with a manageable and practical way of finding solutions to issues that arise in the course of family life. One of the family members identifies a personal problem that they would like help to resolve, such as 'sorting out the mess in my room/office'. The family then brainstorms as many solutions as they can imagine. The person whose problem it is, selects the ideas that have the most potential and considers their possible consequences. These are then placed in order of priority and the first chosen for trial. Problem-solving provides the family with a way of working together on an issue and sharing in the collective responsibility for the solutions that emerge.

> **Case example**
>
> Jackie's problem was how to handle mealtimes when family members did not arrive on time. A brainstorm with the family provided many new ideas. She considered each suggestion in turn and finally decided that the first one to try was 'To give each a warning and, if they paid no attention to it, then the food would be left to get cold and after 10 minutes it would be put in the bin'. She went home to try out this plan. By the next session, she had only had to put one person's meal in the bin, and now they were all turning up more or less on time. The positive impact for the family was that Jackie had stayed calm, communication was much more relaxed and the children were taking responsibility – and facing the consequences of their actions.

Negotiation

This complex communication skill provides another means for parents and children to resolve disagreements. Brainstorms are used to explore what is meant by 'negotiation' and to identify the range of skills that are important. Video exercises and role-play help children and parents to consider alternative ways of tackling everyday issues that cause family conflict, for example children wanting to stay up late, requesting an unnecessary but expensive item or untidy bedrooms. Children are encouraged to think carefully about what they want and how to ask for it, so that they can present thoughtful arguments for why they should be taken seriously. Parents discuss and experiment with ways to encourage their child to think through the implications of their request and, together, they work towards a mutually acceptable compromise. The importance of listening carefully and respecting each other's point of view is discussed and parents are encouraged 'to throw the ball back' to their child and resist the temptation to resolve issues themselves.

> **Case example**
>
> James wanted a new pair of trainers, although he had recently had some. He presented his reasons for making this request, and instead of just saying 'no' his parents listened carefully this time and said they understood but 'wondered' with him how they would find the money to pay for them. James offered to find out how much the trainers cost, to start saving and to do some odd jobs that would help to pay for them. They agreed to talk about it again in three weeks when James would show them how much he had saved. James was pleased that they had taken him seriously and was eager to raise the money. His parents felt they had successfully averted the 'whingeing' that usually accompanied such a request and made them cross. Three weeks later, James no longer wanted the trainers but was busy saving towards a computer game that he now wanted much more.

Speech management

Perhaps the most difficult aspect of stuttering for older children and their parents is its unpredictability, which can leave people feeling helpless and powerless. The goal of speech management strategies is to give the child a sense of competence in managing the stuttering more effectively, and of taking charge of the problem rather than feeling vulnerable or helpless. This is achieved by becoming the expert in their stuttering, learning about what it is, how it works and experimenting with ways of making speaking easier and more manageable.

Knowledge about the mechanics of speech production is often an important precursor to the analysis of the individual characteristics of the stuttering. Anatomical models, charts and line drawings can illustrate the complexity of the mechanism as well as the relationship between breathing, the voice box and the articulators. Exploring the way sounds are made and distinguished usually intrigues, whereas experimenting with changes in rate, intonation and voice quality demonstrates that voluntary control is possible. This increased proprioceptive awareness is a recurring theme as therapy progresses.

Identification and desensitization

In Van Riper's (1973) well-respected approach to stuttering therapy, the identification and desensitization strategies are based on the concept that a large part of the problem is the speaker's struggle to avoid, disguise or minimize the core moments of stuttering. Whether the goal in therapy is to use techniques for shaping fluency or to modify moments of stuttering, it is important to develop a greater understanding of what is mechanically different in stuttered speech compared with normal speech production. Increased awareness and insight into the overt characteristics lead to greater objectivity and 'ownership', both of which are fundamental to behavioural change.

The following is a brief overview of some of the steps used for desensitization:

- tallying, analysing and describing stuttering from videotapes of other people is often a less threatening starting place
- personal characteristics can be identified using a mirror or videotape
- agreed labels for individual characteristics are important
- voluntary or fake stuttering in a variety of situations is a valuable technique.

After each task the child learns to reflect on his or her achievements, both on the surface level of the task and in terms of cognitive and affective components. One 14-year-old, when asked to reflect on which component of the therapy process had been particularly helpful, commented that voluntary stuttering had been the key to reducing the fear of stuttering. For another child it was learning to say what she meant despite the stuttering and to resist the temptation to avoid words and talk 'rubbish'.

Taking this further, children are encouraged to experiment with their own stuttering but also to teach therapists and parents how to do it 'properly'. The children often become demanding teachers, enjoying the role of expert in stuttering, taking their 'pupils' out on stuttering assignments to observe people's reactions. Parents' experience of voluntary stuttering or a slowed rate ensures that they gain insight into the complexity of the mechanism and the effort that behavioural change requires. In terms of their own cognitive cycles, many parents benefit from discovering how their behavioural responses to their child's stuttering can positively influence his or her ability to deal with the problem calmly and objectively.

Management strategies

Different management strategies are discussed, evaluated and practised with each child, most importantly using the knowledge and skills he or she already brings to the clinic. The aim is to help children to choose techniques and goals for themselves. Although fluency-shaping methods often imply that the entire verbal output is manipulated, it is clear that children are more likely to use a technique that is 'normal sounding' and may not want to use it throughout their talking. The following techniques may be used singly or in combination:

• rate control
• judicious pausing or phrasing
• easy onsets to vowels
• soft contacts for consonants
• managing airflow.

These techniques can be used for modifying the stuttering moment before, during or after the block (Van Riper, 1973). These techniques (their tools) are practised to a high level of competence to ensure that the children are able to employ them confidently within the clinic.

Personal choice is emphasized as the children select the particular techniques that are acceptable, functional and user-friendly, and each child establishes a level of control that is 'good enough'. The strategies that children identify for themselves, especially if they are already in their repertoire, are easier to establish in the long term than those that have to be taught, ensuring that they can be generalized effectively. Total fluency control is never the target.

The role of the therapist is to model, guide and offer feedback while facilitating the graded steps for practising and reviewing progress. In a group therapy setting, role-play, speaking circles, presentations and debates are useful ways of practising new skills and developing confidence.

Some children with more severe stuttering benefit from a highly structured way of learning modification strategies, starting with linguistically simple units and building up to longer and more complex tasks as their fluency management skills increase. Occasionally, the use of delayed auditory feedback will help those children with severe stuttering to experience the proprioceptive and kinaesthetic feedback of speech control, which then forms the basis of a structured programme as described above.

Transfer

Transferring these skills into the real world should start immediately with homework tasks related to clinic-based practice. Children are also encouraged to practise fake stuttering, easy stuttering and speech management techniques in a hierarchy of speaking situations beyond the clinic.

There are many texts which describe in more detail the contents and steps of speech management programmes (Van Riper, 1973; Riley and Riley, 1984; Guitar, 1998; Turnbull and Stewart, 1999; Conture, 2001; Manning, 2001; Gregory, 2003).

Parents' role

Parents also need to know about stuttering management techniques and the constructive role they have in supporting their child's progress at home. As parents become aware of their child's increasing ability to take ownership of the stutter, to communicate more confidently and effectively, to problem-solve and negotiate, they too can begin to relax and 'let go' of the responsibility – reinforcing the growth of independence.

Therapists' role

Clients should never be asked to do something that the therapist would be unwilling to do. Therapists should always lead the way in behavioural experiments, for example stuttering openly in a shop while the child watches for reactions, or using speech management strategies during a telephone assignment. Student therapists can have a very supportive role in 'normalizing' fears about public speaking or presenting in front of video cameras.

Resources

Video feedback plays a substantial role in the therapeutic endeavour. Initially, it can seem threatening and unnecessarily confrontational, but introduced thoughtfully as a positive tool, videotaping makes therapy make sense. It offers clients targets to work on, positive reinforcement for the changes that are taking place and actual 'proof' of progress.

A range of reading materials, sequential picture stories, social skills activities, topics for negotiations, games and activities – the bread and butter of any speech and language therapy clinic – are used throughout therapy. Homework tasks are always an integral part of the process of transferring the experience of therapy into real-world experiments. The homework tasks are always based around the topics or exercises covered in the session and are jointly constructed by the therapist and individual members of the family.

The involvement of the family or school is an essential component of successful therapy. Depending on the individual circumstances, sessions will be spent with family members in the clinic and visits made to the school.

Clinical pathways

The Michael Palin Centre for Stammering Children provides an assessment and therapy service to children, teenagers and adults who stammer. The assessment procedures summarized earlier are the means by which decisions are made about the components of therapy that are most relevant to each child and family, and the best context for delivering that therapy.

Therapy at the Centre may be offered through individual sessions and weekly or intensive group sessions. Individual family sessions (where possible, *both* parents with their child) comprise most of our daily clinical activity. These sessions provide an opportunity for families to explore the particular issues relevant to their child. It allows them to work at their own pace and to develop knowledge and skills in managing the stuttering.

The number of sessions per family varies depending on the age and stage of the problem; however, for primary or elementary school children, 7–10 hours of therapy would be the usual pattern. Approximately two-thirds of these will have an additional six sessions of direct speech management. For many families this level of intervention is sufficient.

Some families then benefit from opportunities to continue to practise and consolidate the skills they have learnt, in a more natural social group setting. Six, two-hour parallel sessions are organized for the children and their parents. The aim and content of these sessions is flexible and built around the needs of each group. A group setting offers the chance for both children and parents to learn from and support one another as well as to share experiences and develop alternative coping strategies. For a few families whose problems are longstanding and more complex, 2-week intensive group therapy courses for children are held twice a year with full parental participation.

Summary

The goals of therapy are increased confidence and effectiveness in communicating. The process of achieving these goals is through three distinct, but inter-related components: the cognitive aspects, speech management options and social communication skills.

Children may attend individual sessions, group sessions or a combination. The development of self-help skills is emphasized throughout therapy, with a view to managing relapse more successfully. To this end, it is explicitly predicted that every individual will encounter periods when they feel that things are not going well. Each family completes an action plan that consists of a review of the key aspects of therapy that have been particularly helpful and strategies to use when difficulties are encountered. As well as contributing to a sense of self-efficacy, this exercise underlines the personal responsibility involved for each client in managing stuttering in the future. The ball is in their court!

Research programme

An ongoing treatment effectiveness research programme has been developed and conducted at the Centre over recent years. Quantitative and qualitative methodologies complement each other, offering valuable contributions to our understanding of the nature of stuttering and the effectiveness of therapy. The key issue is to select the method that most appropriately addresses the question being asked. It is this philosophy which is reflected in the broad nature of research studies that have been conducted at the Centre.

Measuring outcome

Measurement of change, as with measurement of stuttering, needs to be multidimensional, particularly when stuttering is persistent. Frequency of stutters, represented as a percentage of syllables stuttered (%SS), the number of syllables spoken per minute (SPM) and optimal speech naturalness, are frequently cited in the literature as evidence of success in therapy. However, it is suggested that these provide a one-dimensional perspective of stuttering behaviour and do not account for the variability that is particularly characteristic of stuttering. Although use of multiple measures and contexts, as recommended by Ingham and Riley (1998), partly addresses this issue, other important changes in individuals' experience of the difficulty and their ability to communicate more effectively, is not reflected. This chapter has emphasized the importance of the family's perspective, and this is reflected in the Centre's research activities. The aim is to evaluate the client's rating of change over a number of variables, not just in frequency of stuttering. However, this presents a considerable difficulty to researchers in this field because there are few assessment tools that adequately address these important issues.

Parents' ratings of outcome

In an attempt to address this dilemma, a recent study (Millard, 2002) was conducted to determine parents' views on the most important elements to consider when measuring outcome. The resulting questionnaire contained a wide range of themes that reflected the broad nature of the therapy they had received. In addition to reductions in stuttering frequency and severity, parents also considered the child's anxiety, frustration and concern about speech, confidence in speaking and turn-taking skills to be important indicators of improvement. They also rated their own level of concern and confidence in managing the stuttering effectively, along with the impact on the family as a whole, to be important outcomes of the therapy programme. The questionnaire consists of a series of visual analogue scales to be rated before and after therapy. This format allows a numerical value to be obtained before, during and after therapy so that change can be evaluated. This questionnaire is used routinely to augment fluency measures at the Centre.

Effectiveness of therapy with young children

Parent–child interaction therapy, a therapy programme for pre-school children who stutter, has already been empirically investigated to evaluate its effectiveness (Matthews, Williams and Pring, 1997; Millard and Nicholas, 2002; Nicholas and Millard, 2002). The aim of therapy with young children is to promote natural recovery where possible, or to significantly reduce stuttering and minimize the impact that it has on both the child and the family.

The recent multiple single-case study by Millard and Nicholas (2002) indicated that parent–child interaction therapy has been successful in reducing the dysfluency of all the children, and the long-term outcome data analysis is close to completion. A significant change was also observed in parents' ratings of stuttering severity, and their own level of concern and confidence. Parents rated their children's stutter as less severe, rated themselves as being less concerned about it and feeling more confident in their ability to manage it. As a result of the positive findings of this study, we are currently in the process of conducting a randomized controlled trial.

Chapter 7
Improving communicative functioning with school-aged children who stutter

KENNETH J LOGAN

Introduction

Speech production can be a frustrating – even humiliating – activity for children who stutter. This chapter discusses the primary activities used at the University of Florida Speech and Hearing Clinic (UFSHC) for helping elementary school-aged children who stutter to speak more fluently, manage speech dysfluencies more effectively, and participate more fully during daily tasks. The UFSHC is part of the Department of Communication Sciences and Disorders at the University of Florida. Like many university clinics in the United States, it serves as the initial clinical site for students who are training to become speech-language pathologists. Thus, the clinical staff has two general missions: to provide patients with effective services, and to ensure that clinicians-in-training become proficient at conducting a range of clinical procedures.

Some school-aged children on our caseload never have participated in fluency therapy before coming to UFSHC. More often, however, the children we serve have received fluency therapy elsewhere, but have realized only minimal or temporary benefit from it. Clinicians at UFSHC usually see children individually, particularly during the early stages of treatment. Parents routinely participate in therapy activities, both in the clinic and at home. When caseload demographics and scheduling allow, clinicians conduct some group activities in which children who stutter interact with one another. Such activities are useful in helping children who stutter to gain a more accurate perspective on their communication challenges.

The treatment approach at UFSHC is organized around several training modules, each of which addresses a particular aspect of communication-related functioning. The treatment techniques that clinicians use are intended to help children who stutter to alter speech production in ways that result in fluent speech and, if that does not happen, to manage the expectation or experience of dysfluent speech in ways that are consistent with the notions of communicating competently and participating fully.

The intervention strategies that we describe are derived from the scholarly efforts of numerous past and present clinicians and researchers. This chapter aims to extend the existing literature by: linking intervention strategies to a conceptual framework that motivates treatment, describing some specific instructional methods we use when teaching children, and describing some of the methods we use for assessing treatment outcomes. In doing so, we hope to provide inexperienced clinicians with a sense of how to conduct fluency intervention with school-aged children who stutter and seasoned clinicians with an opportunity to reconsider their treatment goals and methods.

A conceptual framework for treatment

An overview of the ICF

In recent years, we have used the World Health Organization's *International Classification of Functioning, Disability, and Health* (ICF) (WHO, 2001) as a conceptual framework for treating children who stutter. As its name implies, the ICF is a classification system designed to 'provide a scientific basis for understanding and studying health and health-related states, outcomes, and determinants' (WHO, 2001, p. 6). Several authors have discussed the utility of this and similar frameworks in developing intervention programs for people with communication disorders (Yaruss, 1998b; Eadie, 2003). Our work in this chapter is an extension of their efforts.

The ICF does not specifically address etiologic factors associated with stuttering or any other health condition. Nonetheless, the system is consistent with many theoretical models of stuttering, particularly those that incorporate both intrinsic and extrinsic factors to account for a speaker's fluency (Smith and Kelly, 1997). Given its flexibility and scope, we feel the ICF provides a cogent framework for organizing discussions related to the treatment of people who stutter. This chapter will focus on the use of the ICF as a clinical tool for identifying children's treatment needs, designing treatment plans that address those needs, and evaluating treatment outcomes.

The WHO (2001) structural overview of the ICF is shown in Figure 7.1. As can be seen, information on the ICF is organized into two main parts. The first concerns information pertaining to functioning and disability and the second concerns information pertaining to contextual factors. The functioning and disability part of the ICF features two components: one that deals with body functions and structures, and another that deals with activities and participation. Similarly, the contextual factors part features two components: one that deals with environmental factors and another that deals with personal factors. It is argued that health professionals must consider each of these components when assessing and treating people with disabilities, as they all contribute to an individual's functioning (WHO, 2001).

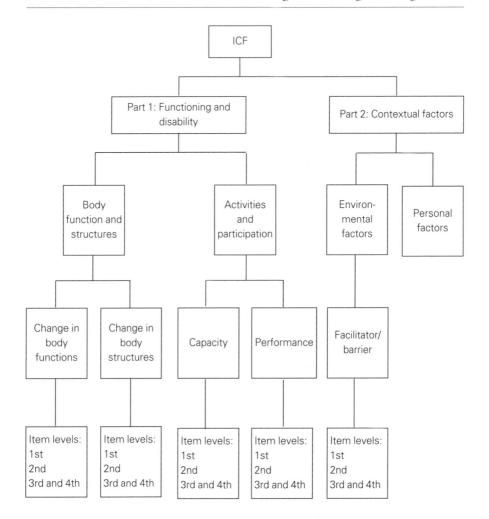

Figure 7.1 Structure of the ICF, from the *International Classification of Functioning, Disability and Health: Short Version* (WHO, 2001, p. 193). (Copyright 2001, WHO. Reprinted with permission.)

Stuttering as an impairment in body function

As its name suggests, the body functions component of the ICF deals with physiological functions of body systems. The ICF lists eight broad domains (not shown in Figure 7.1) under body functions. The WHO (2001, p. 3) defines a domain as 'a practical and meaningful set of related physiological functions, anatomical structures, actions, tasks, or areas of life'. Examples of domains that pertain to body functions include 'Voice and Speech Functions' and 'Mental Functions'. The ICF lists numerous more specific categories under each of the domains. For example, 'Fluency and Rhythm Functions' is listed under the 'Voice and Speech Functions' domain. Other domains are listed under the other ICF components.*

In treatment, healthcare professionals attempt to identify an individual's areas of functioning and impairment through systematic, comprehensive assessment. Within the ICF, impairment is defined as 'a (significant) loss or abnormality in body structure or function' (WHO, 2001, p. 190). Stuttering is classified as an impairment in body function – more specifically, an impairment in the 'fluency and rhythm of speech functions' (WHO, 2001).

Contextual effects

Recall that 'Contextual Factors' comprises the second major part of the ICF. 'Contextual Factors' also contains two components: one that deals with environmental factors and one that deals with personal factors. Environmental factors are defined as 'the physical, social and attitudinal environment in which people live and conduct their lives' (WHO, 2001, p. 218). The ICF lists five broad domains under the 'Environmental Factors' component. Those with particular relevance to stuttering include: 'Support and Relationships', 'Attitudes', and 'Services, Systems, and Policies'. Numerous more specific categories are listed under each of the domains within the 'Environmental Factors' component. For example, 'Individual Attitudes of Immediate Family Members' and 'Individual Attitudes of People in Positions of Authority' are listed under the heading of 'Attitudes'.

Because environmental factors are assumed to affect all components of an individual's functioning (WHO, 2001), clinicians attempt to determine the extent to which various environmental domains facilitate or hinder an individual's functioning. Our treatment plans often target environmental factors that appear to hinder an individual's willingness to speak or an individual's ability to speak fluently. Associated activities are intended to help key conversational partners interact with children who stutter in ways that facilitate speech fluency and participation during treatment activities and everyday tasks.

'Personal Factors' constitutes the second component of the 'Contextual Factors' part of the ICF. 'Personal Factors' encompass 'the particular background of an individual's life and living and comprise features that are not part of a health condition or health states' (WHO, 2001, p. 23). Included here are factors such as gender, race, age, upbringing, habits, and coping styles. Some personal factors have large social and cultural variance. For this

---

*The 'Body Structures' component deals with anatomical parts of the body. As with 'Body Functions', the ICF lists eight domains under the 'Body Structures' component, including 'Structures Involved in Voice and Speech' and 'Structures of the Nervous System'. Although recent research with adults has identified neuroanatomical differences between nonstuttering speakers and some adults who stutter (Foundas et al., 2001), speech-related body structures are not specifically targeted for change during treatment. Thus, we will not discuss this ICF component further.

reason, they are not presently classified in the ICF (*see* Figure 7.1). Nonetheless, because personal factors also are thought to affect all components of an individual's functioning, it is important for clinicians to consider them in treatment (WHO, 2001).

School-aged children differ markedly in their ability to conceptualize, analyze, and monitor speech production and speech fluency (Conture, 2001). Thus, clinicians are careful to present instructional activities in ways that account for individual differences. School-aged children also differ markedly in how they cope with or react to stuttering. Many school-aged children who stutter are aware of their fluency impairment (Ezrati-Vinacour, Platzky and Yairi, 2001). Such children can potentially develop strategies for coping with stuttering, and some coping strategies clearly are more productive than others. With some children who stutter, unproductive coping strategies may hinder communicative functioning to a greater extent than the fluency impairment itself (Manning, 2001). For this reason, many clinicians (Guitar, 1998; Yaruss, 1998a; Neilson, 1999; Manning, 2001) regard coping strategies or, more broadly, reactions to stuttering as a potentially important treatment variable.

Activities and participation

Some children show dissociation between the severity of fluency impairment they present and the extent to which they participate in daily activities (Yaruss, 1998a). Others show considerable variation in functioning across communicative contexts (Yaruss, 1997). Hence, our treatment plans also routinely address the daily tasks and activities that children perform. The ICF lists nine domains under the 'Activities and Participation' component. These pertain to major life tasks and actions, such as 'Communication', 'Interpersonal Interactions and Relationships', 'Community, Social, and Civic Life', and 'Learning and Applying Knowledge'. As with the other components, the ICF lists a number of more specific categories under each of the domains within the 'Activities and Participation' component. By carefully considering these domains and their many sub-categories, clinicians can thoroughly describe the various limitations and restrictions children exhibit. Such information is useful when setting treatment goals and assessing treatment outcomes.

Consistent with the ICF, clinicians attempt to determine children's capacity and performance for executing particular tasks or actions. The construct of 'Capacity' refers to 'the highest probable level of functioning that a person may reach in a domain in the Activities and Participation list at a given moment' (WHO, 2001, p. 192). Assessments of capacity occur in standard environments (such as an in-clinic conversation with the clinician). Thus, they reflect the environmentally adjusted ability of an individual. Alternatively, the construct of 'Performance' refers to what children do in their daily environment.

With the ICF, capacity and performance are considered to determine the presence and extent of activity limitations (that is, difficulties an individual may have in executing activities) and participation restrictions (that is, problems an individual may experience in involvement in life activities). It is well known that 'in-clinic fluency' (capacity) is sometimes a poor predictor of 'out-of-clinic fluency' (performance) for children who stutter. Accordingly, clinicians typically address both capacity and performance when designing treatment programs or assessing treatment outcomes.

Interactions and outcomes

An individual's overall functioning can be understood as the product of complex interactions among one's body structures and functions, levels of activity and participation, and environmental and personal factors. Each of the four primary components in the model can affect the other components (WHO, 2001). With stuttering, changes in communicative functioning often are driven by changes in speech fluency. This is not always the case, however. For example, eliminating classroom teasing (an environmental hindrance) can reduce a child's stuttering frequency (a change in body function), reduce a child's negative emotions toward communication (a change in personal factors), and increase the number of questions the child asks in class (a change in participation).

Interactions between components of the ICF are not always predictable or linear (WHO, 2001). For example, one child may present with moderately severe fluency impairment, but participate in class discussions more often than most classmates do. Another child may present with mild fluency impairment, but consistently avoid participating in classroom discussions. Yet another child may present with moderate fluency impairment, yet teachers and peers consider him a competent public speaker. Such scenarios suggest that there are many variables and a variety of perspectives for clinicians to consider when helping children who stutter improve communication functioning.

Consistent with the ICF, our overarching goal for fluency treatment is to help children who stutter eliminate or, at least, substantially reduce their communicative disability. WHO (2001, p. 190) uses the term 'disability' as 'an umbrella term for impairments, activity limitations and participation restrictions' that an individual exhibits. As such, the concept is broader than that of impairment. Although we always seek to help children eliminate their fluency impairments, we do not feel that such an outcome is essential for a particular treatment program to be regarded as successful. We have seen many clients who exhibit residual stuttering after treatment and who simultaneously report satisfaction with their level of communicative functioning in daily activities. This view is consistent with recent research examining the characteristics of speakers who are described as being 'recovered' from stuttering (Anderson and Felsenfeld, 2003).

An overview of the treatment approach

In Table 7.1, we outline the basic form of our intervention approach. As can be seen, the approach features three basic parts: assessing treatment needs, treating identified needs, and re-assessing treatment needs. We overlay the ICF framework upon these three parts to generate knowledge and skill objectives that clinicians address, as necessary, with children.

Table 7.1 Outline of intervention components

Assessing treatment needs
Determine the child's current level of functioning:
    assess body functions and structures to determine extent of impairment
    assess capacity to perform basic communicative activities
    assess performance during daily activities
Identify contextual factors that facilitate or hinder functioning:
    assess effects of environmental factors
    assess effects of personal factors

Treating identified needs
Implement strategies, as necessary, to improve communicative functioning:
    knowledge and skills to reduce the extent of impairment
    knowledge and skills to reduce activity limitations and participation restrictions
Implement strategies, as necessary, to reduce or eliminate hindrances to functioning:
    knowledge and skills to reduce environmental factors that hinder fluency
    knowledge and skills to reduce personal factors that hinder fluency

Reassessing treatment needs
Assess the extent to which the child's functioning and communicative context change:
    changes in fluency impairment
    changes in capacity to conduct communication activities
    changes in performance and participation during daily activities
    changes in environmental and personal context

Assessing treatment needs

Given the considerable variability that 7 to 12 year olds present, clinicians may have difficulty determining which goals and objectives to address with a child and which methods to use when addressing them. At UFSHC, clinicians individualize treatment programs by addressing a series of organizing questions. The details of these questions and associated assessment activities are beyond the scope of the chapter. Suffice to say that the questions follow from the ICF and are consistent with the American Speech-Language-Hearing Association's (ASHA, 1995) assessment guidelines. Accordingly, they lead to treatment plans that are adequate in breadth, focused on functional outcomes, and considerate of children's and others' perspectives. When posed over time, the questions also provide a framework for revising the content and focus of the treatment plan.

Treating identified needs

The learning activities associated with the intervention strategies outlined in Table 7.1 are designed to result in the attainment of specific short-term goals (such as reducing a child's speech rate). In turn, the short-term goals are intended to help children who stutter realize broader outcomes related to functioning and disability. Given the many differences that 7 to 12 year olds present, clinicians do not follow a rigid treatment protocol. In short, the composition of a child's treatment plan depends upon:

- the nature and extent of his or her disability
- the extent to which the clinician feels a particular concept or skill is necessary for addressing that disability
- the extent to which the child appears able to master a particular concept or skill.

An intervention program for one child might incorporate all four of the knowledge and skill areas listed under 'Treating identified needs' in Table 7.1, whereas an intervention program for another child might be based upon only two or three of these areas. Similarly, two children might address the same treatment objective, with one developing cursory knowledge or skill in the area and the other developing extensive knowledge or skill in the area.

Generally, clinicians first seek to improve children's capacity to communicate. To do this, clinicians usually focus upon teaching children to alter, or at least monitor, aspects of speech production through one or more of the so-called 'fluency-shaping' techniques. These techniques are effective at improving speech fluency in children and adults who stutter (Boberg and Kully, 1994; Ryan and Van Kirk Ryan, 1995; Craig et al, 1996; Onslow et al, 1996).

Clinicians also may help children and significant others develop their knowledge of basic speech production processes and stuttering. With such knowledge, these individuals can participate in intervention activities more fully. Clinicians also typically incorporate treatment activities to manage and help others manage environmental factors that affect communicative functioning. In our experience, such activities are particularly important when children establish fluency management skills and when children generalize in-clinic skills to other settings.

Finally, clinicians incorporate treatment activities that address personal factors (for example, children's reactions to and means for coping with stuttering) when they significantly hinder children's communicative functioning. Through these knowledge and skill activities most children who stutter realize significant improvement in their capacity to communicate (that is, talking during in-clinic activities with clinicians). After children have established these fundamental concepts and skills, they then are poised to tackle the primary goal: improving communicative performance and participation during daily activities.

General instructional principles

Clinicians organize treatment activities around instructional principles described by Hunter (1994). These include practises such as telling children the objective and relevance of learning activities, modeling desired behaviors, providing varied and relevant instructional input, and identifying component behaviors for skills and concepts.

Clinicians conduct guided practise activities in conjunction with each of the primary learning objectives. During guided practise, clinicians control contextual factors that can potentially hinder children's functioning. These include response length, linguistic complexity, speech rate, topic familiarity, audience size, and the number and nature of clinician-based cues provided (Ryan, 1974; Ingham, 1999; Kully and Langevin, 1999).

During guided practise, clinicians provide regular and specific verbal, written, or visual feedback to children about their performance. Children regularly self-assess performance as well. Clinicians conclude guided practise activities by summarizing or asking children to summarize key concepts. Accordingly, summary statements are another way to verify children's understanding of a concept or skill. Initially, most guided practise activities are clinician directed and conducted within the clinic. As treatment progresses, guided practise activities occur elsewhere and are increasingly parent and child directed.

After children perform skills reliably in guided practise settings, clinicians create opportunities for them to employ skills independently. Independent practise is central to the notion of generalization, and clinicians use it at all stages of intervention. Usually, independent practise activities progress from least to most difficult; however, children sometimes address challenging activities early in the generalization process when such activities have personal importance.

Treatment modules

Clinicians organize treatment activities around six semi-autonomous treatment modules, each of which is derived from the ICF and follows from the treatment areas listed in 'Treating identified needs' in Table 7.1. As noted, not all modules are used with all children who stutter, and if a particular module is used, not all knowledge and skills objectives are necessarily addressed. In the sections below, we discuss the rationale, concepts and skills, primary instructional activities, and primary training obstacles associated with the modules.

Module 1: developing children's speech functioning

Overview and rationale

The neurophysiological processes that result in the behaviors known as 'stuttering' are not precisely understood. Studies using electro-physiological and functional neuroimaging techniques suggest involvement of the motor, pre-motor, and auditory-language systems in the disorder (De Nil and Kroll, 2001; Ingham, 2001). On a more superficial level, stuttering – or at least many of the dysfluencies commonly associated with stuttering – can be conceptualized as a disruption in the ability to initiate or co-articulate the movements associated with speech segments (Wingate, 1988). This disruption can occur within or between syllable boundaries. Studies of speech errors suggest that syllables consist of more fundamental units (Jaeger, 1992). The two primary constituents within a syllable are the *onset* and the *rime*, and the rime is further divisible into the *peak* and the *coda* (Bernhardt and Stemberger, 2000). These entities serve as placeholders for phonemes within syllables. The peak slot typically serves as a placeholder for vowels, whereas the onset slot serves as a placeholder for consonants preceding the peak and the coda slot serves the same function for consonants following the peak. In this view, when a child says 'sss- sss- sat' instead of 'sat', he or she is not 'having trouble saying /s/', *per se*. Rather, the child exhibits difficulty moving from the onset to the rime of the syllable. A central goal in fluency intervention, then, is to help children initiate and link syllable constituents smoothly and consistently.

Many techniques have been devised to help people who stutter speak more fluently. These techniques are more similar than different, however, as most require speakers to alter the timing and/or tension of the respiratory, laryngeal, or articulatory musculature when talking (Conture, 2001; De Nil and Kroll, 2001). The process through which these techniques enhance fluency is poorly understood. Broadly, it appears that their use either normalizes or circumvents the neurophysiological processes that underlie stuttered speech (Boberg et al., 1983). The fluency management techniques we describe in this section form the core of most children's intervention programs. Clinicians can teach these techniques to children in several ways: some involving detailed direct instruction and others involving little or no direct instruction.

Knowledge and skills

In Table 7.2, we present an overview of the techniques that clinicians commonly use to help children reduce the expectation or experience of stuttering. Clinicians usually introduce one or more of these techniques during the initial treatment sessions. Each of the techniques requires speakers to deliberately alter speech timing. Consequently, speakers often report that it feels effortful or unnatural to use the techniques, especially when they are first learning them (Perkins, 1992; Finn and Ingham, 1994; Logan et al., 2002).

Table 7.2 Techniques to help children who stutter to improve speech functioning

Technique	Description
Prolonged speech (PS)	Child reduces the rate of articulation by a specified amount across all syllables
Slow, gentle onset (SGO)	For syllables beginning with consonants: child produces the transition between syllable onset and rime at a reduced articulation rate and with 'light' articulatory contact For syllables beginning with vowels: child produces the syllable peak at reduced articulation rate and with 'light' articulatory contact
Slow, smooth transition (SST)	Child reduces rate of articulation to produce slow, deliberate transitions between syllable boundaries
Pausing	Child decreases speech rate by increasing the frequency and duration of pauses within utterances or the duration of pauses when initiating conversational turns
Slow speech	Child reduces articulation rate and increases frequency and duration of pauses, simultaneously

Four of the five techniques listed in Table 7.2 directly involve reducing articulation rate, that is, the rate at which speakers produce speech sounds. The primary difference among the prolonged speech (PS), slow, gentle onset (SGO), and slow, smooth transition (SST) techniques involves when speakers reduce articulation rate. With PS, speakers reduce the articulation rate of every sound within every syllable. With SGO, speakers reduce the articulation rate of syllables located at the beginning of an utterance or immediately following a pause within an utterance. Speakers then produce subsequent syllables at or near their customary articulation rate. With SST, speakers reduce the rate of articulation for syllable constituents that are located at syllable or word boundaries (for example, 'fun movie' → 'funnmmovie') while blending the syllables or words in a seamless way. With SGO and SST, some syllables are produced slowly and others are not. Thus, these techniques are viewed as special cases of prolonged speech.

As with others' protocols (e.g. Ryan 1974; Onslow, 1996), there is some variation in how clinicians present these skills to children. Older children, especially those with moderate or severe stuttering, typically learn three rate-based skills: PS, SGO, and SST. Clinicians may teach a fourth skill, pausing, in some cases as well (*see below*). Younger children typically learn only the 'slow speech' technique, which also features articulation rate reduction and pausing alterations – minus the relatively comprehensive, detailed instruction associated with PS, SGO, SST, and Pausing. Older children routinely master the first four skills listed in Table 7.2 in 7–14 one-hour treatment sessions. At that point, they usually are able to use the techniques to produce highly fluent speech during semi-structured one-on-one conversations in clinic. Additional sessions are needed, of course, to extend that mastery to out-of-clinic contexts. Young children routinely master 'slow speech' in 5–10 sessions, at which point they too typically can communicate proficiently during structured in-clinic activities. As with older children, additional sessions are needed to generalize that mastery to other settings.

Slow, gentle onset: instructional approach and common challenges

Clinicians typically introduce children to the notion of articulation rate reduction through the SGO technique. With some children, stutter-like dysfluencies are restricted almost entirely to utterance-initial contexts (Logan and Conture, 1995). Thus, such children may find that they can rely on SGO as their primary means of improving fluency.

When teaching SGO, clinicians typically begin with isolated vowels or monosyllable words beginning with vowels. After modeling the technique and explaining basic properties of phonation, clinicians encourage children to initiate target sounds or words in a slightly breathy, prolonged (about 1 s) manner. If children have difficulty doing this, clinicians may ask them to 'hold' the vowel sound by stopping airflow at the glottis and gradually relaxing the vocal folds to initiate phonation. Negative practise (that is, purposefully contrasting tense and abrupt vocal onsets with slow, gentle vocal onsets) is sometimes used to supplement these activities. After children produce SGO within V and VC syllables, they proceed to various advanced guided practise activities. We have developed mono- and bisyllabic vowel-initial word lists and lists of short phrases and sentences that begin with these words (for example, 'in the school'). Children practice SGO while reading the target utterances. After producing SGO to criteria (such as 95% accuracy for two consecutive 20-item lists), children practice using the skill in self-generated utterances during question–answer or play-based activities in which utterance length is gradually increased (Ryan, 1974).

As children master SGO on vowel-initial words, clinicians introduce mono- and bi-syllabic words that begin with continuant and nasal consonants. Because these consonants involve only partial obstruction of the vocal tract, children rarely have difficulty prolonging them. When producing CV and CVC words, children are encouraged to move slowly from the syllable onset to the syllable rime. Clinicians introduce syllables that begin with affricate and plosive consonants last. As with vowels, children begin by 'holding' the particular consonant at its place of articulation and then gradually releasing the associated musculature until frication is heard. Children then are instructed to prolong the frication for a specified duration (for example, 1 s) before proceeding to the vowel (for example, 'top' → 'tttooop'). Clinicians then ask children to produce SGO during these words beginning from a neutral articulatory posture.

When children have mastered SGO with vowel- and consonant-initial words at a rate of about 1 syllable per second (SPS), articulation rate is increased to about 2 SPS, and finally to an articulation rate described as a 'slight stretch'. Guided practise, similar to that described for vowel-initial words, is then implemented to further establish SGO at the word, phrase and sentence levels during reading and, later, spontaneously formulated speech.

Problems that may arise when children are learning to produce SGO include:

- failing to prolong speech for the specified length of time
- prolonging only the vowel within a syllable (for example, saying 'noooot' instead of 'nnnooot')
- producing vowel-initial words with excessive breathiness
- relaxing speech muscles so that speech is unintelligible

Most children readily correct these problems when given further instruction and practise.

Slow, smooth transition: instructional approach and common challenges

In contrast to SGO, the SST technique involves making timing and tension adjustments when proceeding from the rime of one syllable to the onset of another (for example, 'tell me' → 'teeelllmmme'). Accordingly, SST is useful for reducing fluency disruption on non-initial syllables within words or utterances. Children who have mastered SGO usually find it easy to produce syllable transitions in this manner.

Beginning guided practise activities are organized around word pairs with 'same sound' transitions (such as 'phone number', 'your room') and then proceed to 'different sound' transitions (for example, 'dish soap', 'brown goat'). After children develop proficiency with word pairs in isolation, they practise them within phrases and sentences (for example, 'Where is the brown wire?' → 'Where is the broowwnnwwiire?'). Initially, clinicians ask children to prolong transitions in an exaggerated way (for example, ~2 seconds per word pair). As children master that rate, articulation rate is increased incrementally to what clinicians describe as a 'slight stretch'. Because clinicians usually introduce SST after SGO, they then may ask children to use both techniques simultaneously. This develops children's ability to alter articulation rate at various points within an utterance.

When learning to produce SST children may fail to reduce articulation rate uniformly across phones at the syllable boundary or pause between syllable boundaries. Most children correct these problems readily when given additional instruction and practise.

Prolonged speech: instructional approach and common challenges

As noted above, PS requires speakers to make temporal adjustments across many syllables. Children who have mastered SGO and SST usually find it fairly easy to master PS. Clinicians often compare PS to slow-motion video clips of sporting activities to emphasize the notion that all movements are produced at a uniform rate.

With PS, clinicians typically target an initial articulation rate of 1 SPS or 60 syllables per minute (SPM). If children stutter often at that rate, which they rarely do, a slower rate is targeted (for example, 30 SPM). Such rates are comparable to those described by others (Shames and Florance, 1980).

Clinicians model PS while saying sentences and reading paragraphs, reminding children of the purpose behind the skill and that the very slow rates will not be used in daily activities. A variety of guided practise activities are used to help children develop proficiency with PS. Some clinicians (Shames and Florance, 1980; Ryan and Van Kirk Ryan, 1995) use delayed auditory feedback (DAF) to establish PS. Clinicians at UFSHC typically use a rather 'low-tech' approach, however. For instance, clinicians and children often produce PS in unison while reading short sentences or paragraphs. Clinicians then may record themselves reading at a desired rate on audiotape before a session. During the session, children attempt to match this rate by reading in unison with the audiotape playback. After mastering that skill, children then talk about other topics while using the taped playback of the clinician's voice as a rate reference. Use of the rate reference is faded gradually as children's competence increases. If necessary, a variety of discrimination and negative practise activities are used to further develop children's ability to prolong speech and identify inappropriate rates.

Some children speak in monotone fashion and others in a 'sing-song' fashion when using PS. In such cases, clinicians provide children with feedback about their speech naturalness (Finn and Ingham, 1994). Listeners tend to regard rate-controlled speech as sounding less natural than spontaneously produced speech (Martin and Haroldson, 1992); thus, clinicians address speech naturalness even in the absence of marked intonational distortion.

Clinicians increase the difficulty of guided practise activities by gradually increasing articulation rate and by manipulating contextual variables that affect an individual's communicative functioning (such as audience size or amount of material spoken). Guided practise activities are conducted until children can reliably produce the targeted rate for roughly 15-minute intervals with little or no stuttering. Speaking activities include short (two- to three-minute) monologues as well as conversations and discussions with clinicians and parents. When children have demonstrated the ability to speak at slower rates for the targeted time intervals, they then are instructed to use a 'slightly slow' rate (and natural sounding speech) during in-clinic monologues and conversations.

Children may exhibit the following problems when learning PS:

- speaking markedly slower or faster than the target rate
- prolonging vowels, but not consonants

- pausing after each word
- using monotone or 'sing-song' intonation.

Most children correct these problems readily when given additional instruction and practise.

Pausing: instructional approach and common challenges

In our experience, pause alterations generally have a less dramatic impact upon children's fluency than PS, SGO, or SST. Nonetheless, the technique can be useful for some children, especially when used in conjunction with the rate-based techniques described above. Because pauses divide utterances into relatively short units, the technique offers a tool for controlling utterance length during connected discourse. As speakers increase the frequency and duration of pauses, they also tend to reduce articulation rate (Logan et al., 2002). Thus, pause alterations offer an indirect way to address articulation rate with children who are not enthusiastic about directly manipulating rate through PS.

Instructional activities for pausing are straightforward. Clinicians first ask children to identify pauses in others' speech. Clinicians then model lengthened pauses by placing slashes at major and minor syntactic boundaries in printed text and reading the passages aloud with about 1 s pauses at each slash. Children then participate in guided practise activities, first with reading and later with monologue and conversation, with and without cues to pause. Older children, especially those who report that they are sensitive to conversational time pressure, also may learn to lengthen turn-switching pauses through activities similar to those described for intra-utterance pauses. Later, children practise the skill during conversations with clinicians and parents and role-playing situations in which clinicians or parents interrupt frequently.

Slow speech: instructional approach and common challenges

Like other clinicians (Zebrowski and Kelly, 2002), we do not employ detailed rate management instruction with all children. The slow speech technique is essentially an amalgamation of the PS and pausing strategies described above. It is similar (perhaps identical) to rate-based strategies described by Ryan (1974) and Zebrowski and Kelly (2002). Clinicians usually implement slow speech with younger children (roughly, those aged less than nine years) or children who have difficulty processing the instructional details associated with SGO, SST and PS. Because slow speech incorporates elements of the other four treatment techniques, clinicians usually introduce it in isolation.

To establish slow speech, clinicians first provide children with a brief description of the technique and its purpose. Clinicians inform children that speakers can slow speech by pausing more often, by pausing longer, or by 'stretching' speech sounds. Clinicians then model these possibilities, at a rate roughly 15% slower than their customary rate. Children are directed to use a similar speech rate at first, but eventually settle upon a speech rate that sounds natural, yet is slow enough to afford a satisfactory level of speech fluency (for example, fewer than 3 stutter-like dysfluencies per 100 syllables).

Guided practise activities progress from sentence imitation to unison and solo reading to spontaneously formulated speech at the word, phrase, sentence and/or narrative levels. Eventually, children participate in 'controlled conversations' during which clinicians attempt to modulate the length of children's speaking turns by mixing close-ended requests with open-ended requests. Eventually, children practise producing slow speech in the presence of environmental factors that typically hinder speech fluency.

Module 2: developing children's knowledge base

Overview and rationale

Most children have a limited understanding of speech and communication. This can result in miscommunication between clinicians and children, and lead children to develop thoughts, feelings or coping behaviors that hinder communicative functioning. Accordingly, many of our intervention plans include activities designed to develop children's background knowledge of speech production or stuttering. Such concepts usually are addressed both at a personal level (that is, children's knowledge of what *they* do) and on a general level (that is, children's knowledge of what *other people* do). Clinicians conduct these activities in parallel with activities from other modules. For children who feel embarrassed or ashamed of their stuttering, clinicians first focus on general knowledge issues, and later move toward personal knowledge issues, as children generally are more willing to discuss others' difficulties and limitations than they are their own.

Basic concepts and skills

Concepts and skills that clinicians can address as part of this module are listed in Table 7.3. The extent to which knowledge objectives are addressed depends upon the child's age, developmental level, and treatment needs. In this section, we primarily focus on learning activities related to general knowledge issues. Personal knowledge issues are discussed in subsequent sections on coping strategies.

Most children have little explicit knowledge of how speech is produced. Thus, clinicians may address some of the speech production concepts that are listed in Table 7.3. These include key concepts or terms that will be used during treatment as well as the structures and processes involved in speech production. Clinicians also typically introduce the concept of speaking rate, helping children to understand what constitutes slow, fast, and typical verbal output. Clinicians also review the distinction between 'smooth' and 'bumpy' speech. For older children, clinicians may also briefly review the various types of dysfluencies that speakers produce, as well as basic concepts pertaining to articulatory phonetics (such as place, manner, or voicing

Table 7.3 Strategies for building children's (and others') knowledge base

ICF component	Knowledge and skill areas (the child will identify, explain or describe)
Body functions	Basic speech-related terminology Structures and processes involved in speech production Dysfluency types and their relative frequencies Articulatory characteristics of consonants and vowels Common questions that people have about stuttering Basic facts and common myths about stuttering Common characteristics of stuttered speech Anatomic or physiologic correlates of speech dysfluencies Treatment approaches, treatment goals, and desired outcomes
Activities and participation	Ways stuttering limits communication Tasks that are often 'hard' or 'easy' to do Ways stuttering affects participation in daily activities Activities that are 'hard' or 'easy' to participate in
Contextual factors	How physical context affects stuttering How social or communicative context affects stuttering How others' attitudes about speech fluency affect stuttering How listeners respond to stuttering Ways that speakers react to or cope with stuttering Feelings speakers have when stuttering Thoughts speakers have when stuttering

characteristics of consonants). The latter information may be useful for children who learn PS-based techniques. With such concepts in place, clinicians can talk more precisely about treatment issues with children during subsequent sessions.

Clinicians also may have children explore the nature of stuttering and its effects upon daily functioning. As seen in Table 7.3, a range of issues potentially can be addressed. Such information helps children to develop an accurate, objective understanding of communicative disability. Such understanding is important in the development of productive attitudes and beliefs toward stuttering. Clinicians may also address issues related to: the effect of stuttering upon communicative performance and participation, environmental factors that commonly hinder speech fluency, and speech-related behaviors, feelings and thoughts that are common among people who stutter. In doing so, clinicians attempt to help children to realize that their communicative experiences and accompanying coping strategies are usually similar to those of others, and that these experiences and coping strategies are quite sensible, given the circumstances of their speech production system. Clinicians may help older children who stutter to evaluate the advantages and disadvantages of various coping strategies and reactions to stuttering. Alternative responses and coping strategies are then devised.

Instructional approaches and common challenges

Clinicians use a variety of instructional materials and activities to help children who stutter attain the concepts and skills outlined in Table 7.3. These include textbook and web-based illustrations, anatomical models, clinician-generated tables and fact sheets, as well as published materials from the Stuttering Foundation of America and the National Stuttering Association. Children (and their parents) participate in locating and reviewing instructional materials. Many of these activities take place outside the clinic. Clinicians provide children with opportunities to solidify what they have learned through making oral presentations, pamphlets, drawings, and the like. Many of these activities will not be appropriate for younger children who stutter. Children who feel ashamed or embarrassed about stuttering may be reluctant to participate in discussions about stuttering. In such cases, clinicians acknowledge children's feelings and adjust the depth or timing of learning activities as necessary. Typically, however, children address the knowledge and skills associated with this module within the first 5-10 treatment sessions, with incidental learning continuing in subsequent sessions.

Module 3: addressing personal factors

Overview and rationale

This treatment module is designed to reduce the impact that children's coping styles and reactions to stuttering have upon communicative functioning. Concepts and skills in this module are particularly relevant for children who demonstrate the capacity to speak with normal or near normal fluency upon learning skills in Module 1, yet continue to stutter at or near pre-treatment levels in generalization activities at home and at school.

Speakers' reactions to stuttering can be viewed from three related perspectives: affective, behavioral and cognitive (Gregory and Gregory, 1999). Affective issues encompass the feelings that one has about an impairment or associated activity limitations and participation restrictions. People who stutter may experience feelings such as fear, anxiety, embarrassment, and shame when speaking (Murphy and Quesal, 2002). Alternately, behavioral issues encompass the various speech-related responses that speakers produce to either ameliorate or conceal the speech impairment. The so-called secondary or associated behaviors of people who stutter have been well documented (Guitar, 1998). Finally, cognitive issues encompass the thoughts or beliefs that speakers have in response to stutter-related behaviors or listeners' reactions to stutter-related behaviors. This was discussed further in Chapter 4. Children who stutter sometimes present with distorted, inaccurate or unconstructive evaluations about their fluency impairment (Manning, 2001). The communication attitudes of children who stutter tend to be more negative than those of their non-stuttering peers, and the extent of the difference between the groups increases with the age (Vanryckeghem and Brutten, 1997).

The impact of personal factors upon fluency varies across children. Thus, the concepts and skills in this module are of primary importance for some children and of secondary importance for others. In our experience, affective, behavioral, and cognitive hindrances to speech fluency sometimes resolve as speakers improve their speech fluency through strategies such as PS, SGO, and SST. Accordingly, clinicians often refrain from addressing personal factors until children have attempted to incorporate fluency-management techniques into daily activities. (There are exceptions to this practise, however, such as when a child is distressed because of being teased about stuttering.)

Table 7.4 presents several concepts and skills relating to affective, behavioral, and cognitive factors that clinicians might address with children who stutter. When personal factors are addressed in therapy, clinicians typically treat behavioral reactions first, because they are more readily observable than feelings or thoughts.

Table 7.4 Strategies for helping children who stutter to address contextual factors that affect functioning

ICF domain	Knowledge and skill areas
Affective	Identifying one's feelings related to speech and stuttering Validating one's feelings Identifying contextual factors associated with feelings Separating feelings from behavior Managing speech-related anger, guilt, fear, anxiety, etc. Recognizing and valuing intermediate successes
Behavioral reactions	Correcting factual information about stuttering Identifying and describing current speech and speech-related behaviors Identifying or evaluating avoidance of words and situations Manipulating physical tension purposefully Using cancellation, pullout, or preparatory set Reducing word and situation avoidance Acknowledging or disclosing stuttering to others Modifying school policies that affect fluency Asserting one's feelings and needs Responding to teasing and bullying
Cognitive	Identifying or evaluating beliefs about speech and stuttering Improving knowledge of stuttering Developing accurate or constructive interpretations of speech-related events

Behavioral reactions: instructional approaches and common challenges

Children who stutter often produce residual stutter-like dysfluencies after learning the rate-based intervention strategies described in Module 1. Activities in this portion of Module 3 are primarily designed to help children minimize the impact of these residual speech dysfluencies upon communicative functioning. When addressing children's behavioral reactions to stuttering, clinicians usually begin with awareness and identification activities, in which children analyze properties of pseudo-stutters produced by the clinician and pseudo-stutters and actual stutters produced by the child. Such activities help children to generate accurate and complete descriptions of their speech behavior. Hence, children are in a better position to understand the limitations of their present coping strategies.

To help children manage residual dysfluencies, clinicians often introduce Van Riper's (1973) cancellation, pullout, and preparatory set sequence. The basic processes involved with these strategies are described in Table 7.5. Each of the techniques entails altering the timing and tension of speech articulators in similar ways to PS, SGO and SST. Because clinicians typically introduce cancellation, pullout, and preparatory set after the PS-based approaches, most children find them relatively easy to do.

Table 7.5 Strategies for modifying actual or expected speech dysfluencies	
Technique	*Description of basic skill(s)*
Cancellation	Child stops after a stuttered word, identifies behaviors incompatible with smooth, fluent speech, and then reproduces the word using slow, gentle onset (i.e. easier stuttering)
Pullout	Child transforms a stuttered syllable (e.g. sound repetition, sound prolongation) into a slow, gentle onset
Preparatory set	Child produces a slow, gentle onset when stuttering is expected at the start of an utterance; child produces a slow, smooth transition when stuttering is anticipated on an upcoming syllable within an utterance

To establish cancellation, clinicians may deliberately produce pseudo-stutters, and ask children to reproduce each of the 'stuttered' words using slow, gentle onset. Clinicians and children then chorally produce dysfluencies on selected words within typed passages and reproduce them with slow, gentle onset. Children then deliberately produce repetitions or sound prolongations on highlighted words within a typed passage and practice canceling the 'dysfluencies'. Similar activities are implemented to help children develop the ability to cancel and, eventually, pull out of actual stuttered dysfluencies. If necessary, children can practice deliberately manipulating the tension level of speech musculature in conjunction with the temporal adjustments (Guitar, 1998).

To develop preparatory sets, clinicians ask children to circle words that they expect to stutter upon before reading a printed passage. Clinicians and children then highlight the word before the anticipated word and practice making a slow, smooth transition between the two words. Children then reproduce the entire passage, 'preparing for' words they expect to stutter upon by approaching them with slow, deliberate transitions. A more advanced activity involves having children identify two or three words they expect to stutter upon prior to producing a narrative and then attempting to approach each instance of those words by reducing articulation rate during the preceding syllable and through the beginning of the expected word. In our experience, children are more variable in their ability to apply the 'preparatory set' technique. The cause for this is unclear, but may relate to differences in children's ability to anticipate speech disruptions. After stuttering modification techniques have been mastered in structured contexts, children apply them in increasingly difficult spontaneous contexts, such as one-minute narratives, with the clinician prompting either cancellation or pull out of selected dysfluencies. In follow-up activities, children again participate in one-minute narratives while attempting to cancel or pull out of a preset number of dysfluencies. (Children who have mastered PS-based techniques usually do not produce much dysfluency in this context.) Children gradually modify a progressively greater proportion of dysfluencies over increasing time periods in more and more challenging contexts. The goal is to help children who stutter to resolve residual dysfluencies promptly and in a controlled and relatively effortless manner, so as to minimize the impact they have upon communication.

All three of the techniques listed in Table 7.5 require speakers to consciously monitor speech. This requires effort, and children vary in their ability to sustain this effort. Thus, the activities described above may not be feasible for some children. Use of the cancellation and pullout techniques also requires children to be willing to stutter publicly. Some children prefer to use concealment strategies (word substitution, circumlocution) when their attempts to manage fluency via strategies such as SGO or PS are unsuccessful. For such children, additional activities that target thoughts and beliefs about stuttering and others' reactions to stuttering will need to be done as well, if the stuttering modification techniques are to be useful.

Clinicians may address other behavioral changes for some children who stutter. Some children routinely avoid words they expect to stutter upon or situations they expect to stutter in, even after learning the fluency strategies in Module 1. Clinicians typically discuss the advantages and disadvantages associated with these coping strategies and develop guided practise activities to help children respond in other ways. Clinicians also may find it necessary to help children respond to teasing or bullying. Simple acknowledgements of stuttering and assertiveness training may be helpful in this regard (Newman,

Horne, and Bartolomucci, 2000; Murphy and Quesal, 2002). If teasing or bullying persists, clinicians enlist the assistance of parents and school-based guidance counselors or speech-language pathologists.

Affective and cognitive reactions: instructional approaches and common challenges

Many of the activities that address behavioral reactions to stuttering also indirectly address issues related to feelings and beliefs about stuttering. However, with some children who stutter, particularly those who are older, clinicians may address stuttering-related affective and cognitive issues directly.* Activities are implemented to help children increase their awareness of communication- and stuttering-related beliefs and feelings, in particular those that appear to hinder communicative functioning. Clinicians identify beliefs and feelings by conversing with children about their speech experiences or by administering writing prompts tailored to elicit such information. When self-limiting beliefs are noted, they often relate to themes concerning competence, approval, fairness, problem persistence and problem pervasiveness (Seligman, 1990; Egan, 1998). Examples of self-limiting beliefs include:

- *No one* (likes, acknowledges, respects) me when I stutter.
- I must *always* communicate in a completely competent manner.
- It is *terrible* when others react to stuttering in ways that I do not like.
- Stuttering is *bad or wrong*, so I should punish myself or apologize to others because of it.
- I am the *only one* in school who has trouble speaking.
- It is *not fair* that I stutter ... I shouldn't have to deal with this.
- Other people *make me* stutter because of what they say or what they do.
- I stuttered in this situation previously; therefore, I will stutter in this situation again.

Some children interpret life events in absolute terms (*always, never, no one*), which are seldom literally true. Other children link their self-worth to speech fluency, and still others do not realize that they can react to stuttering in alternative ways. In such cases, clinicians help children to identify those beliefs that hinder their communicative performance and invite them to consider alternative interpretations of their experiences. Activities that address children's beliefs are drawn from principles of cognitive-behavioral therapy (*see* Seligman, 1990; Egan, 1998). Such approaches have been shown to be effective at altering beliefs and feelings in children with various disorders (Waters et al., 2001; Lumpkin et al., 2002).

As with behavioral reactions, clinicians seek first to validate children's present beliefs. From there, clinicians may use fictional case studies to help children to identify others' beliefs and discover how such beliefs limit

---

*Clinicians follow ethical and scope-of-practise guidelines to determine whether particular children need to be referred for formal psychological counseling.

functioning. Clinicians and children collaborate to develop more accurate or constructive interpretations of these fictional situations. This basic framework is then applied to address children's self-limiting beliefs. Clinicians also may address the feelings that children experience when speaking. The basic approach is to help children who stutter identify what they are feeling and the situations in which such feelings arise. Clinicians then seek to validate these feelings through empathetic statements that take the form of: 'You feel ____ because you ____' (Egan, 1998). One basic goal is to help children realize that one can feel a particular way (for example, anxious) and still conduct a particular activity. Analogies to sports figures are especially relevant to support this notion. As noted above, clinicians are most apt to do such activities with older children, particularly those who demonstrate the capacity for fluent communication (as defined by in-clinic performance), yet continue to stutter significantly when performing daily activities.

Module 4: Developing others' knowledge base

Overview and rationale

Clinicians also aim to help significant individuals in the child's life to improve their knowledge of speech production and stuttering. The concepts addressed in this module are similar to those outlined in Table 7.3 for children, and children and adults sometimes participate in knowledge-building activities together. Such knowledge may result in adults having: greater empathy for children who stutter, a better sense for what to expect and how to assist children during daily activities, improved ability to answer children's questions about stuttering, or greater accuracy in recognizing improvement and relapse.

Instructional approaches and common challenges

Many parents, particularly those with internet access, have conducted at least some research into stuttering before seeking our services. Their efforts provide a useful starting point for discussion. In most cases, clinicians provide parents with informational materials, including booklets and pamphlets published by the Stuttering Foundation of America and the National Stuttering Association and clinician-generated fact sheets. After parents have read the materials, they meet with clinicians to discuss central concepts or ask questions. This process is repeated several times during the beginning weeks of treatment. Typically, parents master the primary knowledge and skills associated with this module within the first five to eight treatment sessions, with incidental learning continuing in activities after that point. Accordingly, parents usually have established a general understanding of the nature and treatment of stuttering by the time clinicians ask them to conduct guided practise activities at home.

Some adults express frustration when children do not apply fluency management skills throughout each day. In most cases, these individuals do not appreciate how difficult it can be for speakers to alter or monitor speech production for extended periods of time. Accordingly, clinicians assign activities to adults (usually parents) that are the same or similar to those the children do (for example, talk/walk 10% slower than usual for 60 minutes per day; monitor the pressure with which your heel strikes the ground when walking for 60 minutes per day). Upon completing the activities, adults discuss their experiences and implications for fluency intervention.

Module 5: Addressing environmental factors

Overview and rationale

It is well known that children's speech fluency varies significantly across speaking tasks and contexts (Yaruss, 1997). In most cases, environmental factors account for at least some of this variability (WHO, 2001). For this reason, we address environmental factors at all stages of intervention. Environmental factors usually are addressed situationally (that is, during particular activities) and temporarily (i.e. until children can function successfully in a particular environment) in conjunction with activities from other modules.

When children are developing their capacity to speak more fluently, the responsibility for managing environmental demands rests principally with the clinicians, who control factors such as articulation rate, utterance length, and audience size when designing treatment activities. Later, when children are attempting to generalize fluency management skills to daily activities, parents, teachers, and children who stutter are involved in managing environmental factors, as well.

Instructional approaches and common challenges

Examples of concepts and skills that can be addressed within this module are outlined in Table 7.6. The particular concepts and skills that clinicians address with a child vary, depending upon how the environment affects communicative functioning. Some environmental factors, particularly those that relate to physical setting, are relatively easy to manage. For example, if it appears that a child stutters more when talking in the presence of background noise, practise activities can temporarily be conducted within quieter settings. People who stutter often report that they have more difficulty speaking fluently when listeners' behaviors suggest impatience, frustration, or disapproval over the speaker's attempts at communication. Therefore, clinicians seek to have parents and others eliminate any such behaviors and replace them with alternate behaviors that are likely to facilitate children's communicative functioning. In addition, clinicians

Table 7.6 Strategies for addressing environmental hindrances to fluency	
ICF domain	*Potential concepts and skills to address*
Support and relationships	Altering verbal responses to stuttered speech
	Altering non-verbal responses to stuttered speech
	Modifying conversational pace
	Modifying turn-taking behavior
	Modifying requests for information
	Modifying audience size or content
	Discussing stuttering with child
	Labeling child's speech-related behaviors or feelings
	Prompting child to retry a dysfluent utterance
	Prompting child to use fluency management skills
Natural or physical environment	Modifying physical setting
	Facilitating time changes (day or night; first or last)
	Altering background noise level
Attitudes	Monitoring or altering others' responses to failure, adversity
	Identifying or altering others' attitudes toward stuttering
	Affirming child's feelings
	Increasing others' understanding of stuttering
	Offering reassurance and encouragement
	Disclosing or modeling others' beliefs and feelings related to challenging situations
	Monitoring or altering others' distorted thinking
	Reducing or eliminating teasing or bullying

conduct role-playing with children to reduce their sensitivity to such listener reactions.

Children tend to stutter more when they participate in fast-paced conversations or when speakers interrupt one another (Yaruss, 1997). Accordingly, clinicians and other significant conversational partners may attend to speech rate and turn-taking dynamics when interacting with children who stutter, particularly during conversation-based guided and independent practise. Conversational partners attempt to slow speech rate slightly (about 10–20% below customary rate) and, if necessary, to reduce the extent to which their speech overlaps the child's by lengthening turn-switching pauses. Most adult speakers can reduce speech rate readily, even when given only basic instruction in how to do so (Logan et al., 2002). Our goal for such activities is not to have clinicians and parents always speak slowly or always lengthen turn-switching pauses when interacting with children who stutter. Rather, we hope to increase adults' awareness of variations in speech rate and interruptions, particularly when children are practicing basic fluency management techniques, and then have adults adjust these temporal dimensions of speech during select guided and independent practise activities, when it appears that conversational pace hinders children's communicative functioning.

Open-ended requests (for example, 'Tell me all about it.') tend to elicit long, relatively complex utterances from children, whereas closed-ended requests (for example, 'Tell me what color it is.') tend to elicit short, relatively simple utterances (Weiss and Zebrowski, 1992). Children, particularly younger ones, tend to stutter more often when they produce utterances that are long or linguistically complex (Logan and Conture, 1995). Accordingly, clinicians and parents attend to the types of requests they pose to children during conversation-based guided and independent practise. Many initial practise activities are designed around request-response routines, in which clinicians or parents pose closed-ended requests to children, and children respond while using one or more of the fluency management techniques they have learned. As children become proficient responding to closed-ended requests, clinicians and parents elicit longer utterances by using more open-ended requests.

The attitudinal environment in which children live can either facilitate or hinder functioning, as well (WHO, 2001). Thus, clinicians and parents attempt to create a learning environment that is conducive to fluent speech and competent communication for each child who stutters. Adults can address this goal in obvious ways, such as by reducing or eliminating teasing or bullying, and in more subtle ways, such as by periodically reassuring children of their unconditional love or support, or by offering verbal encouragement as children face challenging communication situations (Bandura, 1977b; Egan, 1998; Logan and Yaruss, 1999). Children who feel embarrassed or ashamed of stuttering may also find it helpful to operate within an attitudinal environment in which failure, challenges, and adversity are acknowledged as being a part of everyday experience. Toward this end, parents can practice modeling calm and optimistic responses to life challenges (Seligman, 1990).

Parents also can offer support by providing children with feedback about how fluently they are talking. Onslow and colleagues (Onslow, Packman and Harrison, 2003) have incorporated this notion as a central component of their response-contingent approach to intervention with preschoolers who stutter. This is further described by Williams in Chapter 8. With this approach, parents offer straightforward acknowledgments of children's fluent speech and occasionally highlight children's stuttered speech. Praise statements are presented more often than those that highlight stuttering. When highlighting stuttered speech, parents sometimes ask children to recast an utterance, hopefully in a more fluent way. The techniques are simple for parents to learn and they appear to be an effective way to address stuttering with many preschoolers (Onslow, Packman and Harrison, 2003).

When UFSHC clinicians work with school-aged children, they may use these techniques as a supplement to other fluency management strategies, within the context of children's guided and independent practise activities. Clinicians may also train parents to occasionally prompt for children to re-produce specific words using one of the rate-based management techniques described above (that is, prompted cancellation).

Module 6: Performing and participating in daily activities

Overview and rationale

In our experience, most children who stutter are able to master the concepts and skills addressed within the preceding treatment modules to such an extent that they consistently can perform structured in-clinic activities with normal or near-normal levels of speech fluency. Of course, such improvements are meaningful only if they lead to similar improvements during children's daily activities. This section reviews the primary activities that clinicians conduct to help children attain this important goal.

Instructional approaches and common challenges

As children who stutter develop their speaking capacity, clinicians help them to generalize their in-clinic experiences to a variety of out-of-clinic experiences. Generalization activities proceed in a hierarchical fashion (Ingham, 1999), and typically include the following steps:

* conducting non-conversational and conversational activities in the clinic with clinicians and parents
* conducting clinic-based, non-conversational and conversational activities at home with parents
* addressing home-based activity limitations and participation restrictions
* addressing school-based activity limitations and participation restrictions
* addressing activity limitations and participation restrictions associated with other contexts.

Clinicians typically begin the generalization process by training parents of children who stutter to conduct some or all of the in-clinic, guided practise activities and then transport the activities home. Initially, the home-based guided practise activities focus upon non-conversational tasks (such as producing SGO on initial words within short phrases). When possible, parents record home-based activities so that clinicians can assess performance.

After children who stutter master fundamental fluency skills during non-conversational contexts in the clinic and at home, parents help children to develop fluency skills during structured conversational activities at home. For example, parents might ask children who stutter to use 'slow speech' while responding to closed-ended requests about a picture book. Subsequent conversational-level activities might feature a broader range of parent speech acts, with children expected to produce fluency skills at a predetermined level of accuracy or frequency. In some cases, children lose sight of their progress after one or two unsuccessful generalization activities or they dismiss the significance of intermediate or partial successes. In such cases, clinicians or parents review treatment expectations with children. Children and parents also might devise a straightforward method to document accomplishments (for example, a 'success log'). With such an approach, clinicians can help children to recognize and, it is hoped, appreciate progress.

After children can reliably perform contrived guided practise activities to criterion-level, they address home-based activities for which they present genuine activity limitations or participation restrictions. Pertinent activities are identified through assessment activities with the children and their parents. Prior to having children participate in these activities, clinicians and children conduct preliminary activities that incorporate principles of self-efficacy theory (see Bandura, 1977a; Manning, 2001) to maximize children's chances for success. These activities include participant modeling and vicarious modeling, in which children rehearse or watch the clinician or others use the speech-related skills they are attempting to generalize. In addition, clinicians and children review the desired outcomes for the activity. Generally, clinicians help children to set specific, narrowly focused goals or action statements for these activities, so that children are likely to experience success. At this point in treatment, children typically have had ample practise using relevant fluency management skills as well as monitoring and evaluating various aspects of their speech production (such as rate, frequency of speech dysfluency, physical tension, word avoidance). Thus, they usually perform the preliminary activities smoothly.

After successful completion of the preliminary activities, children and parents address genuine activity limitations and participation restrictions as they arise during the week. This goal can be addressed in several ways. One approach is for a parent and child to set aside blocks of time, during which the child seeks to use specified fluency management skills and parents seek to implement specific supportive behaviors. Practise blocks may last anywhere from five to 60 minutes, depending upon a child's age and functioning. A variation on this is to organize practise activities around specific, well-defined family routines such as 'the daily drive to school' or 'the daily after-school snack', or around specific communicative tasks that the child usually has difficulty performing well (for example, 'telling parents about homework assignments'). During these real-life activities, children strive to implement specific fluency management skills. Parents simultaneously strive to support children's efforts by reminding them of task objectives, periodically praising their smooth speech or well-managed stuttering, and occasionally prompting them to use fluency management skills or to react to stuttered speech in productive ways. Following successful completion of these jointly managed activities, older children who stutter then may be directed to assume responsibility for independently performing similar activities as they arise during the week.

As children improve in their ability to independently perform at-home activities, clinicians, parents, children, and (when possible) school personnel collaborate to identify school- and play-based contexts to address. Because parents and clinicians typically are not present in these contexts, children assume proportionately greater responsibility for their communicative functioning at these times. In some cases, clinicians find it helpful to have children complete 'activity planning sheets' prior to participating in these independent practise activities. The planning sheets serve as a form of self-instruction (Egan, 1998), in which children develop a 'game plan' for a task by:

- considering how the task typically unfolds (for example, current activity limitations, participation restrictions, and behaviors, beliefs, or feelings that hinder functioning)
- identifying alternate or preferred ways in which the task might unfold
- identifying specific strategies to realize the preferred scenario
- determining how strategies can be put into action.

Despite their in-clinic and at-home successes, some children still may show reluctance or resistance when asked to participate in necessary, but challenging, activities associated with school, recreation, or socialization. Following principles described by Bandura (1977a) and Egan (1998), clinicians address these situations by:

- verifying the child's ability to perform the requisite communication skills
- verifying the child's ability to manage residual stuttering
- modeling or rehearsing the skills necessary to perform the activity competently
- listening to, empathizing with and, if necessary, attempting to modify the child's activity-related beliefs and feelings
- offering encouragement or exhortations for action
- helping the child to review and, if necessary, revise goals for the activity
- helping the child to review the potential risks and rewards associated with participation and avoidance.

Assessing outcomes

Clinicians assess children's functioning before treatment and at regular intervals during treatment, with comprehensive reassessments typically held following each semester and/or at the termination of treatment. Assessment measures are designed to capture reductions in communicative disability, and they consider the perspectives of the clinician, parents, teachers, and the child, as all are relevant to gauging changes in communicative functioning and estimating the need for further treatment. The primary outcome measures are as follows.

Changes in stuttering severity

Clinicians, parents, teachers and (when appropriate) children who stutter rate stuttering severity using procedures similar to those described by Onslow, Packman and Harrison (2003).

Changes in speech fluency

Clinicians measure speech rate and the frequency (by type) of speech dysfluencies during clinic- and home-based conversations using procedures similar to those described by Conture (2001). Parents, teachers and (when appropriate) children who stutter also complete a multiple-item rating scale to indicate the frequency with which the child produces various stuttering-related behaviors during various activities.

Changes in participation

Parents, teachers, and (when appropriate) children who stutter complete a multiple-item rating scale to assess the frequency and extent with which the child participates in home- and school-based activities and the competence with which the child communicates (for example, the organization, completeness and appropriateness of information).

Changes in contextual factors

Parents, teachers, and (when appropriate) children who stutter complete a multiple-item rating scale to assess the manner in which the child reacts to the expectation or experience of stuttering. Scale items address affective, behavioral and cognitive reactions. Published, norm-referenced attitudinal scales may be used as well.

Terminating treatment

To summarize, our basic approach to treatment with school-aged children is first to increase children's capacity for fluent speech. This is accomplished primarily through principles and activities in Module 1, with principles and activities from Modules 2, 4 and 5 to support. We then help children generalize fluent speech to home- and school-based activities using principles and activities outlined in Module 6, with principles and activities from Modules 2, 4 and 5 to support. This approach usually leads to one of several scenarios, the most common of which are described below.

Communicative functioning is within normal limits

With these cases, the fluency-, communication- and participation-related measures described above suggest that the child is functioning similar to or above peers. When children sustain this level of functioning for several weeks, treatment time is reduced; that is, from weekly sessions, to bi-weekly sessions, to monthly sessions. Bi-weekly and monthly sessions are largely for monitoring purposes; hence, session length is reduced to 30 minutes or less. After several months, direct contact is discontinued, and client progress is monitored via periodic telephone calls to parents for approximately 12 months.

Communication functioning is substantially improved

With these cases, fluency-related assessments suggest substantial improvement from pre-treatment communicative performance; however, residual stuttering remains (that is, mildly dysfluent speech, occasional situational stuttering). If assessment measures indicate that the child is participating fully and communicating competently, and the child demonstrates the ability to cope with or react to residual stuttering satisfactorily, clinicians proceed to reduce treatment time in the manner described above.

Additional sessions may be scheduled in the following circumstances to help a child consistently realize his or her capacity for fluent speech:

• participation restrictions or activity limitations persist in spite of having the capacity to speak fluently
• the child does not cope with or react to residual stuttering effectively
• the child is not satisfied with the post-treatment level of functioning.

Activities during additional sessions include a review of knowledge and skills from Module 1 (and Modules 2, 4 and 5, if necessary) as well as activities that address knowledge and skills from Module 3 (affective, behavioral and cognitive reactions to stuttering). Generalization activities (Module 6) are then re-initiated.

Communication functioning is not significantly improved

With these cases, fluency-related assessments typically indicate that post-treatment fluency performance during out-of-clinic activities is similar to pre-treatment fluency performance, and some or all activity limitations and participation restrictions remain. Additional sessions are scheduled to further establish the child's capacity for fluent speech and to realize that capacity more consistently. These activities include continued practise of knowledge and skills from Module 1 (and Modules 2 and 4, if necessary). Activities relating to contextual factors (Modules 3 and 5) are (re)addressed in detail. Generalization activities (Module 6) are then re-initiated. Subsequent actions for children who do not respond to this remediation are considered on a case-by-case basis.

Conclusion

This chapter outlines some principles and practises that clinicians can consider when treating school-aged children who stutter. Obviously, space did not permit a description of all possible activities that one might consider, or all possible patient profiles that one might encounter when working with this population. The chapter outlines a program that relies principally upon common fluency-shaping techniques. In this regard, our approach is similar to many other behavioral treatments. Although such treatments appear to be effective, in general, at reducing the frequency with which children produce stutter-like dysfluencies, the limitations of this approach are well known. First, not all children improve speech fluency during daily activities through fluency-shaping approaches. Second, one cannot assume that the elimination or reduction of children's stutter-like dysfluencies is equivalent to the elimination or reduction of children's communicative disability. Third, not all children aspire to eliminate all or even most stutter-like dysfluencies. Fourth, some children report that it takes an unacceptable amount of mental effort to realize highly fluent speech, even after extensive practise.

For these reasons, we feel it is important for clinicians to be prepared to augment standard behavioral techniques with intervention strategies that address the frequency and extent with which children participate in daily activities as well as the ways in which they cope with or react to those disruptions in speech fluency that characterize stuttering. Several of these 'augmentative' strategies have been outlined here. With a comprehensive approach such as this, clinicians can look beyond issues concerning fluency impairment to address the broader-based concerns that comprise children's communicative disabilities. In doing so, clinicians should be well positioned to help children transform speech production from a frustrating – even humiliating – activity into one that is performed confidently and competently.

Chapter 8
Use of an adapted form of the Lidcombe Program in conjunction with intensive group therapy

ROBERTA WILLIAMS

Treatment approaches and the involvement of significant others

Any approach to the treatment of stuttering needs to be flexible, as children in this age group vary greatly in their levels of awareness and concern about stuttering. There are growing 'external' demands, such as school, and stuttering itself may have become more entrenched. It is likely that the balance between a treatment approach that addresses the stuttering impairment itself and the approach that deals with its effect on the child and the family needs to be 're-tuned'. The treatment approach described in this chapter is a conjunction between the Lidcombe Program of Early Intervention of Stuttering in Pre-school Children (Onslow, Costa and Rue, 1990; Onslow, Andrews and Lincoln, 1994; Onslow, Packman and Harrison, 2003), adapted for use with children aged between 7 and 12 years, and an intensive group therapy programme used at The Compass Centre, City University, London. The adapted use of the Lidcombe Program of Early Stuttering Intervention has been found to be effective in reducing the frequency or 'impairment' of stuttering, whereas group intensive therapy addresses aspects of activity limitation and participation restriction that can result from stuttering in many children (WHO, 2001). Both approaches involve significant others.

Application of the Lidcombe Program for older children

The Lidcombe Program is a behavioural treatment developed primarily for early intervention for stuttering in pre-school children (Onslow, Costa and Rue, 1990; Onslow, Andrew and Lincoln, 1994; Onslow, Packman and Harrison, 2003). It is administered in the child's natural environment, by a parent or significant other who is guided by a clinician. Administration is based on reinforcing stutter-free speech and extinguishing stuttered speech. In Stage One of the Program, parents carry out therapy each day with their child. Gradually, less-structured, natural conversations are used, and parents visit the clinic each week to report on progress and receive guidance. The parents rate the severity of their child's stuttering each day on a 10-point scale and the clinician measures the percentage of stuttering each week. Once stuttering is no longer present, or is at a very low level, Stage Two is initiated, in which the frequency of the visits and the therapy are reduced but monitoring of stutter-free speech is maintained.

Older children are necessarily different from pre-school children in, for example, their changing levels of attachment or maturing socialization. Therefore, the results of research with pre-school children cannot be generalized to this older age group. Indeed, for this group, the Lidcombe Program may not be considered to be the therapy of choice or the only treatment needed; the decision to use the Program with an older child is dependent on the nature of the individual child and the family. Not only may older children be growing out of the pre-school developmental charac-teristics that respond so well to the Lidcombe Program's essential components, but, in many cases, the stuttering behaviour is more firmly entrenched and children may be starting to react to it as if it is 'a problem'. A study by Lincoln et al. (1996) reports on the use of the Program with older children and describes individualized implementation of the components. These workers found that older children took a longer time and more visits to reduce stuttering frequency. The results were also less durable.

This chapter describes views of a sample of speech and language therapists who have administered an adaptation of the Lidcombe Program to older children, and it includes a detailed description of one client in particular. There is some evidence that the results of Lincoln et al. (1996) are replicated: children respond positively and a reduction in the frequency of stuttering is possible, even though it may not be eliminated.

The Lidcombe Program

The reader is referred to the manual and text for the Lidcombe Program of Early Stuttering Intervention (Onslow, Packman and Harrison, 2003) for a comprehensive description of the treatment itself, but some of the key elements and the essential components are outlined here in order to consider whether the Lidcombe Program might be selected as the approach of choice for the older child. The essential components of the Lidcombe Program involve parental verbal contingencies for stutter-free and unambiguous stuttering, measurement of stuttering, weekly clinic visits, treatment in structured and unstructured conversations and programmed maintenance. The key elements are as follows.

Delivery of the Program by a parent or other significant person in the child's life, who is trained by a clinician

This element appears intuitively powerful for the pre-school child, in whom levels of attachment are high, and Woods, Shearsby and Burnham (2002) found that these levels increased. When making the decision to follow the Lidcombe Program with an older child this may be a key factor to take into consideration. Children of this age vary considerably in the level of approbation they enjoy from a parent and it may be that a significant person, other than a parent, will encourage a greater level of change. Clinical reports have stated that some children respond well to friends who will attend clinic visits and act as a 'buddy' during structured practice, so this may be an adaptation that will produce sustained change.

Therapy is delivered each day

Stuttering has been found to have operant properties in both children and adults (Bloodstein, 1995) and, as with other learning, it would seem self-evident that stutter-free speech needs to be practised regularly. The first concern about daily practice is one of time, as both parents and children describe difficulties in finding space to carry out therapy. Similar concerns also occur among the parents of pre-school children, and resolutions can be found through solution-focused discussion. There is certainly more time when a child is still at primary or elementary school compared with secondary or high school, but working parents and parents with several children express difficulties. More problematic may be motivation for the child who, in many cases, is unable to appreciate the need for the practice, especially when it conflicts with a preferred recreational activity. Positive gains need to take place relatively quickly and need to be made obvious. The use of tangible reinforcement can be effective in encouraging daily practice but the balance is delicate as the effect of the therapy can be slower to see than for the pre-school child. For many school-aged children, weekly visits are essential to maintain motivation, but later on telephone contact can be maintained successfully.

Children are not taught to use a different speech pattern

It is widely considered that the imposition of a different speech pattern to replace stuttered speech is difficult to maintain, and many children at this age are unwilling to adopt it all the time. Even those children who are able to impose fluent speech through rate control and light contacts report that it is impossible to remember techniques when in the playground, football field or at the school disco. The attractiveness of the Lidcombe Program for school-aged children is that it is based on practising the 'normal' part of that child's speech until this becomes the default option. Constant vigilance is not a frustration and the children themselves do not report feeling as if they are odd. Although the social validity study by Lincoln, Onslow and Reed (1997) has not been replicated with older children, this study and practical experience suggests that the stutter-free speech of these stuttering children will be perceptually indistinguishable from that of control subjects.

Treatment should be a positive and enjoyable experience

Another key difference in carrying out the Lidcombe Program with older children is the degree to which they can be involved in the process of therapy, and in decisions about its implementation. This may be the key to increasing older children's motivation as they are encouraged to 'design' their own programmes and invent their own rewards.

Treatment effects are monitored over a long period of maintenance

As with pre-school children, parents and the older child are encouraged to continue with Stage Two of the Program.

To conclude, the advantages are that the Lidcombe Program does not train speech change, it is unlikely to impair speech naturalness and it is conducted by parents or possibly 'buddies' in natural situations.

Theoretical rationale underpinning the approach

Behavioural methodology – the rationale for the use of the Lidcombe Program

It has been recognized for a number of years that stuttering is an operant and will respond to behavioural methodology. Stuttering in school-aged children is more tractable than in older clients (Van Riper, 1973; Martin, 1981; Cooper, 1987; Onslow and Ingham, 1987). The success of the Lidcombe Program depends on the truth of these theoretical statements when supported by an appropriate therapeutic context.

Onslow, Packman and Harrison (2003, p. 6) state that the Lidcombe Program is a behavioural treatment for pre-school children where 'the treatment agent is parental verbal contingencies for stutter-free speech and stuttered speech during everyday life'. Stuttering in small children is an operant, and verbal contingencies are the only treatment agents.

Research with pre-school children has shown that Stage One can be completed in a median of 11 visits (Jones et al., 2000; Kingston et al., 2003), and that treatment gains can be maintained for up to seven years (Lincoln and Onslow, 1997). Woods, Shearsby and Burnham (2002) demonstrated that the children showed no psychological ill-effects, and a study by Lincoln, Onslow and Reed (1997) provided evidence that naïve listeners could not distinguish the speech of children from the experimental group from the speech of children in the control group, that is, the results were socially valid. It appears therefore that the programme's efficacy and efficiency with this younger age group is impressive.

Lincoln et al. (1996) provide the only study to report on the use of the Program with older children, and they describe how individualized implementation of the components is possible. At this time the non-programmed operant treatments that showed promise for pre-schoolers were yet to be used with older children. The results of this investigation showed that a median of 12 one-hour treatment sessions was required to achieve less than 1.5% stuttered syllables (%SS). This was a difference of one session compared with the median %SS achieved by pre-school children, but there was a big difference in the range of sessions (between four and 39). Lincoln et al. (1996) were unable to tell whether this was a random or a systematic variation among clients, although severity, children with complicated histories and longer post-stuttering onset times could have been factors. A number of children failed to meet Stage Two criteria, but all had lower %SS. Surveys also found that parents were satisfied or very satisfied with the Program.

To conclude, it has been shown by both Onslow, Andrews and Lincoln (1994) and Lincoln et al. (1996) that a longer time, or more visits, is required to achieve the same results with school-aged children. The results were also less durable. Starkweather (1993) also links an increase in age with longer treatment times. One of the most interesting aspects of working with this age group, however, is the fact that there is less chance of natural recovery. Long-term reduction in stuttering is more likely to be attributable to the intervention.

Literature on the nature of the attachment bond may shed some light on why the treatment agent (verbal contingencies) is so effective in the Lidcombe Program. Herbert (2003) describes the formation of mutual, interlocking patterns of attachment behaviours as part of the behaviour system whereby responses in the child might produce a change in the environment or a rewarding outcome. Where the behaviours in the parent and the child correlate highly the behaviour is likely to be maintained. To develop as an individual the child must slowly detach him- or herself and by school age this bond is considerably loosened. This may mean that the verbal contingencies have less power to influence behaviour change. The detachment of the bond varies between children, however, and may be one reason why some school-aged children respond better to the Lidcombe Program than others.

Socialization in the 7- to 12-year-old child: the rationale for the additional component of the intensive courses

The development of socialization may be one of the most important differences when considering the possible application of the Lidcombe Program in older children compared with pre-schoolers. To function effectively, children adapt and adjust to changing physical development, social situations and different people. They use intellectual skills flexibly to do this, engage in problem-solving and, in extreme situations, try to alter the situation to suit themselves. Bandura (1969, 1977b) commented that the most fundamental model for learning about socialization by children is through observing and copying examples. But they do not just imitate, but interpret, what they learn from people who have value and meaning for them which, in fact, gives the value to a reward.

This development is relevant both to the development of stuttering and to its management. In the first case, through stuttering, a child may experience a phenomenon he or she does not see in others. Therefore, the role of observational or 'vicarious' learning (Bandura, 1969, 1977b) is not available. It is not possible for the child to learn how to respond through observing how another might do this in the case of stuttering. In terms of management, the opportunity to observe others responding to the phenomenon of stuttering is offered in group therapy.

Fear is discussed in some depth in the literature on socialization, as a child's natural response to something which threatens his or her security and which is vital to adaptation. It has as its base a physiological mechanism. This is important as it contributes to the discussion about why stuttering becomes more serious for the child as he or she grows older and, in turn, why the contribution of group therapy is important.

According to Ollendick and King (1991), fears for school-aged children tend to be anxieties about their ability to succeed in a competitive society, their competence, prestige and lack of significance, all of which can be compromised by stuttering. These authors summarize the childish fears for 7 to 12 year olds as:

- Between 7 and 8: aspects of school, supernatural events and physical danger.
- Between 9 and 11: social fears, fears about wars, health and bodily injury, and school performance.

Worry ensues from fear, and this can be accompanied by restlessness, being easily fatigued, difficulty concentrating, irritability, muscle tension and sleep disturbance. The fact that stuttering is exacerbated by the above physiological conditions may set up a vicious cycle of events.

The most positive feedback from children attending the intensive courses at the Compass Centre focuses on the value of meeting others who stutter and of making friends without the worry of stuttering. Most children, of course, do have friends at school and at home, but many do not talk about stuttering to them. Being able to talk easily and openly to new people may be considered a social skill and children who lack this can lead lonely lives.

Because of stuttering a child may have a restriction in the 'funnels and filters' through which friends are made (Herbert, 2003). One filter is homogamy, which indicates the presence of similar individual characteristics, common interests or values, and a child who stutters may not find someone with similar characteristics. Also, he or she is not able to discover common interests or values if conversation is compromised.

The literature on 'identity' (Reeve, 2002; Watson, 2002) is also relevant to this discussion as the role and impact of stuttering for individuals is very variable. For some people stuttering is a part of how they see or construe themselves; for others it is not central. Most importantly, stuttering viewed as disabling or differentiating may range from being clearly untrue to truly devastating. This is supported by the observation by Herbert (2003) that children make friends with those they believe are similar to themselves not those who necessarily actually are.

The emotional difficulty around friendlessness is known to be a major source of distress. Herbert (2003) describes how many children lack the crucial social skills required to cope with school and friendships, and this may be extrapolated to stuttering. He states that deficits in peer relationships can lead to lack of friends, an inability to be appropriately assertive, victimization or bullying, social withdrawal and aggression. Children who lack peer support are likely to develop internalizing problems, such as poor self-esteem, loneliness, anxiety and depression. Two of the reasons Herbert (2003) gives for socialization problems are:

- A situational model: failure to develop proficiency through lack of opportunity to use or practise skills.
- The interference model: skills are present but are not used because emotional or cognitive factors interfere with performance, for example anxiety, criticism and low self-esteem.

A number of researchers have reported that stuttering can have adverse effects on self-esteem (Starkweather, Ridener-Gottwald and Halfond, 1991; Bajina, 1995). Similarly, Vanryckeghem et al. (2001) report from a study of 143 school children that speech-associated mal-attitude of children who stutter increases significantly with age and stuttering severity. They stress, therefore, that the 'attitudinal and emotional reactions of the person who stutters about his or her speech needs the early and continued attention of the clinician' (Vanryckeghem et al., 2001, p. 9). Conversely, Yovetich, Leschied and Flicht (2000) found no differences in five dimensions of self-esteem compared with normative data. A recent 'friendship' study (Davis, Howell and Cook, 2002) found that children who stuttered were significantly more likely to be bullied, rejected and isolated in school and, although they might form one strong friendship, they were less likely to be included in social groupings. They were less popular than their non-stuttering counterparts and less likely to be leaders. They were more highly regarded socially in the classroom situation compared with situations outside the classroom.

As with so many different areas of stuttering, there is no definite conclusion. It is arguable, however, that stuttering may be involved as a key factor in socialization difficulty for some children. It seems likely that strategies to enhance these skills, which are available through peer-based intensive courses, will benefit them.

Elkind (1967) described the older school-aged child as a pragmatic optimist – concerned with producing things of meaning and value that will receive the approval of others. McClelland (1961) noted that this age group of child will persist in mastering skills and, most importantly, will do so especially if 'fuelled' by parental encouragement or pressure. Erikson (1965) commented that children are as amenable as they are ever likely to be to learning. The combination of peer support on intensive courses, and parental or significant other encouragement from the Lidcombe Program, is of benefit in mastering stutter-free speech.

Intensive group therapy courses

Group therapy is seen as a powerful tool for change within many disciplines, both with children and with adults. For the older child, stuttering has often begun to develop wider implications, and feelings of frustration, anger, anxiety, tension, stupidity and embarrassment are reported. The importance of these factors is considered in more detail in other chapters in this volume. Sheehan (1970, p. 297) clearly articulates that, 'since stuttering … occurs in a social context, group therapy is a natural choice for therapy'.

The Lidcombe Program, adapted for the school-aged child, is supported by intensive group therapy courses at the Compass Centre to address matters such as friendship and meeting others, school issues, parental concern and teasing and bullying. The intensive courses are based loosely on identification and desensitization principles (Van Riper, 1973) as well as the development of communication skills. Children come to the intensive courses from many agencies so they may use a variety of impairment-based approaches. During the intensive courses they are encouraged to use the method of speech fluency control or modification with which they are familiar. Parents or significant others are involved in the courses to some extent, and this is especially the case for families working with their child using the Lidcombe Program.

Ramig and Bennett (1997) provide a checklist for comparing intervention components across a number of interventions, all of which are addressed in the combined intensive course and adapted Lidcombe Program approach. Both accommodate individual differences in stuttering, personality, reactions to stuttering and concomitant speech and language problems. The intensive course particularly addresses the development of avoidance and struggle reactions (Van Riper, 1973), which develop as awareness and concern grow.

The intensive courses at the Compass Centre follow the model of tailored or customized instruction (Ramig and Bennett, 1997) because individuals are encouraged to use their own particular approach to managing their stutter-free speech. This instruction operates within a framework in which three dimensions are borne in mind when planning (Barnes, Ernst and Hyde, 1999).

First, the type of group member: all the children have been referred as having a stutter (with a wide range of severity). In these particular groups they should be able to access levels of discussion consistent with language and maturity of the age group. Children with a learning disability severe enough to disallow this, or those for whom English is a tentative second language, are offered different approaches.

Second, the purpose: the definition of a group is 'a number of people coming together with a common aim'. The purpose of these groups is to deal with features of stuttering common to children aged between 7 and 11 years, through discussion and exercises.

The common aim is stated through three clear, interlinking sectors that, in turn, have their own aims, personal to each member of the group:

* social communication strategies
* overt stuttering management
* discussion of covert aspects of stuttering.

The course focuses on sharing experiences, learning strategies and enhancing confidence.

Third, the type of group: the group is closed, intensive over 4 days and is seen as providing an opportunity for children to learn and practise skills, receive feedback and meet others with similar concerns. It has features of both a dynamic and a skills-based group.

The intensive courses are designed to offer older children an opportunity to consider the nature and role of communication as a whole, and the wider implications of stuttering in a 'safe' environment. The key elements here include the following.

* Socialization with a peer group. For many stuttering children, this may be the first time they have met another child who stutters, and the first opportunity they may have had to interact without 'thinking about' their stuttering.
* The opportunity to consider the 'normal' speaking processes. Not only does this teach the symbiotic and interactive relationship of airflow, voicing and articulation in order to enhance fluency (Williams, 1994), but

it establishes a knowledge base that supports behavioural changes. This removal of the mystery of stuttering (Runyan and Runyan, 1999) by describing it objectively can be a powerful desensitizer, as well as providing children with greater control as they familiarize themselves with their own 'mechanical' behaviours.

- The opportunity for children to understand how they interfere with fluent speech production and to feel the difference through experimenting with negative practice contrasted with stutter-free production.
- Opportunities to practise stutter-free speech in realistic settings, extending this through enactment into a hierarchy of situations. Murphy (1994) talks of encouraging openness and assertiveness through a role play, 'Let's Make a Movie'. In a similar way, the performance for the parents allows the children to inform parents about what stuttering is, to declare the communication approaches from others that they prefer and to demonstrate their identities, and not be overwhelmed by the stuttering stereotype.
- The purposeful use of, and development of, effective communication skills.
- The opportunity to examine feelings about, and attitudes towards, stuttering.

Description of therapy

The group goes through several phases over 4 days.

Formation of the group

The children (known as 'students') are introduced to each other and to the undergraduate clinicians who provide one-to-one support for individuals within the group setting, and are given gelling activities.

Assessment: stuttering self-evaluation assessments and the Situation Profile Assessment (R Williams, S Davis and M Chelidoni, unpublished data) are carried out in the initial phase; this allows students accelerated understanding of each other.

Setting individual communication, speech and attitude goals.

Purpose of the group

Communication skills games, experiments using speech in a variety of individual and social contexts, discussion and role-play are used to enhance communication skills, reduce struggle and ensure students' participation.

The final stage

This is marked by a presentation for the parents – often a short moral play (invented by the students) or a series of role-plays, readings or a summary of a survey about stuttering undertaken during the course.

Group identity and the formation of a naturalistic setting for experimenting with aspects of change are endorsed by opportunities to mix at break times for sport, games and meals. Parents are encouraged to participate, and are updated in their own group at regular intervals about the progress of the young people. This is necessarily more of a social discussion group, but one that has the common theme of worry and concern about their child's speech and how to manage the school situation. The focus is on mutual support and encouragement to use strategies.

Facilitating change through groups

Corey and Corey (1997) describe a list of therapeutic factors in addition to the skills learning that facilitate change in groups.

Self-disclosure

Through discussion and sharing feelings about stuttering, using the 'iceberg' analogy (Sheehan, 1970), group members are encouraged to deepen their self-knowledge and gain a richer, more integrated picture of who they are. For individuals who fear a catastrophic reaction towards themselves or their stutter there is the opportunity to 'test reality'.

Constructive confrontation

This may be one of the first times a group member has received open advice in public (albeit the safe group) from a clinician, or even peers, and it is an opportunity to apply principles openly and also to receive feedback. For children receiving the Lidcombe Program alongside group therapy, this is an opportunity to test out the naturalness of their speech and whether, for example, the use of self-correction is possible in front of other people.

Feedback

As one of the most powerful ways that learning takes place, individuals can begin to learn that they are responsible for creating favourable and unfavourable outcomes, and for changing the style in which they relate to others (Rothke, 1986).

Cohesion and universality

Students often report that the best thing about the group is meeting other people who stutter – a fundamental rationale for the groups, but hard to describe in terms of outcome measures. It appears that students may gain courage by discovering that they are not alone in their feelings. They begin to see commonalities and to recognize the universality of emotions. As Levy (1983, p. 137) states, 'this commonality has little to do with discovering that others stutter in the same way but rather that others have similar feelings about it'.

Hope

During the course the students sustain the belief (which started with the adapted Lidcombe Program) that change is possible and that they are empowered to make decisions about how they might present themselves. For example, employing mature communication skills even when stuttering produces feelings of control and increases confidence. In combination with the Lidcombe Program the combination is self-sustaining.

The cognitive component

Yalom (1983, 1995) cites research evidence that if people are to gain from a group experience they need a cognitive framework to allow themselves to put what they are experiencing into perspective. As Kelly (1955) states, experience only produces change if it is actively reconstrued. The cognitive framework for attitudes to communication, the use of stutter-free speech and the modification of stuttering are built up through explanation, clarification, interpretation and other such mechanisms during the course.

Commitment to change

This essential feature of progress is greatly assisted by a group. Positive peer pressure can facilitate experimentation strategies in graded activities in the life of the group and thereafter in day-to-day life.

Freedom to experiment

The creation of 'ground rules' by the group is important. The rules focus on acceptance of stuttering and the proposition that it is 'what you say and not how you say it'. This establishes the group as a safe place to experiment, where students are encouraged to allow facets of themselves to appear that may normally stay hidden.

Humour

The use of humour can be misunderstood by children even as close as this in age range. Attempts to joke can misfire, and sensitive children can feel that their peers are making fun of them. Acting the 'joker' may also be a strategy to camouflage distress. Open discussion about what humour is can be revealing and strategies to lighten the gravity of stuttering are powerful therapeutic tools.

Willingness to risk and trust

It is essential that thorough preparation is made to invite students to try out the behaviours necessary for change. When they are ready to risk and trust, it is often surprising the extent to which many students will practise letting go of behaviours that are known and secure, and move towards those which are more uncertain.

Caring and acceptance

The group provides support and care for students who find they are expressing feelings publicly.

Power

The feeling that emerges when a student realizes he or she has reserves of energy, courage and strength is likely to give a child confidence and encourage him or her to pursue change and continue to use, for example, stutter-free speech.

A family's point of view

The following case example has been used (with the consent of the child and his mother) to describe how one child combined an adaptation of the Lidcombe Program with an intensive course for stuttering. BL was selected, not because he was the perfect success story, but because he exemplified some of the difficulties and some of the advantages of using the Lidcombe Program in combination with intensive group therapy.

Background to BL

There was no history of stuttering in BL's family. It had begun gradually when BL was three years old, and was accompanied by persistent moderately severe phonological difficulties. BL had previous therapy for stuttering, which his mother reported as being ineffective. He was having no therapy at the time of referral to the intensive course when he was 10 years old. BL lived at home, 15 miles away from the clinic, with his mother, father and younger sister, and he attended the local primary school.

Initial assessment

BL was 10 years old at the time of his application to the intensive course, and at initial assessment he was stuttering for 18% of the time, had poor intelligibility and several concomitant features, such as facial grimacing and loss of eye contact. In isolation, BL's phonological system was within normal limits, but in conversation BL spoke very quickly and quietly, and the constant initial sound repetitions of /mvmv/ made him difficult to understand. It was apparent that his poor intelligibility was a consequence of the stutter and not a separate disability. It was evident from BL's interactions in the group that he was an effective communicator with good listening and attention skills. He was also an interested and enthusiastic member of the group. On a brief stuttering self-perception questionnaire (*see* Apendix I) ('How much do I?'; Williams, clinical tool), BL reported talking and stuttering 'a lot' at home, whereas at school he spoke little (never!) but stuttered a great deal. He stated that he would never read out loud and would try 'not to move a muscle in mouth and jaws'. However, 'it wouldn't work'. BL described his stuttering on the 'iceberg' (Sheehan, 1970) as 'like a CD jumping' and said he felt 'tense', 'nervous', 'scared', 'stupid' and 'different'. The personal goals he had selected for himself for this first intensive course were 'to maintain eye contact, to speak more loudly and clearly, and to stay calm and stand up for myself'.

BL responded enthusiastically to the course and gained from its socialization aspects. However, it was apparent that there had been no changes to his stutter, which remained severe. BL's mother had accompanied him to the course and had worked successfully with him on it, having an encouraging, accepting and perceptive approach to his need for time with her and away from her with new friends. Because BL had such an overtly severe stutter, insight into his speech and was very willing to work with his mother daily on his speech, it was suggested that it might be possible to offer him the Lidcombe Program.

The record of BL's Lidcombe Therapy is told below in percentage syllables stuttered (%SS) over 34 weeks (Figure 8.1). At the first attendance the %SS was again 18%. A great deal of time was taken initially to establish stutter-free speech at the single-word level in conversations with his mother, which was difficult to establish as 'natural'. This came closest when playing board games, which BL liked and which required very short utterances. The programme was fully explained to BL and he was interested in the analogy of 'reprogramming his talking' as this was familiar to him through his enjoyment of computers. He made major contributions to the timing of structured practice at home, to selection of his tasks, his reinforcement schedule and the reinforcement used, which he chose to keep as 'Good Talking'. BL was gradually able to establish stuttering between approximately 1%SS and 3%SS during structured conversation but there was no change to the %SS and severity ratings (SRs) of approximately 7–8 at other times in the day.

During the school holidays (sessions 7–11), BL attended the follow-up of the intensive course. He was still 'worried and nervous' about stuttering. He still said he needed to make eye contact more, thought he should slow down and he should relax and stand tall to stop him feeling nervous. The amount of speaking and stuttering at home and at school remained the same as it had been previously. He was now feeling that others did not understand what stammering was and thought he 'spoke weird'.

The Lidcombe Program restarted and BL and his mother attended regularly for the next 3 months with one gap (sessions 13–22). Structured conversations took place every day, at BL's insistence and with his mother's wholehearted support. During this time the %SS reduced from a consistent 15–19% (as for at least the past 6 months) to between 7%SS and 10%SS over the subsequent 5 weeks, to between 1%SS and 3%SS from weeks 19–20, when conversations had become less structured and 'sessions' eliminated. At first BL missed these sessions, but he gained confidence as stuttering did not return. There were times when SRs rose and at these points BL's mother would offer structured practice. Between weeks 22 and 30, BL and his family were away on an extended holiday. On their return the low %SS had been maintained and BL entered Stage Two for the maintenance part of the Program.

Two months later, BL attended a further 4-day intensive course and, although it was evident that his stuttering was not maintained at less than 1%SS, it was consistently at approximately 3%SS. No observations of unintelligibility were made by naïve listeners and BL was described as a confident participator. On the 'How much do I?' questionnaire he reported talking 'a lot' both at home and at school and not stuttering 'a lot' in both places (less at school than at home). His comments about what others thought of him were that he was 'the same as everyone else'. BL reported that stuttering still made him 'annoyed, frustrated, tired, embarrassed and tense'.

BL has now completed therapy for two years and contact has been maintained irregularly and from a distance as he is now attending secondary/high school. Mother reports that speech has deteriorated but not to pre-treatment levels. She reports it to be at a severity rating of 3. In a telephone conversation with BL, he was assessed at 2%SS and reported that this was at the top end of his stuttering as it might well be on the telephone (reported as his most-feared situation). He was also interviewed and recorded for an independent research study and provided a score of 3%SS. He was described as being very chatty.

BL's reported opinion about the Lidcombe Program was that 'It didn't stress me – it was low pressured and that is a good thing. All I could be asked was to try to say a word again sometimes and that wasn't that bad.' He said he enjoyed practising with the people he knew, and that working every day with his mother was good. As an aside, BL also said he remembered being amused when, even in the middle of an argument with her she would slip in that his talking was going well, or they would break off for his time for structured conversation. According to BL, the best thing about the Program was 'When it started to improve my speech' and the worst thing was 'Not knowing if it (stuttering) would or wouldn't end.' BL had been informed that the Program was normally used in younger children and that it was only possible to make broad projections about changes in the amount and severity of the stuttering.

BL's opinion of the reinforcement 'Good Talking' and later the 'thumbs up' sign was very positive. He said it was very rewarding, 'It was like ... it encouraged'.

BL was asked what he remembered now of the Lidcombe Program, and he said that when he is 'flowing' he does not need to think about it, but, if reading on his own, he will remember to think about it. In good spells BL said that 'It made me really enthusiastic about talking. In school people were surprised and said I don't stop talking.' There were bad spells even when doing the therapy and he said that his Mum would extend their structured conversations by 15 minutes and that helped. He said he looked forward to his daily structured conversations and would recommend it to other people his age. One of the best things about the therapy was 'Not being treated like a baby' – an interesting comment from a boy of 11 who had been undertaking an adapted form of pre-school therapy.

BL also reported enjoying meeting other children on the intensive courses and feeling that his stuttering was only a speech problem which might be fixed rather than something wrong with him. Feedback from BL's mother was that the stutter was very much less and BL was much easier to understand. She found it hard to remember what it had been like originally and while she appreciated that it was much improved she was sorry that the 1%SS level had not been maintained. BL's mother reported that he enjoyed and looked forward to the visits and liked the undergraduate clinicians' involvement. She also noted that he found that the philosophy of 'keeping going' with a therapy was very important to him and that meeting others in the groups was extremely supportive.

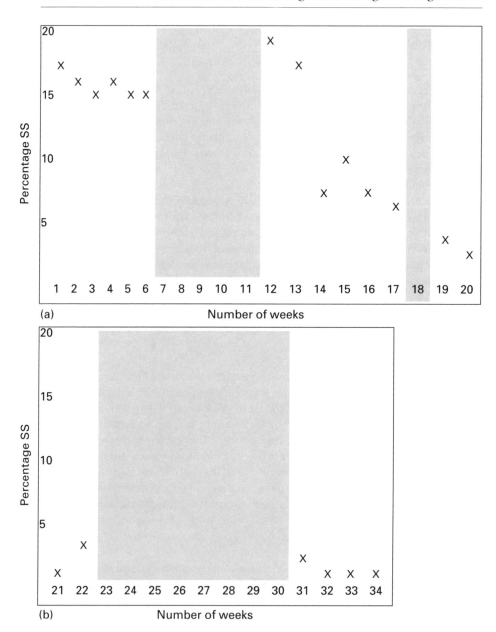

Figure 8.1 Percentage stuttered syllables (%SS) for BL during therapy: (a) progression in the first 20 weeks; (b) through weeks 21–34.

Maintenance activities and length

Stage Two of the Lidcombe Program corresponds loosely to the term 'maintenance', although the authors prefer not to use this term as it implies that the treatment is finished. During this period, speech measures continue to determine whether the child is maintaining treatment benefits and are an integral part of the treatment. Any departure from criteria stimulates a response from the parents in terms of reinstatement of therapy or seeking advice. In the case of the older child, BL, described above, criteria could not be maintained at less than 1%, yet a compromise was necessary to avoid years of therapy. Essentially, by combining work on attitudes, communication skills and the Lidcombe Program, it was decided that irregular contact would continue in the long term but that 3% was the criterion for acceptable stuttering for him.

Maintenance activities for the intensive courses are more flexible. Follow-up days are offered at approximately three- to six-month intervals for two years and are relatively informal since children are also receiving therapy from their referring agencies.

Hancock et al. (1998) highlight the weakness of stuttering treatments for school-aged children as the lack of long-term documentation. Although they noted that few studies considered whether operant treatments worked, the study by Lincoln et al. (1996) did suggest it might be effective but that greater subject numbers and longer follow-up are essential. The study by Hancock et al. (1998) demonstrated the maintenance of the effectiveness of three treatment groups: intensive electromyographic feedback, intensive smooth speech and parent-home smooth speech after four years. This was further elaborated on by Craig in Chapter 5. These results, it is argued, offer evidence for providing therapy in this age group rather than waiting until adulthood despite the motivational concerns arising at this time. The results also argue that children 'can also benefit greatly if treated before or during early adolescence'. Of great importance to this group is the fact that these children had significantly lower levels of anxiety and lower levels of negative communication attitudes after therapy compared with pre-treatment assessments.

Total length of treatment or clinician's time

The total length of Lidcombe Program treatment time is probably longer for school-aged children than for pre-schoolers, as noted by Lincoln et al. (1996). Intensive courses have no fixed period and are available as children grow and experience different concerns in relation to their changing needs and the effect of stuttering on these. Most children reapply to the courses as they reach their mid-teens.

Degree of adherence to protocol and instances of modification

The protocol for the Lidcombe Program is adhered to closely, in that verbal contingencies are the sole treatment agent and constitute the theoretical underpinnings of the therapy. However, a fundamental part of the Lidcombe Program is that it builds in a problem-solving component, although where deviation from the programme is extreme it should not be termed the

Lidcombe Program. Some common differences reported by a number of clinicians when working with school-aged children, which feature in the decision making for this group include the following.

- Children need to take a lead in planning. They may indeed define their desired outcome.
- There must be a 'significant other' who is willing and able to work with the child. If this cannot be the parent then therapists have reported friends acting as 'coaches' or 'buddies' successfully.
- Maintenance needs to continue, with sufficient practice, for at least a year in order to sustain the durability of the therapy.
- There may be a different 'end of therapy' goal, that is, not elimination of stuttering.
- Older children can find verbal contingencies more intrusive and alternative symbols securely 'tagged' to the desired behaviour might be developed in place of these, for example thumbs up, head nod.
- Parents can report a reduction in severity ratings, whereas generalization to school can remain an issue. Occasionally, a teacher is engaged in providing tangible rewards even though they are not used strictly as response contingencies.
- The level of success of the Program can depend on the child's maturity rather than his or her age. Some six-year-olds need more modifications than the occasional eight- or nine-year-old with little awareness of stuttering.
- Where stuttering relates to rapid speech, and stuttering does not appear during visits to the clinic, the child may benefit from a solution-focused approach in addition to the behavioural approach. Children are encouraged to focus on a solution, their stutter-free speech, and then given verbal contingent stimulation to 'use their stutter-free speech more often'.
- Where an older child is blocking, he or she may benefit from an explanation of normal speech processes so that they can understand their problems in becoming stutter free in a similar way as that done in the intensive courses. Following this, parents can be encouraged to offer response-contingent stimulation.
- Children in this age group should be encouraged to self-correct.

Treatment setting

The intensive courses take place within a university setting and have the advantage of a very large clinician:client ratio, or to be more specific, undergraduate clinician:client ratio of at least 1:1. Undergraduate clinicians have already completed their theoretical lectures. The courses are designed to support therapy already being provided to clients, although in some instances this is not possible because of speech and language therapy service shortages within London. Children are not pre-selected according to severity or type of stutter, and they are assessed upon arrival at the Centre as part of the group procedure. Activities are carefully selected to include: focusing on stuttering as the accepted norm for the group while considering strategies for reducing struggle and enhancing communication; experimenting with change through graded, tailored tasks; and simple school-type activities, such as breaks and recreational activities in the lunch hour, in order to maximize opportunities for the children to socialize.

The Lidcombe Program for older children is constructed in a similar way to that for pre-school children, and children are usually selected for this approach from the intensive courses in which the nature of their stuttering and their level of motivation for the programme might be assessed alongside the geographical viability of attending the Centre on a weekly basis. Again, treatment uses undergraduate clinicians, who provide realistic conversation partners for the older children.

Useful outcome measures

Conture and Guitar (1993), Starkweather (1993) and Ramig and Bennett (1997) raise the point that criteria for successful outcomes may no longer be frequency and severity, but increased ability to communicate. This is certainly an important feature for older children who stutter, as therapy which combines the Lidcombe Program with management of other stuttering issues is more likely to have benefits in both areas.

The Lidcombe Program measures the outcome of therapy in %SS and uses as its criterion 1%SS for pre-school children. As discussed above, this may not be possible for all older children, and a compromise needs to be reached with the agreement of the family. Parents and clinicians participate in the measurement of stuttering during treatment through the common framework of severity ratings, and this acts as both another outcome measure and a therapy indicator. Because the Lidcombe Program does not require the child to impose a novel speech pattern on him- or herself, naturalness is an integral part of stutter-free speech.

On the intensive courses, Sheehan's (1970) Iceberg Analogy is used routinely as a descriptive measure of a child's perception of the relative degree of overt compared with covert symptoms and has the advantage of being straightforward to explain and conceptualize. As a group the children are encouraged to discuss what they have described and to seek common features. Repeat Icebergs at follow-up courses are used to evaluate changes in the covert and overt aspects of stuttering.

Because of the short-term nature of the intensive courses, assessment needs to be quick and functional, and targeted at desirable outcomes. The self-perception 'How much do I?' Questionnaire (Appendix I) asks children to rate how much they talk and how much they stutter at home and at school at the start of the course and at follow-up. It is unsurprising that if children state that they stutter little at school; it is often the case that, in fact, they also speak very little. Post-course questionnaires that show a child's perception of stuttering to be less and the amount of talking to be more are considered to be a positive outcome measure and to be desired.

The Situations Profile Assessment (R Williams, S Davis and M Chelidoni, unpublished data) is currently being developed within the Compass Centre. This questionnaire focuses on seven situations:

- social individual
- formal individual
- social group
- formal group
- parents
- telephone
- scripted conversations.

These are rated on eight 'bi-polar constructs', three of which are behavioural, for example:

> I stutter severely here _____ I stutter mildly here

three are cognitive, for example:

> I know why I stutter here _____ I don't know why I stutter here

and two are affective, for example:

> I feel (own descriptor) when I stutter here _____ I do not feel (own descriptor) if I do not stutter here.

Initial results of this assessment, which has now been carried out over three intensive courses, show that children who have attended the intensive courses show significantly fewer negative reactions to situations. An example of the rating scale is provided in Appendix II.

Criteria for ceasing treatment

Children 'stop' treatment on the Lidcombe Program when they have maintained a criterion of 1%SS for approximately two years, although families are encouraged to reinstate therapy should the need arise. For the older child the picture is less clear. Cream et al. (2003) point out that more is at stake in the management of chronic stuttering in adults than the restoration of the perception to all that speech is 'normal' through the control of stuttered speech. It may be likely that treatment will last for longer for older children but that the criterion needs to be agreed when therapy is underway. It is possible that it may need to reflect the 'severity' of the original stutter and the presence or absence of complex covert aspects.

Discussion of maintenance of contact with child/family/school after treatment has stopped, and for how long

Children aged between 7 and 11 are just entering a phase of emotional and physical development when communication faces some of its most severe challenges. In some cases Lidcombe Program visits are regularly fixed; in others, parents are encouraged to keep in touch when the need arises and to maintain a familiarity with the procedures.

Intensive courses not only run for children aged between 7 and 11 years but also for older teenagers so that issues common to this age group can be addressed. Individuals and families are encouraged to view the intensive course as a structure that offers different support at different times in their lives for what might be an ongoing phenomenon. As the likelihood of elimination of stuttering becomes slighter as the child's age increases, so the notion of treatment stopping becomes more emotionally linked to treatment or personal failure. Instead, treatment is designed to foster the facilitation of activity rather than its limitation and the enhancement of participation rather than its restriction.

Appendices

Appendix I: 'How much do I?' stuttering self-perception questionnaire (unpublished)

Name: Date:

Mark the point which you feel is 'right' for you:

How much do I talk at home?

a lot   ☐   ☐   ☐   ☐   ☐   not a lot

How much do I talk at school?

a lot   ☐   ☐   ☐   ☐   ☐   not a lot

How much do I stammer at home?

a lot   ☐   ☐   ☐   ☐   ☐   not a lot

How much do I stammer at school?

a lot   ❏   ❏   ❏   ❏   ❏   not a lot

Finish these sentences:

What I think about stammering is ...

Because I stammer I ...

What other people think about my stammering is ...

What I would like to do on this course is ...

Appendix II: Example of rating form for Situation Profile Assessment

Social individual

1   I would often be in
    this situation   I would hardly ever
                                                be in this situation

2   I would often talk to
    a friend   I would hardly ever
                                                talk to a friend

3   I would not worry if I
    stuttered here   I would worry if I
                                                stuttered here

4   If I were to stutter
    here I would know
    why   If I were to stutter
                                                here I would not
                                                know why

5   I would stutter mildly
    here   I would stutter
                                                severely here

6   If I were to stutter
    here, a friend would
    not be able to tell   If I were to stutter
                                                here a friend would
                                                be able to tell

7   If I were to stutter   Opposite: ...
    here I would feel ...

8   If I were to stutter
    here a friend would
    be understanding   If I were to stutter
                                                here a friend would
                                                not be understanding

Chapter 9
Stuttering and concomitant problems

NAN BERNSTEIN RATNER

How frequently is stuttering accompanied by concomitant problems?

Clinicians are often faced with the challenge of working with children who stutter who additionally present with other communicative disorders. This is not surprising, given the higher likelihood of concomitant problems which accompany any primary diagnosis of a single communicative impairment. For example, epidemiological studies suggest that there is a markedly higher risk that a child who is first documented to have a fluency problem will have an additional language or articulation problem (Blood and Seider, 1981; Homzie et al., 1988; St Louis, Murray and Ashworth, 1991; Arndt and Healey, 2001; Blood et al., 2003), and an accompanying higher risk that children first diagnosed with language or articulation problems will also be found to have an additional relevant clinical communication disorder (Shriberg, Tomblin and McSweeny, 1999). Arndt and Healey (2001) used American state qualification guidelines to define existence of disorders. Using this set of criteria, they determined that almost 45% of children on caseloads who stutter had concomitant communication disorders. Because qualification for inclusion on public school caseload under the Individuals with Disabilities Education Act (1997) is quite stringent, the authors speculated that the true incidence of clinically relevant coexisting disorder might be even higher.

The most recent study of co-occurring disorders in children who stutter (Blood et al., 2003) sampled 2000 American school-based therapists, and narrowly defined coexisting disorders as those which could be documented empirically in case records. This survey found that almost 63% of children who stutter had been diagnosed with at least one coexisting disorder. Of these, approximately 20% had one additional diagnostically relevant disorder, and almost 30% had two. The remainder had more than two additional coexisting speech, language, or non-speech/language/hearing disorders. The authors report that the most common coexisting disorder was articulation/phonology (the authors did not provide distinguishing criteria for these two labels). Almost 50% of children being treated for stuttering were considered to have articulation or phonological disorders. These numbers are slightly higher than those reported by Yaruss, LaSalle and Conture (1998).

It should be noted that the survey by Blood et al. (2003) broke language disorders into numerous overlapping diagnostic labels. When queried specifically about the number of children on their caseloads who stutter, but who had *no* coexisting language disorders, clinicians indicated that only 26.5% met such criteria. It can be inferred, contrary to the authors' interpretation, that the most common coexisting disorder in stuttering is comprehension and/or expressive language disorder, affecting as many as three-quarters of children diagnosed as stuttering. The authors could not determine whether language problems stemmed from fluency disorder (as in avoidance of feared words creating the impression of lexical disorder), or were truly concomitant. The data from the study by Blood et al. (2003) also allow the extrapolation that only 5-6% of such children had coexisting primary disorders, such as autism, mental retardation, cerebral palsy, and so forth, that might place them directly at risk for multiple speech–language deficits. Thus, the reason for such high co-morbidity reports is as yet unclear.

The higher risk ratios reported in an accumulating literature are suggestive of at least three potential and non-exclusionary factors that produce multiple clinical impairments within the same child. The first is genetic – accumulating evidence suggests that fluency disorders, specific language impairment and articulation disorder of unknown etiology may all be transmitted genetically (for a summary, *see* Bernstein Ratner (2004a) and the discussion in Chapter 1). A second, possible explanation for the higher incidence of concomitant problems in children already carrying one primary communicative impairment is that dysfunction in one domain of speech or language ability may cascade to affect other areas of development. For example, a primary language problem may compromise fluency abilities in a child with fragile speech fluency resources. A third possibility is that whatever conditions provoke stuttering in some young children may also predispose them to additional communicative impairments.

The higher risk ratios must also be taken into perspective. Estimates of how often children who stutter carry additional clinical diagnoses vary tremendously (*see* Nippold, 1990, 2002 for critiques), probably because of inconsistent defining characteristics that will be discussed shortly. However, many children who stutter appear to function well within normal limits for speech and language skills (Nippold, 1990; Bernstein Ratner and Silverman, 2000). Even if children who stutter had the same rate of other disorders as the general population, a substantial minority would be likely to require clinical intervention for additional handicapping conditions. The likelihood that the true rate in this group is higher than in the general population argues for the development of appropriate diagnostic and intervention protocols for this group of children. Both prevalence estimates of concomitant impairment and experience from everyday clinical practise suggest the need for more uniform criteria for defining both stuttering and the other disorders that may complicate its presentation. In the next section, I will reiterate some critical criteria that other authors have presented for diagnosis of stuttering, and review pertinent concepts in determination of whether a clinically relevant accompanying disorder exists.

Clinical characteristics of developmental stuttering

At this point in a text, it may seem superfluous to review diagnostic concerns in identification of developmental stuttering. However, there is some evidence to suggest that some children on pediatric speech and language therapy caseloads, in particular those with expressive language impairments, have atypically dysfluent speech (Hall, Yamashita and Aram, 1993; Hall, 1996, 1999; Boscolo, Bernstein Ratner and Rescorla, 2002). Such children demonstrate both a higher level of all types of dysfluencies, and an elevated frequency of stutter-like dysfluencies (SLDs) (part-word repetition, prolongations, broken words) (Hall, 1999; Boscolo, Bernstein Ratner and Rescorla, 2002). Thus, we can take as a given that some children who present to the clinician with atypical fluency patterns require rather thoughtful differential diagnosis. For example, in Boscolo, Bernstein Ratner and Rescorla (2002), almost 80% of children with history of specific language impairment (SLI) produced SLDs during narrative. However, as noted in many places in this text, frequency of dysfluencies is not a universally accepted single standard for diagnosis of stuttering.

As noted by previous contributors, affective and cognitive features are usually relevant in the identification and treatment of stuttering. Stutters are distinguished from normal dysfluencies only partially on the basis of dysfluency type. Although the relative frequency of part-word and whole-word repetitions, consonantal prolongations, blocks, and broken words is typically higher in a person diagnosed with stuttering, effort and awareness during moments of dysfluency are qualitative hallmarks unique to stuttering. Although studies in this area are few, professional and clinical observation of many cases referred for expressive language impairment with concomitant stuttering lack these qualitative features. In other words, while the children are indeed very dysfluent, their dysfluencies lack the characteristic struggle and reactivity seen in stuttering. They typically do not have awareness or self-concept as a person who stutters, and do not demonstrate the situational and linguistic avoidance so common in even relatively young children who stutter. As noted later in this chapter, the probable origin of these children's stutter-like dysfluencies is highly likely to be language-based, and may not respond to traditional stuttering therapy components.

Although it is not clear that all studies examining stuttering and concomitant disorders have used a uniform definition of stuttering, it is clear that quite varied definitions of phonological and language impairment have also complicated our understanding of how often coexisting disorders accompany childhood stuttering. For example, there is no standard definition of phonological impairment. Some studies that have asked whether or not stuttering children are more likely to have phonological impairment have asked for clinical judgement, caseload placement, or evidence of both developmental and atypical phonological processes (*see* Nippold, 2002 for review). Still others have used percentile rankings on normed phonetic inventories (Bernstein Ratner and Silverman, 2000). Similarly, while stuttering children may score more poorly on tests of language skills than fluent peers in some studies (Bernstein Ratner and Silverman, 2000; Anderson and Conture, 2000), few studies that specifically contrast stuttering and non-stuttering children on such tests have identified children with frank language impairment. Differences that have been observed have been, for the most part, sub-clinical.

While the majority of studies examining concomitant problems in children who stutter have not broken subject populations down by etiologic conditions, there is some agreement that certain childhood conditions or syndromes carry with them an increased risk for developmental stuttering. These conditions will be addressed later in this chapter.

Determination of concomitant impairment: diagnostic concerns

Because it is more likely that a child referred for fluency problems has additional concomitant disorders of communication, it is extremely important, in our opinion, that the clinician conducts a very thorough diagnostic evaluation of *all* children referred for stuttering. Some centers do not typically perform such broad-scale evaluations. It is our position, however, that a more thorough diagnostic protocol will make it more likely that stuttering is correctly identified, and not confused with language formulation-induced dysfluency patterns to be discussed later in this chapter. It also allows the clinician to appreciate factors that can have an adverse effect on both therapy planning and prognosis.

Components of the full-scale diagnostic for children who stutter

As detailed in other chapters, and in detail in Chapter 2, it is, of course, very important to gather, at the minimum, the following:

- Relevant case history information.
- Parental concerns about and reactions to the child's stuttering that will influence family counseling.
- Behavioral features of the stuttering problem, including frequency and severity measures. In the case of children who may have concomitant problems or dysfluency that overlaps in characteristics with developmental stuttering, it will also be very important to calculate the ratio of SLDs to total dysfluencies. Although SLDs may be more frequent in children with expressive language problems, these children still have a preponderant pattern of more typical dysfluencies, such as filled and unfilled pauses, word and phrase repetitions, and phrase revisions (sometimes called 'mazes') (Miller and Lall, 2001).
- Affective and cognitive components, using age-appropriate scales such as the Communication Attitude Test (CAT) (Vanryckeghem and Brutten, 1997). Administration of such devices permits more broadly focused therapeutic goals, when appropriate; conversely, lack of speaking or dysfluency avoidance/concern and/or self-concept as a person who stutters may become evident for some children who are better viewed as having dysfluency secondary to language production difficulties.

For all children we see in our clinic, we also add age-appropriate standardized language assessments that minimally target the following domains of language: expressive syntax/morphology; expressive vocabulary; receptive syntax/morphology; and receptive language. As appropriate to the child's age, we use norm-referenced stand-alone devices, or either full-scale or selected sub-tests of 'battery' tests, such as the Clinical Evaluation of Language Fundamentals (CELF) or the Test of Language Development (TOLD). Because of concerns in establishing eligibility for therapeutic intervention, such devices *must* be norm referenced.

We additionally conduct a formal analysis of a dyadic and narrative language sample to gather information about the age-appropriateness of syntax and morphology, using measures such as mean length of utterance (MLU), type:token ratio (TTR), or number of different words (NDW), developmental sentence score (DSS), or index of productive syntax (IPSYN). In each case, we compare the child's performance on the sample to published normative data. We attempt to discern patterns of dysfluency in the child's output that may reflect localized sources of encoding stress. Sometimes such analyses are very informative. For example, there are widely held beliefs that various sounds are difficult for young children who stutter, or that parental questioning may elicit stuttering in children. Both of these beliefs turned out to be false when a sample of speech of young children who stutter was analyzed: in the case of children very close to onset of stuttering, asking their own question tended to provoke stuttering. This makes sense because question formation is an advanced language skill for toddlers. But, because question words in English are heavily weighted toward initial /w/ and /h/, it was relatively easy to surmise wrongly that the sounds themselves were the locus of difficulty (Bernstein Ratner, 2001). Determining whether or not phonology, syntax, or pragmatics affect fluency of output has meaningful ramifications for intervention, as discussed later in this chapter. Lastly, we appraise the pragmatic appropriateness of the child's interaction on an informal level, as well as that of the parents. Because of our growing concern that many patterns of adult input to children who stutter are inappropriately categorized as too demanding (Bernstein Ratner, 2004b), we do not make individualized judgements about the goodness-of-fit of a parent's speech to a stuttering child. We tend to be more concerned about patterns of response to the child's conversation in general, as well as responses to moments of dysfluency.

If any articulation errors are heard during assessment, we administer a norm-referenced phonological inventory, such as the Goldman Fristoe Test of Articulation 2 (GFTA-2) (Goldman and Fristoe, 2000). We do not treat a child for a concomitant phonological problem unless the normed score falls at least 1.5 standard deviations (SD) from the mean, or below standard score cut-offs for the particular measure in question. Because relative phonologic proficiency is quite dynamic during the pre-school and early elementary school years, we re-administer the articulation test at least once a year for children enrolled in fluency therapy, to ensure that children are keeping pace with peers and do not demonstrate persistent residual errors that fall progressively further from normative expectations (Shriberg and Austin, 1997). Research suggests that outcomes in phonological development are not systematically linked to fluency outcomes. Children with persistent stuttering appear to make slower phonological progress, but catch up, for the most part (Paden, Ambrose, and Yairi, 2002); however, some children resolve fluency problems but not phonologic problems and vice versa. Rather than attempt to predict or forestall outcomes, we suggest that clinicians treat the clinically relevant symptoms they see.

Differential diagnosis

Concomitant impairments of phonology and language

Simply put, we would not consider a child to demonstrate a concomitant impairment unless sufficient data were available that would independently classify the child as having the additional disordering conditions. That is, a score that is below normal on one or more language measures is not, in and of itself, confirmatory of a language disorder. The scores must be sufficiently below age expectation or normative range, and must be discrepant from mental age.

We evaluate the test and conversational sample results for the following variables.

Does the child stutter?

We first perform a differential diagnosis of stuttering versus the following possibilities when more than one communicative disorder is suspected.

Dysfluency caused by language impairment

This profile may result from difficulties in word-finding, syntactic formulation or discourse formulation. Numerous recent studies have begun to document dysfluency patterns that appear to stem from expressive language formulation problems. In this regard, decision-making must rely on qualitative assessment of the dysfluency pattern, and consider the following factors.

Is the fluency pattern characteristic of clinical stuttering?

In this regard, we would look past the frequency of whole- and part-word repetitions, which are frequent in speech and language impairment (Hall, Yamashita and Aram, 1993; Hall, 1999; Boscolo, Bernstein Ratner and Rescorla, 2002) and search for confirmatory evidence of blocks and prolongations, which do not appear as frequently in expressive language impairment, but are core behaviors of developmental stuttering. Although a number of studies now attest to the high frequency of SLDs in children with speech and language impairment, it is clear that great homogeneity exists in this population. Not all children with speech and language impairment appear to be more dysfluent than typically developing children (Miranda, McCabe and Bliss, 1998; Lees, Anderson and Martin, 1999; Scott and Windsor, 2000). However, in some other studies, the frequency of SLDs has been sufficient, without consideration of other diagnostic markers, to classify the child with speech and language impairment as a child who stutters as well. Other patterns have been observed as well. For example, Thordadottir and Ellis Weismer (2002) found that children with speech and language impairment produce numerous content mazes, but few filled pauses. When determining how such dysfluencies should be addressed in therapy, reformulation patterns must be distinguished from pragmatic behaviors used to hold the floor. That is, a child may demonstrate dysfluencies in formulation independent of interruptions or hasty attempts to take a communicative turn, which are known to provoke utterance initial dysfluency at all ages.

Does the child have self-concept as a person who stutters?

Is the dysfluency accompanied by awareness, avoidance, struggle, or other reactive responses so classic in developmental stuttering? Does the dysfluency pattern conform to distributional patterns that may suggest it is provoked by word-finding, sentence formulation, or pragmatic processes?

Such an analysis is critical to appropriate intervention planning. Few devices exist for such an appraisal. However, like others, we have noted that some children are dysfluent primarily when asking questions (Weiss and Zebrowski, 1992; Wilkenfeld and Curlee, 1997), others when they attempt complex utterances (Bernstein Ratner and Sih, 1987). Careful observation in the classroom, playground and/or home may suggest precipitators of dysfluency that are not immediately evident in the context of the therapy room.

Although the lack of efficacy data in treating children with concomitant disorders or disorders that may be confused with developmental stuttering has been identified as a critical gap in the clinical literature (Ingham and Cordes, 1999), we take as basic that this subject inherently addresses individual differences among children because the potential mixes among weaknesses and strengths are unlimited. Such individual variability presents both challenges and opportunities to the clinician. For example, we have found it useful to combine standardized analysis of syntactic ability in children who stutter and other children demonstrating fluency problems, with analysis of spontaneous language samples and probes of elicited imitation that progressively challenge levels of sentence formulation (Bernstein Ratner and Sih, 1987; Bernstein Ratner, 2001).

Some children appear to show impairments that may influence their fluency patterns (Anderson and Conture, 2000) and suggest targets for intervention: gaps between expressive and receptive language scores, now quantifiable on the Peabody Picture Vocabulary Test (Dunn and Dunn, 1997) and Expressive Vocabulary Test (Williams, 1997), or delayed/disordered patterns of expressive syntax and morphology.

Developmental dysfluency

A second area of potential confusion is the age-old concern that a presenting fluency problem is not stuttering, but 'developmental dysfluency'. We wish to make the specific comment that evolving research on spontaneous recovery from stuttering has produced some questionable initial diagnoses of young children referred to our clinic. For example, we have seen children between two and four years of age who clearly qualify as having a developmental stutter based upon their behavioral, affective, and cognitive profiles, including SSI-3 scores. However, because the referring clinician understands that as much as 80% of early stuttering resolves spontaneously, we have seen the resulting diagnosis termed 'developmental dysfluency'. The term 'developmental dysfluency' should be reserved for cases in which behavioral profiles lack a reactive component, affective and cognitive components of the dysfluency profile are absent, and expressive language formulation has undergone a recent 'spurt' capable of triggering a high level of sentence production dysfluency (including sequelae to language intervention for older children with expressive speech and language impairment) (Starkweather and Givens-Ackerman, 1997).

Known syndromes accompanied by higher incidence of stuttering

This section notes some specific syndromes and conditions in which stuttering or stuttering-like dysfluency has been noted. In each case, the clinician must ask whether the fluency pattern is that of developmental stuttering or a secondary fluency pattern that derives from a primary problem in other domains.

The frequency with which stuttering has been observed in Down syndrome (Devenny and Silverman, 1990; Ferrier et al., 1991) and in learning disability of unknown etiology (Stansfield, 1990) suggests a genuinely higher risk of concomitant speech–language formulation and stuttering in this population. For example, Boberg (1978) suggests a roughly doubled risk in some students with learning disabilities. Some treatment concerns for this population are outlined in Preus (1990). We suggest the following case planning process:

- to what extent is the child capable of conceptualizing and employing traditional components of fluency shaping therapy? (goal: improved fluency skills)
- to what extent does dysfluency appear to be triggered by language formulation issues that may be addressed by strengthening language skills? (goal: fewer triggers for dysfluency)
- to what extent is dysfluency accompanied by secondary and struggle behaviors that the child is capable of addressing through stuttering-modification therapy components? (goals: fewer triggers for dysfluency; ability to move through dysfluent moments).

For most of the conditions we report on next in this section, stuttering or abnormal fluency patterns have been reported, but there is little to guide the clinician in establishing specific treatment objectives or methods. They are included here mainly because of the often-heard question at meetings, 'What do you know about (condition such-and-such) and stuttering?' What we do know is that a number of disorders have been linked to atypical patterns of fluency; thus encountering a child with such symptoms would not be unexpected. However, the resemblance of such symptoms to classic developmental stuttering, and responsiveness of symptoms to typical stuttering intervention techniques is very poorly documented.

Fragile X syndrome is characterized by rate variability, stuttering-like sound, and syllable repetitions that may reflect a combination of speech-motor and language formulation problems (Ferrier et al., 1991; Abbeduto and Hagerman, 1997; Belser and Sudhalter, 2001). We note that the literature does not provide an in-depth analysis of the dysfluencies in this population, in particular whether affective or cognitive components of developmental stuttering are present.

Gilles de la Tourette syndrome has been likened to stuttering in many ways (van Borsel and Vanryckeghem, 2000; Ludlow and Loucks, 2003). Importantly, there is some evidence that the stutter-like dysfluencies in Gilles de la Tourette syndrome are exaggerated by linguistic loading (*see* Ludlow and Loucks, 2003 for summary). For the practicing clinician, it is important to note that some Gilles de la Tourette syndrome appears to emerge from a history of developmental stuttering (Ludlow, 1993), and will thus require change in treatment planning. Ludlow (1993) also notes that some fluency-inducing conditions for people who stutter, such as masking or delayed auditory feedback, do not usually facilitate fluency in those with Gilles de la Tourette syndrome. There is limited evidence of behavioral (SLP) treatment efficacy in controlling the vocal tics characteristic of Gilles de la Tourette syndrome. Van Borsel and Vanryckeghem (2000) reported some success in moderating symptoms in a teen, using slowed and syllable-timed speech, as well as self-monitoring of tic behaviour.

Other conditions in which fluency disorder has been specifically discussed among symptoms include *Turner syndrome*. Roughly one-quarter of one group of people with Turner syndrome were being treated for stuttering, articulation and/or language problems (Van Borsel et al., 1999). In a large study of people with *spina bifida/hydrocephalus*, prolongations, part-word repetitions, larger linguistic revisions and mazes were noted in affected children's speech. Although there was little evidence of reactivity (Huber-Okrainec et al., 2002), the frequency of dysfluency appeared to increase over the lifespan. Speech in *Prader–Willi* syndrome may be characterized by dysfluencies that are not fully compatible with stuttering (Defloor, van Borsel and Curfs, 2000). Lastly, in *Landau–Kleffner* syndrome, an acquired receptive and expressive aphasia accompanied by seizure activity in children, typically having an onset between the ages of 4 and 7 years, one case study suggested that dysfluency arose after discontinuation of seizure medications (Tutuncuoglu, Serdaroglu and Kadioglu, 2002). The authors suggest that late-onset stuttering should be evaluated for differential diagnosis of Landau–Kleffner syndrome, since medications and immunoglobulin therapy markedly improved symptoms.

Stuttering is reported to coexist with *attention deficit hyperactivity disorder* (ADHD) (Healey and Reid, 2003). Chapter 10 discusses ADHD and stuttering in detail.

Atypical fluency patterns (for example, word-final stuttering: Camerata, 1989; Lebrun and von Borsel, 1990; Stansfield, 1995) have also been identified in populations with coexisting problems, primarily phonological disorder or more global learning disability. There is some, but not universal, agreement that a proportion of these behaviors represent compensation for underlying problems (such as word-final deletion or substitution inappropriately compensated for or poorly modeled, as in an adult who responds to the child's production of /ki/ for 'keep' by modeling, 'say /kip-p-p/', something we have observed in parental and clinician correction of errors). This would imply that such behaviors are learned; Stansfield (1995) notes that the literature on this phenomenon does not identify the affective and cognitive components typically associated with developmental stuttering.

Intervention concerns for the stuttering child with concomitant disorders

Despite Ingham and Cordes' (1999) dissatisfaction with the evidence basis for recommendations in treating children who stutter and have concomitant disorders, we note that careful study in this area is difficult. Stuttering is a low-incidence disorder, and splitting populations into controlled behavioral sub-groups and treatment plans will inevitably produce few statistically significant outcomes, in part because of diminished power to detect meaningful differences (Jones et al., 2002).

In the study by Blood et al. (2003), in a nationwide sample, respondents identified no fewer than 30 concomitant disorders potentially associated with stuttering and noted that a proportion of children had from two to six concomitant conditions. With such variability within a population, we prefer to emphasize careful, individualized problem-solving to manage the child who stutters with concomitant problems. However, the management of each individual child must reflect the assessment of treatment outcomes, with re-appraisal and re-evaluation of those therapeutic techniques that do not appear to be producing measurable changes in the behavioral, affective, and/or cognitive features of the disorders, and progressive refinement of those that appear to be beneficial.

General principles of management should include establishing therapeutic priorities and recognizing potential trade-offs that may pit progress in one domain against regression in another. In terms of broad intervention models, Bernstein Ratner (1995b) identified sequential, componential, and cyclic options. Sequential therapy essentially prioritizes one or more of the child's goals over the others, and organizes them linearly, so that secondary goals are not worked on until primary goals have been met. Organizing sequentially can be problematic. In some conditions, such as developmental language disorder, there is growing awareness that children require long-standing management, and it may be difficult to determine when a problem has been addressed sufficiently to 'move on' (Bernstein Ratner, 2004a). Coupled with a well-recognized sense of insecurity that many American and British clinicians have in feeling that they can treat fluency disorder effectively (St Louis and Durrenberger, 1993; Crighton-Smith, Wright and Stackhouse, 2003), sequential planning may delay treatment of the stuttering program unacceptably.

In componential approaches, part of the therapy session or sequence is devoted to each of the child's identified areas of weakness. The value of such an approach is that it leaves no area unaddressed, but may result in either too little time devoted to particular skill development, or programming of tasks that interfere across disorder domains, as will be discussed in detail in the next section. In evaluating the utility of either of these approaches, Logan and LaSalle (2003) suggest that the clinician should ask: How severe are the concomitant impairments? How do they affect everyday functioning? How do others react to the specific behavioral problems that are created by the disorder? Whether either disorder will resolve without treatment? (the likelihood of spontaneous recovery).

Finally, in cyclic approaches, each disorder area is worked on for a specified amount of time during a term, semester, or other calendar period, with programmed alternation to other goals and return to prior targets on a pre-established schedule. This approach to intervention borrows from the cycles approach in phonological intervention (Hodson and Paden, 1991), which has been shown to produce some spontaneous gains during times when a specific target is temporarily dropped from the therapy schedule after initial skills have been taught. Arndt and Healey (2001) found that all of these approaches were being employed across a 10-state American sample.

Trading relationships and their implications for concurrent therapy targets

Despite the high incidence of coexisting fluency and phonologic disorders, there is little support for the notion that fluency is compromised by levels of phonological demand. That is, we have little empirical support for the hypothesis that work on phonological targets will aggravate an existing fluency pattern (Throneburg and Yairi, 1994; Bernstein Ratner, 2001). Concern has been voiced that specific phonologic intervention strategies might be incompatible with fluency-shaping (for example, overarticulation of targeted phonemes or increases in metaphonological awareness) (Ramig and Bennett, 1995).

Wolk (1998) suggests some principles for concurrent phonologic and fluency therapy. These include the use of indirect approaches to phonological intervention, use of processes to more efficiently group phonological targets and speed phonological remediation, use of direct fluency-shaping components, such as reduced speech rate, and soft articulatory targets, which can improve speech naturalness. She advises concurrent therapy for both disorders, the instruction and use of conceptual contrasts for both disorders (easy/hard sounds, front/back sounds), but also suggests avoidance of overt correction of speech errors to maintain the child's sense of self-efficacy in speaking. Finally, she recommends the use of groups, to maximize friendly competition, and the ability to monitor the speech of others, as prerequisites to monitoring one's own output.

Language formulation difficulties and fluency, conversely, are known to interact. An abundant literature now links increased length of utterance, and, specifically, linguistic demand, with increased levels of dysfluency and stuttering (Bernstein Ratner, 1997b). This strongly suggests that children's fluency targets need to be carefully monitored, so that activities designed to teach fluency-enhancing or fluency-modifying skills do not stress the child's current level of linguistic ability. For an individual child, it is likely that fluency may be compromised during work on emerging target structures, whereas carefully designed fluency activities should require linguistic responses well below those being worked on in language therapy.

All clinicians are concerned about generalization of within-session fluency and language goals; such concerns are amplified in the case of co-existing disorders. As other chapters in this text indicate, transfer of fluency goals is aided by programming of fluency-challenging activities that replicate real-world interactions. The same is true of language targets. Most programmed materials for fluency enhancement adequately incorporate early stages of language challenge (single words, multiple word chains, carrier phrases, and so forth), but do not overtly address fluency practise in language targets with increased levels of developmental demand (Bernstein Ratner and Sih, 1987). In fact, most fluency programs equate increased demand with increased length of utterance in words, a poor predictor of children's fluency (Brundage and Bernstein Ratner, 1989; Bernstein Ratner, 1997b).

A surprisingly large number of children in the survey by Blood et al. (2003) were thought to demonstrate clinically relevant problems in pragmatics and higher-level language processing. Estimates ranged from 9% to 12%, with unknown overlap between children having both expressive and/or receptive pragmatic difficulties. In the child with concomitant disorder, discourse-level concerns may relate to language functioning and/or to affective/cognitive components of fluency disorder. For example, even in normally fluent speakers, fillers are elevated by both cognitive load and the need to take role as lead in conversational interactions, which sometimes provokes the speaker into attempting to 'take the floor' before the message has been adequately planned (Bortfeld et al., 2001). Subtle cues are used to regulate turn-taking and to prevent precipitous turn-taking – even normally fluent speakers are more dysfluent on the telephone when they cannot co-ordinate feedback (Oviatt, 1995). This suggests the value of using real-world discourse activities to regulate the speed of inter-speaker turn-taking latencies, which are highly correlated with fluency failure in children (Newman and Smit, 1989).

Pragmatically impaired and fluency-disordered children share certain consequences of their disorders that have important social correlates. Both disorders may require responses to bullying and teasing; stuttering often appears to benefit from self-disclosure. Few studies of self-efficacy and self-image have been done with children who have specific communicative impairment, but research suggests that stuttering and voice-disordered children show more negative attitudes toward speech than typically developing or articulation-disordered children (De Nil and Brutten, 1990). It seems reasonable to assume, however, that multiple disorders will compound problems. Suggested intervention targets that are relevant to children with expressive language problems, pragmatic problems, and fluency include turn-taking, responsiveness, and directness. For children with language impairment and children who stutter, self-efficacy, locus of control and self-monitoring are also important skills to develop in order to generalize treatment within the therapy room to outside environments. In all cases, bringing real-world interaction into the therapy room, and therapy goals out to the real world, are important in maintaining and expanding use of skills (Finn, 2003).

Treatment concerns in the real world

One of the most sobering statistics about treatment of the child who stutters and has additional concomitant disorders was provided recently by Blood et al. (2003). Their national survey specifically asked how much time was accorded for treatment of fluency and accompanying disorders in the school setting. Results suggested that the average American school child who stutters was seen for about 45 minutes per week for all diagnostically relevant conditions, with time almost equally divided between treatment of the fluency disorder and the other problems. Given the length of the typical American child's school year, the authors surmised that children were receiving only about 15 hours of therapy per year devoted to fluency remediation (and a similarly dismal equivalent amount of time for all other relevant speech-language goals). We would concur with their comment that it is not surprising if children do not make progress toward their communicative goals given such limited therapeutic attention.

In this vein, it is important to note that many American school districts insist on grouping children for treatment to maximize caseload efficiency. Only 30% of the children reported in the survey by Blood et al. (2003) appeared to receive group therapy. However, because stuttering is a low-incidence disorder, and may occur in fewer than two children on clinicians' individual caseloads (ASHA, 2003; Blood et al., 2003), it is not uncommon for

American children who stutter to spend a large part of this limited therapy time in treatment with children having very different therapy goals (Cirrin et al., 2003).

Group therapy can be very efficient for children having fluency goals (Ramig and Bennett, 1995), but this recommendation is predicated upon the children in the group having similar needs and objectives. Roberta Williams expands further on this in Chapter 8. Otherwise, the child who stutters is an observer while the other children work on specific goals, as they are when he or she works on fluency targets. Given that many clinicians 'split' therapy times among component disorders in children with concomitant problems, it may be of value to consider whether or not such an arrangement best serves the child with disordered functioning across multiple domains. There are few data to contrast individual therapy with group therapy involving homo-geneously disordered children; however, recent evidence suggests that articulation skills improve more rapidly in the context of individualized therapy (Schooling, 2003).

Conclusion

The rather high rate of documented concomitant problems in children who stutter suggests the need for very thorough assessment across domains of functioning whenever a child is referred for suspected fluency disorder. Careful assessment can differentiate primary stuttering from fluency failure that stems from other primary conditions, particularly expressive language formulation. Further, understanding of the child's relative strengths and weaknesses across domains of functioning can lead to principled choices in the order and nature of goals for areas needing remediation. Because children vary in their individual profiles across multiple domains of ability and weakness, it is imperative that clinicians create individualized goals that reflect the weight of the behavioral, affective, and cognitive components of the fluency disorder, as well as ancillary areas of strength and weakness that will affect the ability to utilize therapy objectives to gain and maintain fluency.

Chapter 10
Treating children who stutter with coexisting learning, behavioral or cognitive challenges

E CHARLES HEALEY, ROBERT REID AND JOE DONAHER

Introduction

Most clinicians who are employed in an elementary school will encounter and plan treatment programs for a child who stutters. However, when a child who stutters also exhibits a broad range of learning, behavioral, or cognitive disabilities that coexist with the stuttering, the clinician is faced with more difficult decisions about treatment. First, the clinician must determine the extent to which the child's stuttering is influenced by a concomitant disorder. Second, decisions must be made relative to the focus and form of treatment that will be provided. The purpose of this chapter is twofold:

- To provide information on characteristics of children who stutter who also exhibit concomitant learning, behavioral or cognitive challenges.
- To provide an overview of treatment decisions and recommendations that we have found useful in our clinical practise and others have documented as being successful when managing children who stutter who also have coexisting speech, language, learning and/or behavioral disorders.

Categories of concomitant disorders

Three specific categories of children will be discussed in this chapter. Children with 'learning difficulties or disabilities' (LD), children with attention deficit hyperactive disorder (ADHD), and children with cognitive delays (that is, mental retardation* and Down syndrome). The following are

---

*Referred to as 'learning disability' in the UK.

definitions, terminology, and descriptions of the disorders as the terms are used in this chapter.

Learning disability

Because of the lack of consistency of terminology used around the world to describe children with disabilities, it is important to set forth definitions of terms used in this chapter. One of the most variable terms used by professionals to describe a child's learning difficulty is the term 'learning disability' (LD). Even within the USA, 'learning disability' can refer to a wide variety of symptoms and disorders (for example, dyslexia, reading disabled, developmental aphasia). Conceptually, the term refers to children who evidence a marked disparity between their measured intelligence and their academic achievement. Put simply, these are children who despite normal intelligence have difficulty learning for no readily apparent reason. The current American legal definition of learning disability notes that learning disabilities refer to:

> those children who have a disorder in one or more of the basic psychological processes involved in understanding or in using language, spoken or written, which disorder may manifest itself in imperfect ability to listen, think, speak, read, write, spell, or to do mathematical calculations. The term includes such conditions as perceptual handicaps, brain injury, minimal brain dysfunction, dyslexia, and developmental aphasia. The term does not include a learning problem which is primarily the result of visual, hearing or motor handicaps, of mental retardation, of emotional disturbance, or of environmental, cultural, or economic disadvantage. (Individuals with Disabilities Education Act 1997)

There is no single identification procedure for LD, which can cause difficulty in defining which children have the disorder. In the USA, different states are allowed to set their own standards and criteria for which children qualify for services. In general, children are classified as having a learning disability if they evidence a discrepancy of 1.3–1.5 standard scale units between an intelligence test score and a standardized academic achievement test. For example, a child with a measured IQ score of 115 and a written language standardized test score of 92 could be classified as having a learning disability in written language. Note that the deficit does not need to occur across all academic areas. For instance, a child might be learning disabled in reading but not in math. Also, because a large percentage of children with a learning disability have language disorders, some professionals prefer the term language-learning disabilities (Shames and Anderson, 2002). For the purposes of this chapter, the term 'learning disabilities' will be used but includes children who also have language impairments with the learning disability.

Estimates of the prevalence of LD in school-aged children vary widely because of a slight difference in identification criteria, with the most widely accepted estimates at around 5% of the school-aged population. In the USA, children diagnosed as learning disabled constitute approximately 50% of the special education population, with LD being the single largest group of children in special education (Lerner, 2000). Children with LD are an extremely heterogeneous group and it is impossible to describe a 'typical' child with LD. However, there are some areas of difficulty that are very common among children with LD. The most common academic problem is in the area of reading. Approximately 80% of children with LD have problems with reading (Lyon and Moats, 1997). Language problems associated with children with LD include difficulties with phonological awareness, delayed speech development, difficulty with grammar and syntax, vocabulary deficiencies, and difficulty comprehending spoken language (Lerner, 2000). Pragmatic issues frequently manifest in difficulties with social skills and interactive abilities. Unfortunately, documentation of the dysfluency characteristics of children with LD in the literature is limited at best.

Attention deficit hyperactive disorder

Attention deficit hyperactive disorder (ADHD) is a disorder that has been recognized for decades but the exact terminology has changed often when describing children with difficulty moderating activity or who have problems with attention and impulsivity. Terms such as hyperkinetic, hyperactive, minimal brain dysfunction, and attention deficit disorders have all been used to describe children with ADHD-like behaviors (Barkley, 1998). In 1980, the third edition of the *Diagnostic and Statistical Manual of Mental Disorders* (DSM-III) used the term attention deficit disorder (ADD), which included two categories: ADD with hyperactivity and ADD without hyperactivity. In 1987, the DSM-IIIR combined the attention and hyperactivity dimensions into a single term, which is referred to now as attention deficit hyperactivity disorder (ADHD). Just as terminology has changed over the years, so too have the diagnostic criteria. Additional changes in diagnostic criteria for ADHD were released in 1994 as DSM-IV guidelines (APA, 1994). The primary impact of these diagnostic changes has been an increase in the number of children who would be diagnosed with ADHD (Baumgaertel, Wolraich and Dietrich, 1995).

Currently, ADHD is subdivided into three categories: ADHD combined type; ADHD predominantly inattentive type; and ADHD predominantly hyperactive–impulsive type. ADHD combined type occurs when at least six symptoms each of inattention and hyperactivity–impulsivity are present and it is the most common form of ADHD. The predominantly inattentive and predominantly hyperactive–impulsive types of ADHD are diagnosed when at least six of nine symptoms are present from each respective category but not from the other.

When diagnosing a child with ADHD using these symptoms, one must also understand there are exclusionary clauses that are often overlooked. First, some of the ADHD symptoms have to become manifest prior to age seven but usually appear around age three. Thus, it is common to have the symptoms of ADHD first appear in the pre-school years. Children are not considered to have ADHD if the symptoms initially occur when children reach middle or high school age. Second, children must exhibit ADHD symptoms in two or more environments, such as school, home and other social settings. Third, the symptoms must result in clinically significant impairment in academic, social, or occupational functioning. Typically, a child with ADHD will experience severe difficulties in school, will have serious social problems (for example, few or no friends), will not be able to do uninterrupted work, and will be unpopular. Fourth, anxiety disorders, mood disorders, or a traumatic life event (such as divorce, death in the family) may result in problems with attention or impulsivity (Reid and Maag, 1994; Sabatino and Vance, 1994). Moreover, ADHD is not the result of any mental disorder, learning disability, developmental disorder, or anxiety and depression. One should be able to rule out these disorders before an ADHD diagnosis is made.

Another feature of ADHD is that these children, as a group, are highly variable in terms of their performance and behavior (Barkley, 1998). It is common to find other disorders such as oppositional defiant disorders, conduct disorders, or LD in addition to a diagnosis of ADHD (Barkley, 1998; DuPaul and Stoner, 2002). It has also been reported that language deficits are present in the majority of children with some form of diagnosable attention disorder (Giddan, 1991). Thus it is difficult to speak of a 'typical' child with ADHD. However, there is one theme that occurs regularly with all children with ADHD – they are consistently inconsistent. Professionals will not see the same kind of performance pattern displayed by a child from one day to the next (DuPaul and Stoner, 2002). For example, one day the child will do well in completing assignments but the next day the child struggles to finish any task. Therefore, clinicians, parents, and teachers must expect the unexpected from this type of child. Unfortunately, some children have one good day, which then becomes the expectation and the thought is that 'He could do it if he really wanted to' (Reid, 1999). Practitioners should remember that inconsistent performance and behaviors are hallmark symptoms of ADHD.

Little is known about the specific characteristics of stuttering in children with ADHD other than the patterns of dysfluencies are consistent with children who only stutter. Because most children who have ADHD will be placed on medication to help them manage their behavior, it is unclear how the medication will affect stuttering. Most documented evidence is that the same medication can cause an increase or decrease in a child's frequency of stuttering. Thus, the effects of medications on stuttering behaviors are unpredictable (Healey and Reid, 2003).

Children with mental retardation and Down syndrome

The last category of children discussed in this chapter includes a broad range of children with mental retardation and other forms of developmental cognitive delays that prevent them from progressing at normal rates of speech and language abilities. Children with developmental delays often exhibit more than typical instances of stuttering, particularly in children with Down syndrome (Manning, 2001).

In the USA the current legal definition of mental retardation refers to significantly sub-average intellectual functioning that occurs in conjunction with deficits in adaptive behavior which is manifested during the developmental period and which adversely affects a child's educational performance (Individual with Disabilities Education Act 1997). Mental retardation is divided into four levels based on the severity of impairment: mild (IQ approximately 55–70); moderate (IQ approximately 40–55); severe (IQ approximately 25–40); and profound (IQ below 25) (Grossman, 1983). Children with mild and moderate retardation are most likely to be involved in speech and language therapy.

More than 250 causes of mental retardation have been identified. However, for a significant proportion of individuals, the exact cause of mental retardation is unknown (McLaren and Bryson, 1987). One of the better-known and most thoroughly researched causes of mental retardation is Down syndrome. Down syndrome is caused by a chromosomal abnormality. There are three major types of Down syndrome with the most common being trisomy 21 where the twenty-first set of chromosomes contains three rather than two chromosomes. This typically results in moderate mental retardation. Children with Down syndrome account for approximately 5-6% of all cases of retardation.

Children with mental retardation will exhibit difficulties in learning. There are a number of common problem areas, such as problems with both short-term and long-term memory. As a result children with mental retardation will have difficulty storing and retrieving information (Merrill, 1990; Bray, Fletcher and Turner, 1997). This in turn results in a decreased rate of learning. Problems maintaining sustained attention are also common and exacerbate learning problems (Zeaman and House, 1979). Generalizing knowledge, a skill that occurs naturally among most children, may not occur for children with mental retardation. As a result, they may not be able to apply skills across settings.

There is inconclusive evidence that children with Down syndrome exhibit stuttering behaviors, as they are typically defined. Conture (2001), reporting the findings of a study by Preus (1981), stated that of 47 children with Down syndrome, 34% had symptoms of stuttering while 31% had dysfluencies similar to cluttering (that is, minimal awareness and reaction to the dysfluency, intelligibility difficulties, and a rapid speech rate). Devenny and Silverman (1990) found that 42% of their sample of adults with Down syndrome exhibited involuntary repetitions and prolongations of sounds, effort, and tension during dysfluent moments, and secondary symptoms such as facial grimacing and eye closure. Similar dysfluent speech symptoms were identified in a small group of Down syndrome children. Willcox (1988) discovered that three of five children with Down syndrome she tested produced multiple-unit, part-word repetitions and sound prolongations of more than one second. However, two of the five children in her sample did not exhibit stuttering-like behaviors. Their nonfluencies resembled those of normally developing children.

Other nonfluent speech characteristics of individuals with Down syndrome include long pauses between words within an utterance, pauses in inappropriate places within an utterance usually accompanied by a sudden production of words that might be difficult to understand (for example, 'I'm going shop … 'in t'morrow'), use of multiple interjections of words before an utterance (for example, 'um … um … er … er … a … it's mine') (Bray, 2001). The nature of these dysfluencies could be the result of slower developing speech and language processes, which contributes to the presence of nonfluent, unintelligible speech. It has been shown that children with mental retardation and Down syndrome frequently struggle with their language abilities. Most notably, these children often experience difficulty with speech production, including phonologic competence secondary to physiologic complications, syntactic and morphological knowledge, and social-interaction skills (Paul, 2001). The demands of language functioning for a person with a disabled cognitive system could contribute to the lack of proper idea formulation, word-finding difficulties, and syntactic processing of an utterance (Starkweather, 1987).

Prevalence of concomitant disorders in children who stutter

A consistent finding in the literature on stuttering is that a small but significant percentage of children who stutter exhibit concomitant speech and/or language disorders in addition to their stuttering. The expected number of children who stutter and who have a concomitant disorder is somewhat unclear and seems to vary considerably among studies, and can be best explained by methodologic differences in studies (Nippold, 1990). Arndt and Healey (2001) suggest that one major methodologic difference among studies is the way in which the concomitant disorder is defined. The wide variety of criteria used to identify the number of dysfluent children who have a concomitant speech and language disorder makes it difficult to compare results among past studies. For example, Blood and Seider (1981) did not appear to provide their survey respondents with criteria for determining the presence of a concomitant disorder. In comparison, Riley and Riley (1979) and St Louis and Hinzman (1988) used specific definitions of stuttering and concomitant disorders when selecting children for their studies, although some disorders appeared to have been broadly defined. For example, the children with fluency and phonologic disorders in the St Louis and Hinzman (1988) study had moderate or severe stuttering. These authors stated that 'some of these subjects would have been classified by speech-language clinicians primarily as articulation or language-disordered children rather than stutterers' (St Louis and Hinzman, 1988, p. 351). Further information on the diagnosis of children with stuttering and language problems has been provided by Bernstein Ratner in Chapter 9.

Blood and Seider (1981) conducted a survey of 358 school-based speech-language pathologists to determine the percentage of children who stutter and who have various concomitant disorders. However, the definitions of each coexisting condition were not specified. In their study, they discovered that 68% of 1060 children who stutter had at least one concomitant disorder. The concomitant disorders reported most often by the clinicians were articulation disorders (16%), language disorders (10%), learning disabilities (7%), and reading disabilities (6%). Arndt and Healey (2001) found different percentages for these types of disorders in children who were identified as having a fluency disorder. Clinicians in that study were asked to specify the number of children who were suspected of having some type of concomitant disorder. A survey of 241 school-based clinicians from a cross-section of states within the USA revealed that of 109 children who stutter, the percentage of children with a suspected coexisting disorder included 13% with articulation disorders, 20% with language disorders, 24% with a learning disability, and 14% having a reading disability. Another combined 17% had emotional disorders, mental retardation and ADHD (Arndt and Healey, 2001). Specifically, they found that 4% of the children who stutter had ADHD. By contrast, Conture (2001) suggested that between 10% and 20% of children who stutter might exhibit ADHD, whereas Riley and Riley (2000) reported that 26% of the children who stutter whom they sampled had ADHD symptoms.

The specific incidence of dysfluent speech in children with cognitive delays has been studied in various populations of people with mental retardation and in those with Down syndrome. The percentage of occurrence of stuttering in people with cognitive delays was studied several decades ago and ranged from less than 1% (Martyn, Sheehan and Slutz, 1969) to as high as 20% (Schlanger, 1953). Chapman and Cooper (1973) reported that the incidence of stuttering in a sample of 1467 institutionalized people with mental retardation was 2%. In the population of individuals with Down syndrome, estimates of the prevalence of stuttering range from 7% to 60% (Manning, 2001). Differences in percentages appear to be related to how stuttering was defined in earlier studies and whether or not individuals were exhibiting symptoms of cluttering instead of stuttering (Willcox, 1988). Clearly, too, these individuals have a high occurrence of speech and language disorders and neuropathologies that complicate the diagnosis of stuttering

Nonetheless, it can be concluded that the prevalence of stuttering in individuals with Down syndrome is unusually high (Manning, 2001).

Key assessment issues

From a clinical perspective, the presence of concomitant disorders in children who stutter is important because these subgroups of children require a different type of treatment than those who only stutter (Wolk, Edwards and Conture, 1993). Concomitant disorders with stuttering presents certain challenges for the clinician in designing and implementing treatment programs (Logan and LaSalle, 2003). However, before implementing any treatment program for children who stutter and have a concomitant disorder, it is important for clinicians to consider two major assessment questions.

Which disorder negatively affects communication the most, stuttering or the concomitant disorder?

A clinician needs to consider the severity of the fluency disorder or the speech and/or language disorder associated with the concomitant problem within the context of the child's communicative and social functioning. Because effective and functional communication is the goal of any speech-language treatment, efforts should be made to address the most problematic speech or language disorder. Given that language problems are common with LD children and significant delays in speech and language development are typical for children with mental retardation and Down syndrome, treating the language deficits first may indirectly improve fluency skills. Bray (2001) notes that children with Down syndrome are particularly dysfluent as their language and expressive vocabulary are expanding. Specifically, speech nonfluencies such as interjections or word-fillers (e.g. uh, um, er), revisions, false starts, and self-interruptions (such as 'You need some, well, first get some') are characteristic of children with language impairments. These types of disruptions in the fluent production of an utterance are directly influenced by grammatical complexity and the child's constrained language formulation requirements (Scott Trautman, Healey and Norris, 2001). Thus, treatment aimed at facilitating improved linguistic competence would contribute to the perception of improved fluency.

On the other hand, if the child's stuttering interferes most with communication, that is the disorder that should be addressed first. It is the clinician's responsibility to focus on improved fluency or the use of strategies that will encourage the management of the stuttering. In the next section of this chapter, we will discuss how a treatment program for children who stutter who have learning, behavioral, or cognitive challenges will need to be modified to accommodate the needs of these populations.

Which model of intervention will be used when stuttering and a

concomitant disorder coexist?

There are a number of ways that clinicians have approached treatment when a concomitant disorder coexists with stuttering. Guitar (1998) stated that treating the coexisting speech and language problem does not necessarily increase the frequency of a child's stuttering. He recommends a clinician to integrate the treatment of stuttering with the concomitant speech or language disorder. In an effort to assist clinicians in making clinical decisions about how to treat children who stutter with concomitant disorder, Bernstein Ratner (1995b) suggested four specific approaches for how this could be accomplished. These included the following.

- A 'blended approach' (simultaneously treating stuttering and the concomitant disorder, such as incorporating stuttering and language targets simultaneously within a therapy session).
- A 'cycles approach' (treating each disorder for specific periods of time during the course of therapy).
- A 'sequential approach' (treating stuttering near completion followed by the initiation of language or articulation training).
- A 'concurrent approach' (parallel treatment of stuttering and other speech/language targets for equal amounts of time within the context of the lowest phonologic and linguistic demands).

The sequential approach, which delays treating the other impairment until some time in the future, appears to be the least desirable option (Bernstein Ratner, 1995a, b). The blended, cycles, and concurrent approaches appear to be viable options for treatment aimed at facilitating increased fluency and remediation of the speech/language disorder associated with the concomitant problem.

Louko, Conture, and Edwards (1999) proposed that stuttering and a concomitant phonologic problem can, and should, be treated simultaneously. This is supported by data from Arndt and Healey (2001). They found that the majority of clinicians treating a fluency disorder and a concomitant phonologic and/or language disorder used a blended approach in which both disorders were addressed simultaneously in the treatment program. Clearly, though, there are other approaches to treating a dysfluent child's concomitant disorder. Arndt and Healey (2001) also found that many clinicians used a concurrent approach when treating stuttering and a concomitant disorder. With the concurrent approach, Bernstein Ratner (1995b) recommended that fluency training be placed within linguistic and phonologic contexts that the child can manage. For example, when treating a phonologic disorder, a clinician could focus on treating the fluency disorder while the clinician models the correct sound production without direct reference to the child's sound production during each session. In this approach, both problems are addressed but only the fluency disorder is treated directly. Louko, Conture and Edwards (1999) take a slightly different approach by combining simultaneous treatment of stuttering and disordered phonology from a speech-language pathologist and the parents of the child.

Interestingly, only a few school-based clinicians in the study by Arndt and Healey (2001) used a cycles approach, and even fewer applied a sequential approach in which treatment continued with one disorder until all goals were met. As Bernstein Ratner (1995b) suggested, a clinician's choice of treatment depends on a careful analysis of the child's needs and may require changes in programming if progress is impeded through one particular approach. This might be particularly true for young children (that is, kindergarten through third grade) and for those with learning, behavioral, and cognitive challenges. Logan and LaSalle (2003) suggest that young children may have difficulty remembering or being able to separate stuttering management techniques from other speech and language concepts being taught. We believe the same difficulties exist for children who stutter who also have LD, ADHD, or mental retardation.

Therefore, one recommendation is to approach the treatment of stuttering and any other speech/language problem using a cycles approach. Treatment would involve using specific time intervals during the treatment program – treating one of the impairments for several weeks followed by treating the second impairment for the next several weeks. Or, a clinician could use a slightly different cycles approach (criterion-based) in which treatment of one impairment would continue until a specific criterion level of performance had been reached, which is then followed by treatment for the second impairment until specific performance criteria had been met (Logan and LaSalle, 2003). For example, the clinician could start the first treatment cycle for a child with Down syndrome by encouraging the child to use a prolonged speech pattern while producing single words or short phrases, using pausing between phrases, and focusing on proper turn-taking (Guitar, 1998). Once a criterion level of fluency is established at these simple levels of a linguistic context, a gradual increase in utterance length and complexity could be implemented to include sentences or short monologues as well as an increase in the speech rate and reduction of pauses between utterances (Ryan and Van Kirk Ryan, 1995). The second criterion-based cycle might use rhymes and jingles or some other simple expressive language task as a way to promote the child's learning of predictable language structures (Bray, 2001). The third and fourth cycles of the program would be focused on reviewing previously learned fluency management skills and language skills together with the introduction of new techniques or strategies that fall within the child's abilities to manage the demands of a speaking situation. This type of cycles approach could include the parents by having them provide indirect support/modeling of behaviors being addressed by the clinician.

Logan and LaSalle (2003) also recommend that clinicians should not require a child to integrate stuttering and articulation/language skills within the same speech activity until he or she can demonstrate successful management of the techniques or skills at simple linguistic levels. However, eventually the child needs to be able to implement all learned fluency and speech/language strategies simultaneously. Guitar (1998) also suggests that clinicians should reward children's responses with verbal and/or tangible reinforcement. However, reinforcing correct fluency and speech/language behaviors at the same time by saying 'good job' after the child produces an utterance might cause some confusion for the child. Because both problems have been addressed in therapy, care must be taken to ensure the child understands which correct behavior is being reinforced. For example, he recommends that clinicians use a phrase such as 'That was nice and smooth (or easy)' when reinforcing fluent responses or less severe stuttering behavior. When correct sounds are produced, the clinician might say, 'That was a good ___ (sound) on the word ___'. A syntactically correct utterance might be reinforced verbally with a phrase such as 'That was a good sentence'. Being careful to clearly state what behaviors are correct and being reinforced should help the child understand which aspects of the response were correctly produced.

Preliminary treatment considerations for children who stutter who have concomitant LD or ADHD

Given that a clinician has addressed the two issues above, there are a host of other treatment considerations that should be integrated into a clinician's blended, cycles, sequential, or concurrent treatment approach. A clinician needs to consider a variety of environmental and behavioral strategies in order to effectively treat stuttering when LD and ADHD coexist. Unfortunately, specific strategies regarding the management of children who stutter and have LD and ADHD cannot be found in the literature, although some information on treating children who stutter who also have ADHD can be found in an article by Healey and Reid (2003). However, there are a number of similarities in treating children with these disorders that a clinician will want to bear in mind. The co-morbidity of LD and ADHD is approximately 20–40% and includes problems with attention, persistence, and impulsivity (DuPaul and Stoner, 2002).

A clinician will want to consider the management process within the context of well-established environmental and behavioral interventions that have been developed to improve the performance of LD or ADHD children in the classroom. Paul (2001) suggests that the most effective treatments for children with ADHD include a combination of pharmacologic, environmental and behavioral interventions. Healey and Reid (2003) point out that much of the evidence-based research on how to manage children with ADHD in the school environment can be applied to treating stuttering children with these concomitant problems. For example, intervention strategies for ADHD children in the classroom have been applied to a general intervention program for communication disorders (Damico and Armstrong, 1996). This next section is a description of these principles of intervention as they apply to treating children who stutter and have concomitant LD or ADHD.

The first consideration is environmental accommodations that a clinician can provide within the treatment setting. Ideally, children with LD or ADHD should be taught in a room rather than in hallways, open classroom environments, or a corner of a classroom. For instance, research has shown that for children with ADHD, various types of distractions in an environment other than a room can result in decreases in time on task and other problem behaviors (Whalen et al., 1979). However, it is not necessary or even desirable to conduct individual treatment in a room with four plain walls (Abramowitz and O'Leary, 1991). Rather, a clinician should be sensitive to any types of distraction and minimize their potential effects. For example, clinicians could make sure that they have children's attention before speaking by making eye contact, keeping the conversation focused on the main points by minimizing tangential comments, and avoiding talking over competing noise (Michon, 1999).

Consideration of whether the child will be treated individually or as a member of a treatment group is another important decision about therapy. Typically, children with LD and ADHD often do better in one-to-one situations or very small groups with well-behaved students. For example, Damico and Armstrong (1996) suggest that if the speech-language pathologist collaborates with the classroom teacher to provide interventions with ADHD students, then co-operative learning might be an effective strategy to use. The same would be true for children with LD. Within this context, the clinician could encourage a child who stutters to work on basic social skills, which may be problematic for many people who stutter. The combination of struggling with interpersonal communication secondary to stuttering and attention issues associated with ADHD could result in maladaptive social behaviors. These unproductive patterns can be pointed out, analyzed, and worked on with the assistance of the clinician and other members within the same treatment group. Working in groups also allows the clinician to obtain a more realistic view of how an individual performs in social contexts outside the therapy room. This information is vital when considering carry-over of learned skills into future social arenas (Guitar et al., 2000).

Another environmental consideration specifically for children with ADHD is permitting physical movement within the classroom or clinical setting to control restlessness or fidgeting. Allowing children to move, stand during lessons, or interspersing activities that may require physical activity may help maintain attention to the tasks (Reid, 1999). For a child who stutters, this could involve having children move objects, draw a line slowly on a piece of paper, or use some form of gross body movement (such as walking or tossing a ball) while talking with a prolonged speech pattern. Additionally, children with ADHD are more likely to display behavior problems when they are not actively responding and/or receiving frequent feedback on performance (DuPaul and Stoner, 2002). Providing students with frequent opportunities to respond, rather than having them spend time sitting passively while waiting for an opportunity to respond, is a crucial component for keeping a student with ADHD engaged. If a student with ADHD sits too long, tuning out or other inappropriate behavior typically will occur. Thus, children with ADHD usually perform best when they receive frequent and immediate feedback on their performance (Barkley, 1998). Children with LD also should be rewarded for asking questions and seeking clarification on assignments or for why certain strategies assist them in talking with greater fluency.

Relative to instruction and intervention planning, the length and difficulty of individual sessions is an important consideration. For children with ADHD, Healey and Reid (2003) recommend that it may be better to schedule treatment for short periods of time (that is, 10–15-minute segments) rather than one 30-minute treatment session. Long sessions could lead to boredom, noncompliance, and reluctance to practice strategies. If longer sessions are needed, or the student tolerates longer sessions, it is a good idea to break up the activities within the session. For example, rather than doing two 15-minute activities, it would be better to do four seven-minute activities and allow brief breaks in between activities (Reid, 1999). In this way, reviewing material more often could increase the child's ability to retain and implement any management techniques.

Treatment for children who stutter who have LD or ADHD

It is noteworthy that any approach to treatment will depend on factors such as the child's language abilities, and the cognitive difficulty of the task (Westby and Cutler, 1994). Given that approximately one-third of children who stutter also have language impairments (Arndt and Healey, 2001), a clinician should be aware of the links between stuttering, language impairment, LD and ADHD. Children with these characteristics would be at risk for developing the necessary cognitive skills necessary to self-evaluate and self-regulate behaviors (Abikoff, 1985). Therefore, the standard treatment approaches to stuttering when no concomitant disorders are present will have to be adapted to fit the needs of the child with LD or ADHD.

Therapy for children who stutter generally focuses on helping them to achieve a greater level of fluency, manage stuttered moments more effectively, and modify negative cognitive (thoughts, perceptions, and awareness) and affective (emotions and attitudes) elements that affect or influence effective communication in a variety of social contexts. Fluency-shaping techniques, such as easy or gentle onsets of phonation and prolonged speech and/or use of phrasing of an utterance to reduce speech rate, are usually combined with stuttering-modification strategies. A stuttering-modification approach uses pseudo-stuttering to increase children's awareness of what happens during a real stuttering moment and to reduce their need to hide the stuttering (that is, desensitization to stuttering). Actual modification of stuttered moments is accomplished through the use of cancellations and pullouts. Additional treatment strategies in a basic treatment program include increasing a child's awareness of stuttered moments and identification of behaviors that characterize the stuttering behavior. Any negative feelings, attitudes, and emotional reactions that the child and others have toward stuttering also need to be addressed. Finally, systematic manipulation of the length and complexity of the utterance are critical to a child's management of newly learned fluency skills (Ryan and Van Kirk Ryan, 1995; Guitar, 1998; Manning, 2001; Logan and LaSalle, 2003).

Given this basic structure of an integrated treatment program, modifications need to be made in the program to accommodate children who stutter with LD or ADHD. The following is a list of possible modifications or considerations the clinician might want to bear in mind when implementing a program for these children.

- Explain the specific goals of therapy to the child in simple, age-appropriate language. Children should feel some ownership in setting goals and the gains that will occur as a result of work on specific skills and target behaviors. Also, have the child understand the goals of therapy and why those goals will facilitate remediation (Daly and Burnett, 1999).
- Ask the child a question to see whether he or she can describe what has been learned in therapy in their own words (Michon, 1999). By asking children to organize the ideas and express the concepts using their own language, the clinician is increasing the chances of long-term retention of the material (Guitar et al., 2000).
- Make all instructions and directions clear and concise but don't give too many directions at once. Repeat the directions multiple times and have children repeat what they heard and understood. Attention-getting strategies might include lightly touching the child's hand or arm and/or making eye contact with the child prior to the instruction (Michon, 1999). Once attention is achieved, directions can be short and direct. Long involved directions are difficult for the client to remember and could cause a child to lose focus and become distracted (Reid, 1999). An example of an instruction that might be given to a child is, 'Talk about the picture using your stretched speech' rather than, 'Look at the picture and

keep your voice on continuously and blend the words together the whole time you are talking about the picture'. The clinician would also give verbal directions to use a particular speech strategy and then model the strategy for the child. Before responding, the child should be asked to repeat what he or she is to do and then demonstrate that understanding by using the desired strategy within a specific speech context (Healey and Reid, 2003). Also, it is important to give concrete examples of all techniques. Clinicians can encourage children to use artwork, schematics or any visual reminders to increase comprehension of difficult concepts (Pfiffner, 1995).

- Select a topic that is highly interesting to the child, or about which the child has considerable knowledge (for example, sports, hobbies, curricular topics). This topic then provides a theme for therapy. Most or all treatment activities and materials used to teach new skills will be based on this theme. Children and/or their families or teachers can contribute ideas, information, and materials related to the theme so that the topic stays within the realm of the child's prior knowledge. Numerous materials for most themes can be obtained from toy sets, books, magazines, newspaper articles, and various websites (Healey, Scott Trautman and Panico, 2001).

- Use concrete examples and contextualized materials (objects, pictures, drawings, printed materials) as much as possible during therapy as a means of controlling the length and complexity of utterances. Clinicians need to consider how much contextualization the child will need to support talking and account for the child's cognitive-linguistic capabilities. To make this decision, the clinician should determine if the child is more dysfluent when talking in contextualized or in decontextualized situations (no supportive communication materials). If the clinician is unsure whether the degree of contextualization affects the child's fluency, he or she should probe by collecting brief speech samples at various levels of linguistic complexity. For example, speech sampling could occur by asking the child to talk while engaged in pretend play or retelling a story with pictures about getting ready for school. A little more difficult speaking situation might involve retelling their own experiences getting ready for school, or retelling a scene from a favorite movie or television program without contextual support. The clinician could limit linguistic complexity of a response by targeting single-word or phrase-level productions, asking the child to label or describe materials or objects associated while using a fluency-enhancing or stuttering-modification strategy. For instance, if a child has just learned a new fluency-enhancing skill, the clinician might probe the child's ability to use it across several utterances by asking the child to recall three things that happened in therapy that day (Healey, Scott Trautman and Panico, 2001).

- Increase the child's awareness and self-monitoring. Many LD and ADHD children show poor awareness of stuttering or self-monitoring skills. Strategies for achieving greater awareness and self-monitoring include video and audio recording to provide immediate feedback on performance or correct behavior. Self-correction through self-cues to reduce speech rate, self-rating of task performance, and/or use of one of the strategies taught in therapy will assist in improving awareness and self-monitoring (Daly and Burnett, 1999).

Treatment of children who stutter who have mental retardation or Down syndrome

Cooper (1986) suggests that the management of stuttering in children who are mentally retarded and have Down syndrome is primarily a behavioral modification program. Little attention is given to modifying or shaping attitudes and feelings that may inhibit the development of improved fluency. The focus of therapy is for the clinician to use concepts and explanations for instruction that account for the child's limited conceptual and linguistic skills. Language training in the form of vocabulary development may be as much of a focus of therapy as stuttering (Bray, 2001).

Many of the suggestions described above for children who stutter and have LD or ADHD are relevant to modifications of treatment with children who are dysfluent and mentally retarded or have Down syndrome. In addition to those suggestions, the following is a list of recommended procedures for treating this population.

- Determine the child's awareness of stuttering or nonfluent speech that disrupts communication. Perhaps the child is no more aware of stuttering than he or she is aware of knowing when to speak or not, and the need to have good listening skills, taking conversational turns, and maintaining eye contact during a conversation (Bray, 2001). If the child is aware of his or her nonfluencies, then one of the first steps is to help the child create a list of the types of stuttering that are produced. For example, it might be helpful to have part-word repetition displayed graphically exactly like the child stutters. Thus, if the child says 'b-b-b-ball', the child can recognize a written version of one form of stuttering he or she produces. For a whole-word repetition, like 'it's ... it's ... it's a ball', a similar written example could be used.
- Discuss in simple language what techniques the child will use to enhance a fluent response and reduce the need to produce dysfluency. These might include a number of fluency-enhancing techniques, such as slow speech rate and gentle onsets of phonation (Cooper, 1986; Manning, 2001). It is important for the clinician to model a slow pace of talking by elongating the syllables within the utterance or by using a greater number of pauses between words in order. This also slows the pace of the

conversation, which might allow the child more linguistic processing time (Bray, 2001). Cooper (1986) notes that improvements in speech intelligibility, rate of speech, and voice quality can ensue as a result of having the child use fluency-enhancing gestures.

- Modify the linguistic length and complexity of the utterance, which is consistent with an approach advocated by Ryan and Van Kirk Ryan (1995). Adaptations of this approach, as shown above by Healey, Scott Trautman and Panico (2001), also should work well with this population. As the length and complexity of the utterance increases, it will be important to allow the child greater time in planning and processing the utterance (Bray, 2001).

- Encourage the child to master the use of learned fluency strategies. For this population, it is important to have the child use learned strategies extensively within and outside of therapy. Clinicians need to encourage the client through a reinforcement schedule to practice new speech patterns in as many structured (treatment session) and unstructured (at home, classroom, and so forth) situations as much as possible. In order to accomplish the extended use of newly learned strategies, the clinician should enlist the support of parents, teachers, communication aids, and resource personnel to assist in the practise and maintenance of basic fluency skills (Cooper, 1986).

- Clinicians should work with the child to set tangible goals and reasonable timelines for completing those goals. Students should be rewarded often for both the work completed and their behaviors during the therapy process (Blazer, 1999). Clinicians should ensure that the child fully understands what they are being reinforced for by clearly and repeatedly modeling the desired behaviors (Conture, 2001).

Supporting family and teachers of children who stutter who also have LD, ADHD or mental retardation

It is important for clinicians to garner the assistance of family members and teachers in the treatment process. Parents and teachers can be extremely effective in helping children to manage the disorder and serving as raters of severity of the stuttering and the concomitant problem. However, clinicians need to assess the desirability of asking parents to assist with treatment in the home. Our experience has shown that parents want to carry over the treatment in the home but find that doing so is stressful for them and their child. Nevertheless, there are a few things a clinician could consider as a means of supporting the role of the family and teachers in the treatment process for children who stutter and have LD, ADHD or mental retardation.

- Educate the parents and the entire family about the diagnosis and how that will affect the child's ability to perform certain tasks. Frequently parents receive a diagnosis (or two) but never receive a functional explanation of what that means to the child and the family in everyday situations. The clinician should also stress how the child's cognitive, emotional, psychosocial and physical abilities will affect his fluency in a variety of speaking situations.

- The family should become well-versed in strategies used to decrease the environmental demands placed on the child (Starkweather, 1987). These include interaction strategies, such as:
  - reducing the rate of speech in the house
  - allowing more pause time before speaking
  - using less complex language and vocabulary
  - providing increased listening time
  - decreasing interruptions from all family members
  - reducing competition for attention between all family members
  - avoiding demands for speech.
- The family and teachers should also be informed about the rationale for strategies that the clinician is using to accomplish the goals of treatment. They should also understand why their child might experience difficulty utilizing techniques or completing assignments especially in light of their coexisting issues. Parents and teachers must understand that the child is undertaking something extremely difficult and could easily experience feelings of frustration, doubt, shame and insecurity (Pfiffner, 1995).
- Clinicians should explain, demonstrate, and model everything that they want the family and teachers to do at home. If possible, the clinician should observe the parents and teachers using the strategies with the child. If they have a firm understanding and comfort level with the strategies, they will be more likely to use them at home or at school.
- The clinician could offer suggestions if persistent stuttering leads to teasing. Even if the child is not being teased, this will make the teacher aware that it may happen and make him or her more alert in case it does happen (Murphy, 2000).

Summary

When children who stutter have a coexisting learning, behavioral or cognitive disability, the clinician will be faced with the task of developing an appropriate treatment program for them. Understanding the nature of a child's stuttering and concomitant disorders begins with careful assessment. Once a clinician is familiar with each child's unique characteristics, abilities, and challenges, he or she will need to decide on the design of the treatment program for the stuttering and the concomitant disorder. The prevailing opinion is that children who stutter who also have a concomitant disorder should receive simultaneous treatment for both disorders, and variations in this approach have been suggested by Bernstein Ratner (1995b) and, more recently, by Logan and LaSalle (2003).

Unfortunately, there are no studies reported in the literature that have documented the effectiveness of an approach to treating children with stuttering and concomitant problems. Given this, we have attempted in this chapter to outline some of the key elements a clinician should bear in mind when treating a child who stutters and has learning, behavioral or cognitive impairments. A number of issues that have been found to be effective in working with children with LD and ADHD in the classroom also appear to have particular relevance to clinicians treating these children who also stutter. A number of suggestions were presented in helping clinicians work with children with mental retardation and Down syndrome. Teachers and family members also become important adjuncts to the treatment process so there is continuity and coherence for these children.

Chapter 11
Conclusions

CAMERON STARK AND ROBERTA LEES

Stammering in school-aged children is both common and serious. Ashley Craig and Tran demonstrates that, although stuttering will resolve spontaneously in many children, it persists or begins in others, with a prevalence in young school-aged children of about 1.4%. It can take some time for children to pass through the system to arrive at therapy. Slightly older children may already have undergone unsuccessful treatment. As several of the authors in this volume report, awareness of stuttering and ensuing reactions can also make treatment challenging.

There are differences between the treatments described, both in relation to their theoretical underpinnings and in the method of delivery of the treatments. There are, however, as many similarities as differences. This chapter explores some of the similarities, and discusses possible common ground on which to build future treatment developments.

The population studied

This text has highlighted some of the complexities of treating the school-aged child who stutters. Although stuttering is a common disorder in population terms, the spontaneous recovery of many children means that the point prevalence (the number of children who stutter at any one point in time) suggests that stuttering will not be the most common disorder treated by clinicians working with school-aged children, unless of course the clinician is a specialist in this disorder. Generalist clinicians then are faced with the problem of treating a complex disorder which they may treat infrequently. To complicate the situation still further, some of this group of children also have concomitant problems which may be linguistic, learning, behavioural, cognitive or physiological. Bernstein Ratner (Chapter 9) focuses particularly on linguistic problems, and on syndromes that are accompanied by a higher incidence of stuttering. She has stressed the importance of accurate diagnostic procedures to differentiate between stuttering and dysfluency as a result of a language disorder. This is an important distinction and one that will be useful to clinicians for treatment planning. Numerous clinicians ask about stuttering in certain known syndromes and Bernstein Ratner has expanded on this topic. This is an area worthy of much further investigation to try to explain why some syndromes are more often accompanied by stuttering. Further study of cognitive, linguistic and motoric functioning in these syndromes might shed further light on this.

In recent times there has been a growing awareness of attention deficit hyperactivity disorder (ADHD) and clinicians have often remarked on the co-occurrence of stuttering in this disorder. Healey, Reid and Donaher have expanded on this in Chapter 10, and, of course, the question of why stuttering occurs frequently in this disorder merits further study. There has been an awareness for some time of stuttering occurring in cognitive conditions such as Down syndrome, and this is also further discussed in Chapter 10.

Population approaches

Considered from a public health perspective, stuttering is important because of its impact, and its prevalence. The demonstration by Bernstein Ratner (Chapter 9), and by Healey, Reid and Donaher (Chapter 10), raises important issues of inclusion. If some children with other disorders also stutter, then the chance of their being isolated from their peer group, and disadvantaged in the educational process, is clear.

To clinicians, the need to treat stuttering is self-evident. There are, however, necessary public health considerations. Measurement of effectiveness is discussed in more detail by Stark and Lees (Chapter 3), but it is helpful to consider the challenges as they relate to future research. In younger children, the benefits of treatment have to be balanced against the costs and burden of treatment. Speech and language therapy services in the UK often have long waiting lists. As work by Yairi and colleagues (Yairi, 1993; Yairi and Ambrose, 1993, 1999) and Craig (Chapter 5) demonstrates, most pre-school children will improve spontaneously. As well as making treatment effectiveness more difficult to measure, this also means that most children treated are receiving an intervention that offers them little or no benefit. If 75% of children would have improved with no intervention, then in effect three children are being treated in order to benefit a fourth.

The treatment equation depends, then, on the gains from treatment against the losses by not treating, compared with other possible uses of the speech and language therapy resource. Early treatment appears to be particularly effective, and it may be that intervention at the pre-school stage would avoid much of the treatment required by young school-aged children. Appropriate cost-effectiveness studies, using the available epidemiological and effectiveness information, may strengthen the argument services can mount for investment in earlier intervention.

At present, however, children who already stutter are not always identified in pre-school years. Even if they are identified, no referral may be made (Lees et al., 2000). It therefore seems that there is no immediate prospect of a marked reduction in school-aged children who require treatment. The cost-benefit equation is clearer in this age group, given the reduced number of children who are likely to improve spontaneously. Craig (Chapter 5) demonstrates the social and mental health burden that falls on children who stutter. Given this impact, it is obviously important that the treatments delivered are as effective as possible. The scarcity of speech and language therapy resources, in the UK at least, also argues for the delivery of interventions in the most efficient way possible, to maximize the gain from the available therapist time.

The descriptions of therapy in this volume make clear the wealth of treatment possibilities. There are broad themes within the treatments offered. The commonality of method between some of the treatments is perhaps clearer when they are presented side by side, as in this textbook, than is always apparent from discussion of separate methods. In effect, this volume provides a masterclass, with extremely experienced clinicians offering details of their treatments in a way that should promote their use by others.

Expert opinion is very important, and the experience of the clinicians and researchers writing in this volume deserves careful attention. Craig (Chapter 5) discusses the idea of evidence-based healthcare. This requires the welding of research evidence with clinical experience and the needs of the particular child and family. Much of the skill of clinicians is in applying research evidence to practical situations. The underpinning requirement, however, is that there is good-quality research supporting the value of interventions. We discussed in an earlier chapter the distinction between effectiveness and efficacy. Demonstrating that treatments work in the 'best' situation, when delivered in research conditions by specialist units with particular experience of the techniques, is a necessary prerequisite to their use in local, non-specialist units.

The presentations of effectiveness discussed in the relevant chapters permit pointers to future implementation research. Most approaches have available research evidence of their value in specialist settings. There are several ways in which routine care may vary from specialist care (*see* boxed text on p. 200). The effect of these influences is that the effect of treatments in routine practice may not be the same as that under research conditions. Not all treatment approaches have this information available at present, and developing this would be important supporting evidence for the widespread adoption of some approaches.

Limits to the applicability of research to routine practice

Differences in case mix
Research protocols often require the exclusion of children who do not meet strict diagnostic criteria, and may exclude children with co-existing problems. Specialist centres may also be referred children who have had a range of previous treatments, sometimes over many years.

Training of therapists
Therapists engaged in research will often be either those who originated the treatment or those who have ready access to experts. They will often receive specialist training in the technique, and their competence may be assessed before they commence treatments. By contrast, clinicians in routine practice may acquire details of techniques from textbooks or papers, videos or conferences. This may be a substantially different grounding in the techniques from those of the clinicians conducting the research on which the adoption of the technique is based.

Adherence to protocols
In research studies, a treatment protocol will often be used, detailing what component of treatment is to be offered at what stage. This may include details of what has to be achieved before the next component of therapy is offered. Adherence to the protocol will often be monitored, for example by video or tape recording of treatment sessions. In routine practice, clinicians often introduce components from other therapies which seem to suit the particular child or family with whom they are working. In a research study, this would usually be specifically discouraged.

Time for treatment
Research projects will often have carefully set out treatment times, over a set number of sessions. In clinical practice, the time available may be considerably less.

Study size can be a barrier to interpretation of research findings. In some cases, the size of a study can be such that it is difficult to be sure if lack of effect is related to ineffectiveness of the treatment, or to inadequate study size. Similarly, the most extreme result will often tend to be reported first, with later studies identifying smaller effect sizes. One way of representing information is to use a systematic review and meta-analysis process, where the results of smaller studies are combined (Stark et al., 2004). The process depends on the existence of studies to include, however, although it can identify gaps in the research knowledge, which may then act as a stimulus to future research.

The following section discusses some of the similarities and differences in the approaches described in this volume.

Treatment processes

Before treatment commences all the contributors in this volume would assess the child who stutters fully to gain a better understanding of both the child and the context in which he or she is stuttering. In order to reduce repetition, contributors on treatment were asked to concentrate on their treatment programmes. A few have commented briefly on their assessment schedule. Bernstein Ratner (Chapter 9) discusses the importance of assessment leading to an accurate diagnosis of the problem, and Lees (Chapter 2) describes a typical assessment of the child.

For children who stutter, with no concomitant problems, there is a general agreement that fluency-shaping techniques can be useful. There is almost universal agreement on the nature of these fluency-shaping techniques. They often involve slowing of speech rate, gentle onsets, managing airflow and soft contacts. Craig (Chapter 5) describes the use of EMG feedback to assist with the acquisition of smooth speech. Some also give children some information on how speech is produced to help them understand the basis of the fluency techniques. These modifications to the speech process do produce an increase in fluency but the clinician must ask, at what cost? Children can be taught to speak fluently in clinic but the transfer and maintenance of this fluency is much more difficult.

Lees (Chapter 4) comments on the need for a greater understanding of the psychology of change. Change is difficult for everyone, and it is particularly difficult for adults to change the way they speak. For children, who have less experience of stuttering, it can be made fun by a competent, skilled clinician. However, the impact of this new fluency on listeners' reactions, particularly from their peer group, cannot be underestimated. Children also need to be motivated to maintain some vigilance when they speak. Craig (Chapter 5), Cook and Botterill (Chapter 6) and Logan (Chapter 7) discuss the value and format of maintenance activities. For clinicians, time must be built into any treatment programme for such activities, and the importance of these should also be stressed to the children and their carers/parents. If there are some residual dysfluencies after a fluency-shaping programme Logan describes the use of stuttering modification techniques to reduce these and their impact.

Williams (Chapter 8) describes reducing stuttering without changing the way the child speaks. This certainly must reduce the fears of adverse listener reactions. Although not describing them as 'maintenance' procedures, Williams does elaborate on how contact is maintained with the child to ensure that treatment benefits are maintained.

As would be expected in any text on stuttering, there is variation in the amount of attention paid to affective and cognitive aspects of stuttering. All authors on treatment do acknowledge that there is a link between thoughts, feelings and stuttering behaviour. Some, for example Cook and Botterill and Logan, describe the cognitive and affective aspects of treatment in some depth providing examples of how they explore these areas with their clients. Williams discusses the use of the group setting to approach such issues. The variation in the amount of attention paid to affective and cognitive aspects of stuttering has a long history. Long-term studies are required to show if dealing with the affective and cognitive aspects of stuttering along with treating the stuttering symptom are superior to treatment of the symptom alone. How 'superiority' of treatment can be measured will be discussed later in this chapter.

Treating the child who stutters and has a concomitant disorder can be challenging. If the child who stutters also has a linguistic disorder both Bernstein Ratner (Chapter 9) and Healey, Reid and Donaher (Chapter 10) discuss ways of treating both problems, sometimes concurrently. The latter elaborate on additional aspects of stuttering treatment if the child has a learning disorder, cognitive disorder or ADHD. These additional aspects sometimes involve modifying the environment. For some clinicians this will be straightforward and for others it will require negotiation with colleagues in the school or clinical setting. These authors do, however, acknowledge that there is really no information on the effectiveness of treatment with this client group, and Bernstein Ratner reminds us of the inherent difficulties in achieving this.

There is a general agreement that parents and teachers should be involved in the child's treatment. Parents and teachers may now be much more knowledgeable about stuttering than in the past, partly because of access to Web-based information. Despite this, providing advice for family and teachers is generally regarded as good practice. It seems appropriate to provide parents with information on the treatment being proposed for their child and to answer questions they might have on stuttering. This is required good practice for healthcare professionals, and also offers the opportunity to engage parents or guardians in their child's treatment, sometimes as co-therapists.

Much of this will involve the clinician in understanding not just the treatment process but also the theoretical underpinning of the approach they have chosen. All contributors on treatment approaches have included information on this in their respective chapters. The problem for all clinicians is how to answer the parents' questions about stuttering without making them feel guilty that they have somehow caused this problem. Some clinicians give advice on ways of interacting with the child which are conducive to fluency. Much more information is needed on the parents' viewpoint. How do they feel about the advice given and how helpful have they found it?

An additional problem faced by some clinicians is when they are referred a child who stutters, whose parents give permission for treatment but wish no part in this treatment. We may assume that the prognosis in this case is much poorer, although effective working with teachers might compensate for this. Little is known about the effects of this. With legislators often having policies of social inclusion, teachers now have many children in their classrooms with very different problems. Teachers cannot devote all their time and energy to the child who stutters, but a skilled clinician enlisting the help of the teacher seems to progress the treatment more effectively. Research is still required to elucidate the effects of teacher involvement in treatment and the most effective type of involvement.

Relapse

If stuttering is part of the human condition then relapse can be expected in some cases. Treatment of stuttering in children often involves changing behaviour, and efforts to change any behaviour in humans usually leads to relapse by some. Of course, much depends on how relapse is defined, for example the child is now stuttering at an unacceptable level for the clinician, the parents or the child. Craig (Chapter 5) and Logan (Chapter 7) focus on strategies for the management of relapse. The reasons for relapse are ill understood but are likely to be multiple. Craig (1998b) has initiated investigations into this problem and further study would be beneficial to elucidate those children likely to relapse following treatment. If they do relapse should they have 'more of the same' or is an entirely different approach to be recommended?

Outcome measures

During the 1970s and 1980s there was much reliance on obtaining data on the stuttering symptoms, for example frequency of stuttering, measured as a percentage of stuttered syllables. Measures of speech rate were also taken. At this time the emphasis was on quantitative data, and many professional journals favoured this type of data. It is time-consuming for clinicians to collect these data unless the measures are taken 'live' by direct counting of the percentage of stuttered syllables and/or speech rate, with no transcription of the child's speech. Many clinicians do use this type of 'live' counting of stuttered syllables and speech rate, and today these are still acceptable outcome measures, but most authors in this text do not consider that they are sufficient in themselves.

There seems to be growing acceptance that qualitative measures also have a place when assessing outcomes. These qualitative measures take account of more than the stuttering behaviour. This theme of a more holistic assessment of children who stutter is apparent throughout this text. When discussing outcomes Cook and Botterill (Chapter 6) describe the measurement of change as multidimensional, involving measurement of stuttering and the parents' viewpoint on change. Logan (Chapter 7) and Williams (Chapter 8) also describe the use of scales to evaluate the amount of participation of the child, the amount of stuttering and the reactions of the child towards stuttering. This is reflecting a growing awareness of the need to take into account the consumer's viewpoint when evaluating the success of any treatment programme. The problem now for the clinician is to find a series of assessments which adequately reflect all of these features, but which are not too time-consuming. Efficiency of the clinician's time and adequate assessment of treatment effectiveness need to be married. Much remains to be done to assess the effectiveness of the various treatment programmes that exist, and Stark and Lees (Chapter 3) discuss some of the possible research designs which would achieve this. They also stress the importance of undertaking this type of research in an age of evidence-based practice. It is likely that financial considerations will play a growing part in determining treatments and it is necessary that clinicians know roughly how long treatments would be expected to take, though there will be great variation, and the types of outcome to expect.

In order to determine outcomes there are some difficult variables to be taken into account, such as the personality and enthusiasm of the clinician. This is difficult to measure but it seems likely that this will play a part in the effective delivery of any treatment programme. The amount of help given by parents and by teachers, and possibly by the child's friends, is also likely to have some influence on the results.

This text is intended to give clinicians enough information to treat, with increased confidence, children who stutter. There have been many reports of clinicians and student clinicians feeling uncomfortable about treating stuttering (St Louis and Lass, 1981; Kelly et al., 1997). The reasons for this are unclear, but the information contained in this text is intended to encourage clinicians to work much more with children who stutter and to evaluate their treatment programmes. Obtaining a good database on the effectiveness of different treatment approaches will serve clinicians well in the future.

References

Abbeduto L, Hagerman R (1997) Language and communication in fragile X syndrome. Mental Retardation and Development Disabilities Research Reviews 3: 313-322.

Abikoff H (1985) Efficacy of cognitive training interventions in hyperactive children: a critical review. Clinical Psychology Review 5: 549-512.

Abramowitz AJ, O'Leary S (1991) Behavioral interventions for the classroom: implications for students with ADHD. School Psychology Review 20: 220-234.

Alderson P, Groves T (2004) What doesn't work and how to show it: ineffectiveness is hard to prove and accept. British Medical Journal 328: 473.

Ambrose NG, Cox NJ, Yairi E (1997) The genetic basis of persistence and recovery in stuttering. Journal of Speech, Language and Hearing Research 40: 567-580.

American Psychiatric Association (1994) Diagnostic and Statistical Manual of Mental Disorders (4th edn). Washington DC: American Psychiatric Association.

American Speech-Language-Hearing Association (1995) Guidelines for practise in stuttering treatment. ASHA 37 (Suppl. 14): 26-35.

American Speech-Language-Hearing Association (2003) ASHA 2003 Omnibus Survey. Rockville MD: ASHA.

Anderson J, Conture E (2000) Language abilities of children who stutter: A preliminary study. Journal of Fluency Disorders 25: 283-304.

Anderson TK, Felsenfeld S (2003) A thematic analysis of late recovery from stuttering. American Journal of Speech-Language Pathology 12: 243-53.

Andrews J, Andrews M (1990) Family Based Treatment in Communicative Disorders: A Systematic Approach. Dekalb, IL: Janelle Publications.

Andrews G, Craig AR (1988) Prediction of outcome after treatment for stuttering. British Journal of Psychiatry 153: 236-240.

Andrews G, Cutler J (1974) Stuttering therapy: the relationship between changes in symptom level and attitude. Journal of Speech and Hearing Research 39: 312-319.

Andrews G, Harris M (1964) The Syndrome of Stuttering. London: Heinemann Medical Books.

Andrews G, Ingham R (1971) Stuttering: considerations in the evaluation of treatment. British Journal of Disorders of Communication 6: 129-138.

Andrews G, Craig AR, Feyer AM, Hoddinott S, Howie P, Neilson M (1983) Stuttering: a review of research findings and theories circa 1982. Journal of Speech and Hearing Disorders 48: 226-246.

Andrews G, Morris-Yates A, Howie P, Martin N (1991) Genetic factors in stuttering confirmed. Archives General Psychiatry 48: 1034-1035.

Aneshensel CS, Frerichs RR, Clark V, Yokopenic PA (1982) Telephone versus in-person surveys of community health status. American Journal of Public Health 72: 1017–1021.

Ardila A, Bateman JR, Nino CR, Pulido E, Rivera DB, Vanegas CJ (1994) An epidemiologic study of stuttering. Journal of Communication Disorders 27: 37–48.

Argyle M, Furnham A, Graham J (1981) Social Situations. Cambridge: Cambridge University Press.

Arndt J, Healey EC (2001) Concomitant disorders in school-age children who stutter. Language, Speech and Hearing Services in Schools 32: 68–78.

Aron ML (1962) The nature and incidence of stuttering among a Bantu group of school going children. Journal of Speech and Hearing Disorders 27: 116–128.

Australian Bureau of Statistics (1998) Estimated Resident Population by Age and Sex in Statistical Local Areas in NSW 30 June 1991. Sydney: Australian Bureau of Statistics.

Backer K, Brutten G, McQuain J (1995) A preliminary assessment of the validity of three instrument-based measures for speech rate determination. Journal of Fluency Disorders 20: 63–75.

Bajina K (1995) Covert aspects associated with the 'stuttering syndrome': focus on self-esteem. In: Fawcus M (ed.), Stuttering from Theory to Practice. London: Whurr Publishers, pp. 99–110.

Baker L, Cantwell DP (1987) A prospective psychiatric follow-up of children with speech/language disorders. Journal of American Academy of Child and Adolescent Psychiatry 26: 546–553.

Bandura A (1969) Principles of Behavior Modification. New York: Holt, Rinehart & Winston.

Bandura A (1977a) Self-efficacy: toward a unifying theory of behavioral change. Psychological Review 84: 191–215.

Bandura A (1977b) Social Learning Theory. Englewood Cliffs, NJ: Prentice Hall.

Barkley RA (1998) Attention Deficit Hyperactivity Disorder: A handbook for diagnosis and treatment, 2nd edn. New York, NY: Guilford Press.

Barnes B, Ernst S, Hyde K (1999) An Introduction to Groupwork: A Group Analytic Experience. London: Macmillan.

Baumgaertel A, Wolraich ML, Dietrich M (1995) Comparison of diagnostic criteria for attention deficit disorder with and without hyperactivity defined by research criteria. Journal of Consulting and Clinical Psychology 58: 580–588.

Beaglehole R, Bonita R, Kjellstrom T (2002) Basic Epidemiology. Geneva: World Health Organization.

Beck S (1995) Cognitive Therapy: Basics and beyond. New York: Guilford Press.

Beitchman JH, Brownlie ER, Inglis A, Wild J, Ferguson B, Schachter D (1996) Seven-year follow-up of speech/language impaired and control children: psychiatric outcome. Journal of Child Psychology and Psychiatry 37: 961–970.

Beitchman JH, Wilson B, Johnson CJ, Atkinson L, Young A, Adlar E, Escobar M, Douglas L (2001) Fourteen-year follow-up of speech/language impaired and control children: psychiatric outcome. Journal of American Academy of Child and Adolescent Psychiatry 40: 75–82.

Belser R, Sudhalter V (2001) Conversational characteristics of children with Fragile X syndrome: repetitive speech. American Journal on Mental Retardation 106: 28–38.

Bernhardt BH, Stemberger JP (2000) Workbook in Nonlinear Phonology for Clinical Application. Austin, TX: Pro-Ed.

Bernstein Ratner N (1981) Are there constraints on childhood disfluency? Journal of Fluency Disorders 6: 341–350.

Bernstein Ratner N (1993) Parents, children, and stuttering. Seminars in Speech and Language 14: 238–249.

Bernstein Ratner N (1995a) Language complexity and stuttering in children. Topics in Language Disorders 15: 180–186.

Bernstein Ratner N (1995b) Treating the child who stutters with concomitant language or phonological impairment. Language, Speech and Hearing Services in Schools 26: 180–186.

Bernstein Ratner N (1997a) Stuttering: a psycholinguistic perspective. In: Curlee R, Siegal G (eds), Nature and Treatment of Stuttering: New Directions. Needham Heights, MA: Allyn & Bacon, pp. 99–127.

Bernstein Ratner N (1997b) Leaving Las Vegas: clinical odds and individual outcomes. American Journal of Speech-Language Pathology 6: 29–33.

Bernstein Ratner N (2001) The phonology of early stuttering: some reasons why there isn't one. In: Bosshardt H, Yaruss JS, Peters HFM (eds), Fluency Disorders: Theory, Research, Treatment and Self-help. Nijmegen: Nijmegen University Press, pp. 203–205.

Bernstein Ratner N (2004a) Atypical speech and language development. In: Berko Gleason J (ed.), The Development of Language, 6th edn. Boston, MA: Allyn & Bacon, pp. 324–395.

Bernstein Ratner N (2004b) Caregiver–child interactions and their impact on children's fluency: implications for treatment. American Journal of Speech and Language Pathology 35: 46–56.

Bernstein Ratner N, Sih C (1987) The effects of gradual increases in sentence length and complexity on children's dysfluency. Journal of Speech and Hearing Disorders 52: 278–287.

Bernstein Ratner N, Silverman S (2000) Parental perceptions of children's communicative development at stuttering onset. Journal of Speech Language and Hearing Research 43: 1252–1263.

Bhopal R (2002) Concepts of Epidemiology. Oxford: Oxford University Press.

Birdwhistell R (1970) Kinetics and Context. Philadelphia, PA: University of Pennsylvania Press.

Blazer B (1999) Developing 504 classroom accommodation plans: a collaborative systematic parent–student–teacher approach. Teaching Exceptional Children 32: 28–33.

Block S (2004) The evidence base for the treatment of stuttering. In: Reilly S, Douglas J, Oates J (eds), Evidence-based Practice in Speech Pathology. London: Whurr Publishers, pp. 83–109.

Blood G (1995) A behavioral-cognitive therapy program for adults who stutter: computers and counseling. Journal of Communication Disorders 28: 165–180.

Blood G, Seider R (1981) The concomitant problems of young stutterers. Journal of Speech and Hearing Research 46: 31–33.

Blood G, Blood I, Tellis G, Gabel R (2001) Communication apprehension and self perceived communication competence in adolescents who stutter. Journal of Fluency Disorders 26: 161–178.

Blood G, Ridenour V, Qualls C, Hammer C (2003) Co-occurring disorders in children who stutter. Journal of Communication Disorders 36: 427–448.

Bloodstein O (1960) The development of stuttering: II. Development phases. Journal of Speech and Hearing Disorders 25: 366–376.

Bloodstein O (1995) A Handbook on Stuttering, 5th edn. San Diego, CA: Singular Publishing.

Bloom C, Cooperman DK (1999) Synergistic Stuttering Therapy: A holistic approach. Boston, MA: Butterworth-Heinemann.

Boberg E (1978) Stuttering in the retarded. II. Prevalence of stuttering in EMR and TMR children. Mental Retardation Bulletin 6: 67–76.

Boberg E (1981) Maintenance of fluency. In: Boberg E (ed.), Maintenance of Fluency: Proceedings of the Banff Conference. New York: Elsevier North Holland, pp. 71–111.

Boberg E, Kully D (1985) Comprehensive Stuttering Program. San Diego, CA: College Hill Press.

Boberg E, Kully D (1994) Long-term results of an intensive treatment program for adults and adolescents who stutter. Journal of Speech and Hearing Research 37: 1050–1059.

Boberg E, Yeudall LT, Schopflocher D, Bo-Lassen P (1983) The effect of an intensive behavioral program on the distribution of EEG alpha power in stutterers during the processing of verbal and visuospatial information. Journal of Fluency Disorders 8: 245–263.

Bortfeld H, Leon S, Bloom J, Schober M, Brennan S (2001) Disfluency rates in conversation: effects of age, relationship, topic, role and gender. Language and Speech 44: 123–147.

Boscolo B, Bernstein Ratner N, Rescorla L (2002) Fluency of school-aged children with a history of specific expressive language impairment: an exploratory study. American Journal of Speech-Language Pathology 11: 41–49.

Botterill W, Cook F (1987) Personal construct theory and the treatment of adolescent dysfluency. In: Rustin L, Purser H, Rowley D (eds), Progress in the Treatment of Fluency Disorders. London: Taylor & Francis, pp. 147–165.

Boyle CA, Decoufle P, Yeargin-Allsopp M (1994) Prevalence and health impact of developmental disabilities in US children. Pediatrics 93: 399–403.

Brady WA, Hall DE (1976) The prevalence of stuttering among school-age children. Language, Speech and Hearing Services in Schools 7: 75–81.

Bray M (2001) Down's Syndrome and Stuttering (brochure). Memphis, TN: Stuttering Foundation of America.

Bray NW, Fletcher KL, Turner LA (1997) Cognitive competencies and strategy use in individuals with mental retardation. In: Maclean WW Jr (ed.), Ellis' Handbook of Mental Deficiency, Psychological Theory, and Research, 3rd edn. Mahwah, NJ: Erlbaum, pp. 197–217.

British Stammering Association (1995) Bullying and the Dysfluent Child. London: British Stammering Association.

British Stammering Association (1996) A Chance to Speak. London: British Stammering Association.

Brook R, Lohr K (1985) Efficiency, effectiveness, variations and quality. Medical Care 23: 710–722.

Brundage S, Bernstein Ratner N (1989) The measurement of stuttering frequency in children's speech. Journal of Fluency Disorders 14: 351–358.

Brutten G, Dunham S (1989) The Communication Attitude Test. A normative study of grade school children. Journal of Fluency Disorders 14: 371–377.

Burns K (2005) Focus on solutions: A health professional's guide. London: Whurr Publishers.

Camerata S (1989) Final consonant repetition: a linguistic perspective. Journal of Speech and Hearing Disorders 54: 159–162.

Cannell CF (1985) Overview: response bias and interviewer variability in surveys. In: Beed TW, Stimson RJ (eds), Survey Interviewing: Theory and techniques. New York: George Allen & Unwin, pp. 1–23.

Cantwell DP, Baker L (1997) Psychiatric disorder in children with speech and language retardation. Archives of General Psychiatry 34: 583–591.

Caruso A, Max L, McClowry M (1999) Perspectives on stuttering as a speech motor disorder. In: Caruso A, Strand E (eds), Clinical Management of Motor Speech Disorders in Children. New York: Thième, pp. 319–344.

Chapman AH, Cooper EB (1973) Nature of stuttering in a mentally retarded population. American Journal of Mental Deficiency 78: 153–157.

Chodron P (2001) Start Where You Are: A guide to compassionate living. Boston: Shambhala Publications.

Cirrin F, Bird A, Biehl L, Disney S, Estomin E, Rudebusch J, Schraeder T, Whitmire K (2003) Speech–language caseload in the schools: a workload analysis approach to setting caseload standards. Seminars in Speech and Language 24: 155–180.

Conture EG (1982) Stuttering in young children. Journal of Developmental and Behavioral Pediatrics 3: 163–169.

Conture EG (1990) Stuttering, 2nd edn. Englewood Cliffs, NJ: Prentice Hall.

Conture EG (1996) Treatment efficacy: stuttering. Journal of Speech and Hearing Research 39: 518–526.

Conture EG (2001) Stuttering: Its nature, diagnosis, and treatment. Needham Heights, MA: Allyn & Bacon.

Conture EG, Guitar B (1993) Evaluating efficacy of treatment of stuttering: school-age children. Journal of Fluency Disorders 18: 253–287.

Conture EG, Melnick KS (1999) Parent-child group approach to stuttering in pre-school children. In: Onslow M, Packman A (eds), The Handbook of Early Stuttering Intervention. San Diego, CA: Singular Publishing Group, pp. 17–53.

Conture E, Wolk L (1990) Stuttering. Seminars in Speech and Language 11: 200–211.

Conture E, Louko L, Edwards ML (1993) Simultaneously treating stuttering and disordered phonology in children: experimental treatment, preliminary findings. American Journal of Speech–Language Pathology 2: 72–81.

Cooper EB (1965) Structuring therapy for therapist and stuttering child. Journal of Speech and Hearing Disorders 30: 75–78.

Cooper EB (1986) The mentally retarded stutterer. In: St Louis K (ed.), The Atypical Stutterer: Principles and practices of rehabilitation. Orlando, FL: Academic Press, pp. 123–154.

Cooper EB (1987) The chronic perseverative stuttering syndrome. Journal of Fluency Disorders 12: 381–388.

Cooper EB, Cooper C (1985) Cooper Personalized Fluency Control Therapy – Revised. Allen, TX: DLM.

Cooper EB, Cooper C (1995) Cooper Assessment for Stuttering Syndromes: Children's Version. San Antonio, CA: The Psychological Association.

Cooper JA (1990) Research Needs in Stuttering: Roadblocks and Future Directions. American Speech and Hearing Association Report no. 18. Rockville, MD: ASHA.

Cordes A (1998) Current status of the stuttering treatment literature. In: Cordes A, Ingham R (eds), Treatment Efficacy for Stuttering: A search for empirical bases. London: Singular, pp. 117–144.

Corey G, Corey MS (1997) Groups: Process and Practice, 5th edn. Pacific Grove, CA: Brooks/Cole Pub. Co. International Thomson Pub.

Corey MS, Corey G (2001) Groups, Process and Practice, 6th edn. Pacific Group, CA: Brooks/Cole Wadsworth Group.

Costello J (1983) Current behavioral treatments for children. In: Prins D, Ingham R (eds), Treatment of Stuttering in Early Childhood. San Diego, CA: College-Hill Press, pp. 69–98.

Costello J, Ingham R (1985) Assessment strategies for stuttering. In: Curlee R, Perkins W (eds), Nature and Treatment of Stuttering: New Directions. London: Taylor & Francis, pp. 303–333.

Costello Ingham J (2003) Evidence-based treatment of stuttering: definition and application. Journal of Fluency Disorders 28: 197–207.

Costello Ingham J, Riley G (1998) Guidelines for documentation of treatment efficacy for young children who stutter. Journal of Speech, Language and Hearing Research 41: 753–770.

Craig A (1990) An investigation into the relationship between anxiety and stuttering. Journal of Speech and Hearing Disorders 55: 290–294.

Craig A (1998a) Treating Stuttering in Older Children, Adolescents and Adults: A guide for clinicians, parents and those who stutter. Gosford: Feedback Publications Press.

Craig A (1998b) Relapse following treatment for stuttering: a critical review and correlative data. Journal of Fluency Disorders 23: 1–30.

Craig A (2000) The developmental nature and effective treatment of stuttering in children and adolescents. Journal of Developmental and Physical Disabilities 12: 173–186.

Craig A, Andrews G (1985) The prediction and prevention of relapse in stuttering: the value of self-control techniques and locus of control measures. Behavior Modification 9: 427–442.

Craig A, Calver P (1991) Following up on treated stutterers. Studies of perceptions of fluency and job status. Journal of Speech and Hearing Research 34: 279–284.

Craig A, Cleary P (1982) Reduction of stuttering by young male stutterers using EMG feedback. Biofeedback and Self-Regulation 7: 241–255.

Craig A, Hancock K (1995) Self reported factors related to relapse following treatment for stuttering. Australian Journal of Human Communication Disorders 23: 48–60.

Craig A, Hancock K (1996) Anxiety in children and young adolescents who stutter. Australian Journal of Human Communication Disorders 24: 29–38.

Craig A, Chang E, Hancock K (1992) Treatment success for children who stutter: a critical review. Australian Journal of Human Communication Disorders 20: 81–92.

Craig A, Feyer AM, Andrews G (1987) An overview of a behavioural treatment for stuttering. Australian Psychologist 22: 53–62.

Craig A, Franklin J, Andrews G (1984) A scale to measure locus of control of behaviour. British Journal of Medical Psychology 57: 173–180.

Craig A, Hancock K, Cobbin D (2002) Managing adolescents who relapse following treatment for stuttering. Journal of Speech Language and Hearing: Asia Pacific 7: 79–91.

Craig A, Tran Y, Craig M (2003) Stereotypes towards stuttering in those who have never had direct contact with people who stutter: a randomized and stratified study. Perceptual Motor Skills 97: 235–245.

Craig A, Hancock K, Chang E, McCready C, Shepley A, McCaul A, Costello D, Harding S, Kehren R, Masel C, Reilly K (1996) A controlled clinical trial for stuttering in persons aged 9 to 14 years. Journal of Speech and Hearing Research 39: 808–826.

Craig A, Hancock K, Tran Y, Craig M, Peters K (2002) Epidemiology of stuttering in the community across the entire lifespan. Journal of Speech, Language, and Hearing Research 45: 1097–1105.

Craig A, Hancock K, Tran Y, Craig M (2003) Anxiety levels in people who stutter: a randomized population study. Journal of Speech, Language, and Hearing Research 46: 1197–1206.

Cream A, Onslow M, Packman A, Llewellyn G (2003) Protection from harm: the experience of adults after therapy with prolonged speech. International Journal of Language and Communication Disorders 23(4): 379–395.

Crighton-Smith I, Wright J, Stackhouse J (2003) Attitudes of speech and language therapists toward stammering: 1985 and 2000. International Journal of Communication Disorders 38: 213–234.

Crowe TA (1997) Emotional aspects of communicative disorders. In: Crowe TA (ed.), Applications of Counseling in Speech-Language Pathology and Audiology. Baltimore, MD: Williams & Wilkins, pp. 30–47.

Cullinan WL, Prather EM, Williams DE (1963) Comparisons of procedures for scaling severity of stuttering. Journal of Speech and Hearing Research 6: 187-194.

Dalton P (1987) Some developments in personal construct therapy with adults who stutter. In: Levy C (ed.), Stuttering Therapies: Practical Approaches. London: Croom Helm, pp. 61-70.

Dalton P (1994) Counselling people with communication problems. In: Dalton P (ed.), Counselling in Practice. Thousand Oaks, CA: Sage Publications, pp. 15-28.

Daly DA, Burnett ML (1999) Cluttering: traditional views and new perspectives. In: Curlee R (ed.), Stuttering and Related Disorders of Fluency, 2nd edn. New York: Thième Medical Publishers, pp. 222-254.

Damico SK, Armstrong M (1996) Intervention strategies for students with ADHD: creating a holistic approach. Seminars in Speech and Language 17: 21-36.

Davis S, Howell P, Cook F (2002) Sociodynamic relationships between children who stutter and their non-stuttering classmates. Journal of Child Psychology and Psychiatry 43: 939-947.

Defloor T, van Borsel J, Curfs L (2000) Speech fluency in Prader–Willi syndrome. Journal of Fluency Disorders 25: 85-98.

Dell C (1989) Treating the School Age Stutterer: A guide for clinicians. Memphis, TN: Speech Foundation of America.

Dell C (1993) Treating school age stutterers. In: Curlee RF (ed.), Stuttering and Related Disorders of Fluency. New York: Thième Medical.

De Nil LF, Brutten G (1990) Speech-associated attitudes: stuttering, voice disordered, articulation disordered and normal speaking children. Journal of Fluency Disorders 15: 127-134.

De Nil LF, Kroll RM (2001) Searching for the neural basis of stuttering treatment outcome: recent neuroimaging studies. Clinical Linguistics and Phonetics 15: 163-168.

De Nil LF, Kroll RM, Kapur S, Houle S (2000) A positron emission tomography study of silent and oral reading of single words in stuttering and nonstuttering adults. Journal of Speech, Language and Hearing Research 43: 1038-1053.

De Nil LF, Kroll RM, Houle S (2001) Functional neuroimaging of cerebellar activation during single word reading and verb generation in stuttering and nonstuttering adults. Neuroscience Letters 302: 77-80.

De Nil LF, Kroll RM, Lafaille SJ, Houle S (2003) A positron emission tomography study of short- and long-term treatment effects on functional brain activation in adults who stutter. Journal of Fluency Disorders 28: 357-380.

De Shazer S (1985) Keys to Solution in Brief Therapy. New York: Norton.

De Shazer S (1986) Words Were Originally Magic. New York: Norton.

Devenny DA, Silverman WP (1990) Speech dysfluency and manual specialization in Down's syndrome. Journal of Mental Deficiency Research 34: 253-260.

Dickson S (1971) Incipient stuttering and spontaneous remission of stuttered speech. Journal of Communication Disorders 4: 99-110.

Dillman DA (1978) Mail and Telephone Surveys. New York: John Wiley.

Doust J, Del Mar C (2004) Why do doctors use treatments that do not work? For many reasons, including their inability to stand idle and do nothing. British Medical Journal 328: 474-475.

Dunn LM, Dunn LM (1997) Peabody Picture Vocabulary Test, 3rd edn. Circle Pines, MN: American Guidance Service.

Dunn LM, Dunn LM, Whetton C, Pintilie D (1982) The British Picture Vocabulary Scales. Windsor, Berks: NFER-Nelson.

DuPaul G, Stoner G (2002) ADHD in the Schools: Assessment and Practise, 2nd edn. New York: Guilford Press.

Eadie TL (2003) The ICF: a proposed framework for comprehensive rehabilitation of individuals who use alaryngeal speech. American Journal of Speech-Language Pathology 12: 189-197.

Egan G (1998) The Skilled Helper, 6th edn. Pacific Grove, CA: Brooks Cole.

Elkind D (1967) Egocentrism in adolescence. Child Development 38: 1025-1034.

Erikson E (1965) Childhood and Society. Harmondsworth: Penguin.

Evesham M (1987) Residential courses for stutterers: combining technique and personal construct psychology. In: Levy C (ed.), Stuttering Therapies: Practical approaches. London: Croom Helm, pp. 61-72.

Evesham M, Fransella F (1987) Stuttering relapse: the effect of combined speech and psychological reconstruction programme. British Journal of Disorders of Communication 20: 237-248.

Ezrati-Vinacour R, Platzky R, Yairi E (2001) The young child's awareness of stuttering-like disfluency. Journal of Speech, Language, and Hearing Research 44: 368-380.

Faber A, Mazlish E (1980) How to Talk so Kids will Listen and Listen so Kids will Talk. New York: Avon Books.

Felsenfield S (1997) Epidemiology and genetics of stuttering. In: Curlee R, Siegal G (eds), Nature and Treatment of Stuttering: New directions (2nd edn). Boston, MA: Allyn & Bacon, pp. 3-23.

Ferrier L, Bashir A, Meryash D, Johnston J, Wolff P (1991) Conversational skills of individuals with fragile-X syndrome: a comparison with autism and Down syndrome. Developmental Medicine and Child Neurology 33: 776-788.

Finn P (2003) Addressing generalization and maintenance of stuttering treatment in the schools: a critical look. Journal of Communication Disorders 36: 153-164.

Finn P, Ingham RJ (1994) Stutterers' self-ratings of how natural speech sounds and feels. Journal of Speech and Hearing Research 37: 326-340.

Fitzgerald HE, Djurdjic SD, Maguin E (1992) Assessment of sensitivity to interpersonal stress in stutterers. Journal of Communication Disorders 25: 31-42.

Foundas AL, Bollich AM, Corey DM, Hurley M, Heilman KM (2001) Anomalous anatomy of speech-language areas in adults with persistent developmental stuttering. Neurology 57: 207-215.

Fox PT, Ingham RJ, Ingham JC, Hirsch TB, Downs JH, Martin C, Jerabek P, Glass T, Lancaster JL (1996) A PET study of the neural systems of stuttering. Nature 382: 158-162.

Fox PT, Ingham RJ, Ingham JC, Zamarripa F, Xiong JH, Lancaster JL (2000) Brain correlates of stuttering and syllable production. A PET performance-correlation analysis. Brain 123: 1985-2004.

Franck A, Jackson R, Pimentel J, Greenwood G (2003) School-age children's perceptions of a person who stutters. Journal of Fluency Disorders 28: 1-15.

Fransella F (1972) Personal Change and Reconstruction: Research on a treatment of stuttering. London: Academic Press.

Fransella F, Dalton P (1990) Personal Construct Counselling in Action. London: Sage.

Gaines ND, Runyan CM, Meyers SC (1991) A comparison of young stutterers' fluent versus stuttered utterances on measures of length and complexity. Journal of Speech and Hearing Research 34: 37-42.

German DJ (1986) Test of Word Finding. Allen, TX: DLM Teaching Resources.

Giddan J (1991) School children with emotional problems and communicative deficits: implications for speech-language pathologists. Language, Speech and Hearing in the Schools 22: 291-295.

Gillespie SK, Cooper EB (1973) Prevalence of speech problems in junior and senior high schools. Journal of Speech and Hearing Research 16: 739–743.

Goldman R, Fristoe M (2000) Goldman–Fristoe Test of Articulation-2. Circle Pines, MN: AGS Publishing.

Gottwald S (1999) Family communication patterns and stuttering development: an analysis of the research literature. In: Bernstein Ratner NE, Healey EC (eds), Stuttering Research and Practice: Bridging the gap. Mahwah, NJ: Lawrence Erlbaum, pp. 175–191.

Gottwald S, Starkweather C (1995) Fluency intervention for pre-schoolers and their families in the public schools. Language, Speech and Hearing Services in Schools 26: 115–126.

Gottwald S, Goldbach P, Isack A (1985) Stuttering prevention and detection. Young Children 41: 9–14.

Gregory HH (1979) Controversies about Stuttering Therapy. Baltimore, MD: University Park Press.

Gregory H (1991) Therapy for elementary school age children. Seminars in Speech and Language 12: 323–335.

Gregory HH (2003) Stuttering Therapy: Rationale and procedures. Boston, MA: Allyn & Bacon.

Gregory HH, Gregory CB (1999) Counseling children who stutter and their parents. In: Curlee RF (ed.), Stuttering and Related Disorders of Fluency, 2nd edn. New York: Thième Medical Publishers, pp. 43–64.

Greig H (1999) Normal non-fluency in 8 and 9 year old children. Unpublished report for the Carnegie undergraduate vacation scholarship.

Grossman H (1983) Classification in Mental Retardation. Washington DC: American Association on Mental Deficiency.

Guitar B (1998) Stuttering: An integrated approach to its nature and treatment, 2nd edn. Baltimore, MD: Williams & Wilkins.

Guitar B (2002) Emotion, temperament and stuttering: some possible relationships. In: Baker KL, Rustin L, Cook F (eds), Proceedings of the Fifth Oxford Dysfluency Conference. Windsor: Kevin L Baker, pp. 1–6.

Guitar B (2003) Acoustic startle responses and temperament in individuals who stammer. Journal of Speech, Language and Hearing Research 46: 233–240.

Guitar B, Grims S (1977) Developing a scale to assess communication attitudes in children who stutter. Poster session presented at the American Speech–Language–Hearing Association Convention, Atlanta, Georgia, November 1977.

Guitar B, Donaher JG, Otto-Montgomery C, Reville J (2000) Group Therapy as an Effective Tool for Fluency Intervention. Paper presented at the annual convention of the American Speech-Language-Hearing Association. Washington, DC, November .

Hall N (1996) Language and fluency in child language disorders: changes over time. Journal of Fluency Disorders 21: 1–32.

Hall N (1999) Speech disruptions in pre-school children with specific language impairment and phonological impairment. Clinical Linguistics and Phonetics 13: 295–307.

Hall N, Yamashita, T, Aram D (1993) Relationship between language and fluency in children with language disorders. Journal of Speech and Hearing Research 36: 568–579.

Hancock K, Craig A (1998) Predictors of stuttering relapse one year following treatment for children aged 9–14 years. Journal of Fluency Disorders 23: 31–48.

Hancock K, Craig A (2002) The effectiveness of re-treatment for adolescents who stutter. Asia-Pacific Journal of Speech, Language and Hearing 7: 138–156.

Hancock K, Craig A, Campbell K, Costello D, Gilmore G, McCaul A, McCready C (1998) Two to six year controlled trial stuttering outcomes for children and adolescents. Journal of Speech and Hearing Research 41: 1242-1252.

Harrison E, Onslow M (1999) Early intervention for stuttering: the Lidcombe Program. In: Curlee RF (ed.), Stuttering and Related Disorders of Fluency. New York: Thième, pp. 65-79.

Hayhow R (1983) The assessment of stuttering and the evaluation of treatment. In: Dalton P. Approaches to the Treatment of Stuttering. London: Croom Helm, pp. 15-46.

Hayhow R, Levy C (1989) Working with Stuttering. Bicester: Winslow Press.

Haynes B (1999) Can it work? Does it work? Is it worth it? British Medical Journal 319: 652-653.

Healey EC, Reid R (2003) Stuttering and ADHD: a tutorial. Journal of Fluency Disorders 28: 79-93.

Healey C, Scott L, Ellis G (1995) Decision making in the treatment of school age children who stutter. Journal of Communication Disorders 28: 107-124.

Healey EC, Scott Trautman L, Panico J (2001) A Model for Manipulating Linguistic Complexity in Stuttering Therapy. International Stuttering Awareness Day Online Conference, Mankato State University, Mankato, MN.

Herbert M (2003) Typical and Atypical Development: From Conception to Adolescence. Oxford: BPS Blackwell.

Hodson B, Paden E (1991) Targeting Intelligible Speech: A Phonological Approach to Remediation. Austin, TX: Pro-Ed.

Hogg J (1994) Developments in further education for adults with profound intellectual and multiple disabilities. In: Watson J (ed.), Innovatory Practice and Severe Learning Difficulties. Edinburgh: Murray House Publications, pp. 163-181.

Homzie M, Lindsay J, Simpson J, Hasenstab S (1988) Concomitant speech, language and learning problems in adult stutterers and in members of their families. Journal of Fluency Disorders 13: 261-277.

Huber-Okrainec J, Dennis M, Brettschneider J, Spiegler B (2002) Neuromotor speech deficits in children and adults with spina bifida and hydrocephalus. Brain and Language 80: 592-602.

Hulstijn W, Peters H, van Lieshout P (1997) Speech Production: Motor Control, Brain Research and Fluency Disorders. Amsterdam: Elsevier Press.

Hunter M (1994) Enhancing Teaching. New York: Macmillan College Publishing Company.

Individuals with Disabilities Education Act (IDEA) (1997) Amendment of 1997, PL 105-17. 105th Congress, 1st Session.

Ingham JC (1999) Behavioral treatment of young children who stutter: an extended length of utterance method. In: Curlee RF (ed.), Stuttering and Related Disorders of Fluency, 2nd edn. New York: Thième Medical Publishers, pp. 80-109.

Ingham R (1976) Onset, prevalence, and recovery from stuttering: a reassessment for findings from the Andrews and Harris study. Journal of Speech and Hearing Disorders 41: 280-281.

Ingham R (1984) Stuttering and Behaviour Therapy: Current Status and Experimental Foundations. San Diego, CA: College Hill Press.

Ingham R (1998) On learning from speech-motor control research in stuttering. In: Cordes A, Ingham RJ (eds), Treatment Efficacy for Stuttering: A search for empirical bases. San Diego, CA: Singular Press Publishing, pp. 67-102.

Ingham R (2001) Brain imaging studies of developmental stuttering. Journal of Communication Disorders 34: 493-516.

Ingham R, Cordes A (1992) Interclinic differences in stuttering-event counts. Journal of Fluency Disorders 17: 171-176.

Ingham R, Cordes A (1997) Self-measurement and evaluating stuttering treatment efficacy. In: Curlee R, Siegel G (eds), Nature and Treatment of Stuttering. London: Allyn & Bacon, pp. 413-437.

Ingham R, Cordes A (1999) Reflections on watching a discipline shoot itself in the foot. In: Bernstein Ratner N, Healey EC (eds), From Research to Practise. Mahwah, NJ: Erlbaum, pp. 211-230.

Ingham R, Riley G (1998) Guidelines for documentation of treatment efficacy for young children who stutter. Journal of Speech, Language, and Hearing Research 41: 753-770.

Ingham R, Ingham JC, Finn P, Fox PT (2003) Towards a functional neural systems model of developmental stuttering. Journal of Fluency Disorders 28: 297-318.

Jaeger JJ (1992) 'Not by the chair of my hinny hin hin': some general properties of slips of the tongue in young children. Journal of Child Language 19: 335-366.

Johnson W, Moeller D (1972) Living with Change: The semantics of coping. New York: Harper & Row.

Jones M, Onslow M, Harrison E, Packman A (2000) Treating stuttering in young children: predicting treatment time in the Lidcombe Program. Journal of Speech, Language and Hearing Research 43: 1440-1450.

Jones M, Gebski V, Onslow M, Packman A (2002) Statistical power in stuttering research: a tutorial. Journal of Speech, Language and Hearing Research 45: 243-255.

Kadi-Hanifi K, Howell P (1992) Syntactic analysis of the spontaneous speech of normally fluent and stuttering children. Journal of Fluency Disorders 17: 151-170.

Kelly G (1955) The Psychology of Personal Constructs. New York: WW Norton.

Kelly EM, Conture EG (1992) Speaking rates, response times latencies, and interrupting behaviours of young stutterers, nonstutterers, and their mothers. Journal of Speech and Hearing Research 35: 1256-1267.

Kelly EM, Martin JS, Bajer KE, Rivera NJ, Bishop JE, Kriziske CB, Stettler DB, Stealy JM (1997) Academic and clinical preparation ad practices of school speech-language pathologists with people who stutter. Language, Speech and Hearing Services in Schools 28: 195-212.

Kingston M, Huber A, Onslow M, Jones M, Packman A (2003) Predicting treatment time with the Lidcombe Programme: replication and meta-analysis International Journal of Language and Communication Disorders 38: 165-177.

Koivunen P, Uhari M, Luotonen J, Kristo A, Raski R, Pokka T, Alho OP (2004) Adenoidectomy versus chemoprophylaxis and placebo for recurrent acute otitis media in children aged under 2 years: randomised controlled trial. British Medical Journal 328: 487-490.

Kully D (2002) Venturing into telehealth: applying interactive technologies to stuttering treatment. ASHA Leader 7: 6-15.

Kully D, Boberg E (1991) Therapy for school-age children. In: Perkins E (ed.), Seminars in Speech and Language: Stuttering: Challenges of therapy. New York: Thième Medical Publishers.

Kully D, Langevin MJ (1999) Intensive treatment for stuttering adolescents. In: Curlee RF (ed.), Stuttering and Related Disorders of Fluency, 2nd edn. New York: Thième Medical Publishers, pp. 139-159.

Langevin M, Kully D (1997) Self Rating of Effects of Stuttering; Children (SRES-C). Unpublished questionnaire. Edmonton, Alta: Institute for Stuttering Treatment and Research.

Langevin M, Kully D (2003) Evidence-based treatment of stuttering: evidence-based practice in a clinical setting. Journal of Fluency Disorders 28: 219-236.

Last JM (2001) A Dictionary of Epidemiology, 4th edn. Oxford: Oxford University Press.

Leavitt RR (1974) The Puerto Ricans: Culture Change and Language Deviance. Tucson, AZ: University of Arizona Press.

Lebrun Y, von Borsel J (1990) Final sound repetitions. Journal of Fluency Disorders 15: 107–113.

Lees R (1994) Of what value is a measure of the stutterer's fluency? Folia Phoniatrica et Logopaedica 46: 223–231.

Lees R (1999) Stammering children in schools. In: McCartney E (ed.), Speech/Language Therapists and Teachers Working Together. London: Whurr Publishers, pp. 135–149.

Lees R, Anderson H, Martin P (1999) The influence of language disorder on fluency: a pilot study. Journal of Fluency Disorders 24: 227–238.

Lees R, Stark C, Baird J, Birse S (2000) Primary care professionals' knowledge and attitudes on speech dysfluency in pre-school children. Child Language Teaching and Therapy 16: 241–254.

Lerner J (2000) Learning Disabilities: Theories, Diagnosis, and Teaching Strategies. Boston, MA: Houghton Mifflin.

Levy C (1993) Group therapy with adults. In: Dalton P, Hardcastle W (eds) Approaches to the Treatment of Stuttering. London: Croom Helm, pp. 136–162.

Lincoln M, Onslow M (1997) Long-term outcome of early intervention for stuttering. American Journal of Speech-Language Pathology 6: 51–58.

Lincoln M, Onslow M, Reed V (1997) Social validity of an early intervention for stuttering: the Lidcombe Program. American Journal of Speech-Language Pathology 6: 77–84.

Lincoln M, Onslow M, Wilson L, Lewis C (1996) A clinical trial of an operant treatment for school-age stuttering children. American Journal of Speech-Language Pathology 5: 73–85.

Logan KJ, Caruso AJ (1997) Parents as partners in the treatment of childhood stuttering. Seminars in Speech and Language 18: 309–327.

Logan KJ, Conture EG (1995) Length, grammatical complexity, and rate differences in stuttered and fluent conversational utterances of children who stutter. Journal of Fluency Disorders 20: 35–61.

Logan KJ, Conture EG (1997) Selected temporal, grammatical, and phonological characteristics of conversational utterances produced by children who stutter. Journal of Speech Language and Hearing Research 40: 107–120.

Logan K, LaSalle L (2003) Developing intervention programs for children with stuttering and concomitant impairments. Seminars in Speech and Language 24: 13–20.

Logan KJ, Yaruss JS (1999) Helping parents address attitudinal and emotional factors with young children who stutter. Contemporary Issues in Communication Science and Disorders 26: 69–81.

Logan KJ, Roberts RR, Pretto AP, Morey MJ (2002) Speaking slowly: effects of four self-guided training approaches on adults' speech rate and naturalness. American Journal of Speech-Language Pathology 11: 163–174.

Louko L, Conture E, Edwards M (1999) Treating children who exhibit co-occurring stuttering and disordered phonology. In: Curlee R (ed.), Stuttering and Related Disorders of Fluency (2nd edn). New York: Thième, pp. 124–138.

Ludlow C (1993) Speech tics in Tourette's syndrome. In: Blanken G, Dittman J, Grimm H, Marshall J, Wallesch C (eds). Linguistic Disorders and Pathologies: An international handbook. Berlin: de Gruyter, pp. 504–509.

Ludlow C, Loucks T (2003) Stuttering: a dynamic motor control disorder. Journal of Fluency Disorders 28: 273–295.

Lumpkin PW, Silverman WK, Weems CF, Markham MR, Kurtines WM (2002) Treating a heterogeneous set of anxiety disorders in youths with group cognitive behavioral therapy: a partially nonconcurrent multiple-baseline evaluation. Behavior Therapy 22: 163-177.

Lyon R, Moats L (1997) Critical conceptual and methodological considerations in reading intervention research. Journal of Learning Disabilities 30: 578-588.

McCauley RJ (1996) Familiar strangers: criterion referenced measures in communication disorders. Language, Speech and Hearing Services in Schools 27: 122-131.

McClelland D (1961) The Achieving Society. Princeton, NJ: Van Nostrand.

McLaren J, Bryson SE (1987) Review of recent epidemiological studies of mental retardation: prevalence, related disorders, and etiology. American Journal of Mental Retardation 92: 243-254.

Manning WH (1996) Clinical Decision Making in the Diagnosis and Treatment of Fluency Disorders. New York: Delmar.

Manning W (2001) Clinical Decision Making in Fluency Disorders, 2nd edn. London: Singular Thomson Learning.

Mansson H (2000) Childhood stuttering: Incidence and development. Journal of Fluency Disorders 25: 47-57.

Martin RR (1981) Introduction and perspective: review of published research. In: Boberg E (ed.), Maintenance of Fluency. New York: Elsevier, pp. 1-30.

Martin RR, Haroldson SK (1992) Stuttering and speech naturalness: audio and audiovisual judgments. Journal of Speech and Hearing Research 35: 521-528.

Martyn M, Sheehan J, Slutz K (1969) Incidence of stuttering and other speech disorders among the retarded. American Journal of Mental Deficiency 74: 206-211.

Matthews S, Williams R, Pring T (1997) Parent-child interaction therapy and dysfluency: a single case study. European Journal of Disorders of Communication 32: 346-357.

Menzies RG, Onslow M, Packman A (1999) Anxiety and stuttering: exploring a complex relationship. American Journal of Speech-Language Pathology 8: 3-10.

Merrill EC (1990) Attentional resource allocation and mental retardation. In: Bray NW (ed.), International Review of Research in Mental Retardation, Vol. 16. San Diego, CA: Academic Press, pp. 51-88.

Meyers S, Woodford L (1992) The Fluency Development System for Young Children. Buffalo, NY: United Educational Services.

Michon LB (1999) Language and the child with attention deficit/hyperactivity disorder. In: Jones C, Searight H, Urban M (eds), Parent Articles about ADHD. San Antonio, TX: Communication Skill Builders, pp. 85-86.

Millard S (2002) Therapy outcome: parents' perspectives. In: Baker KL, Rustin L, Cook F (eds), Proceedings of the Sixth Oxford Dysfluency Conference. Windsor: Kevin L Baker, pp. 89-98.

Millard S, Nicholas A (2002) Evaluating the Effectiveness of Therapy with Young Children Who Stammer. Paper presented at ASHA Treatment Effectiveness Conference for People with Communication Difficulties. London: City University.

Miller J, Lall V (2001) Documenting age-related changes in language production. ASHA Leader 6: 122.

Miller SM, Watson BC (1992) The relationship between communication attitude, anxiety and depression in stutterers and nonstutterers. Journal of Speech and Hearing Research 35: 789-798.

Minuchin S (1974) Families and Family Therapy. London: Tavistock.

Miranda A, McCabe A, Bliss L (1998) Jumping around and leaving things out: a profile of the narrative abilities of children with specific language impairment. Applied Psycho-linguistics 19: 647-668.

Montgomery BM, Fitch JL (1988) The prevalence of stuttering in the hearing-impaired school age population. Journal of Speech and Hearing Disorders 53: 131-135.

Mooney S, Smith P (1995) Bullying and the child who stammers. British Journal of Special Education 22: 24-27.

Moscicki EK (1984) The prevalence of 'incidence' is too high. Proceedings of the American Speech Hearing Association, August; pp. 39-40.

Moscicki EK (1993) Fundamental methodological considerations in controlled clinical trials. Journal of Fluency Disorders 18: 183-196.

Mosley L, Mead D (2001) Considerations in using the Delphi approach: design, questions and answers. Nurse Researcher 8: 24-37.

Mowrer D (1998) Alternative research strategies for the investigation of stuttering. Journal of Fluency Disorders 23: 89-97.

Murphy B (1994) Helping children who stutter: a potpourri of clinical ideas. In: Stuttering Therapy: Practical ideas for the school clinician. Workshop sponsored by SFA & University of Colorado. Colorado: University of Colorado.

Murphy B (1999) A preliminary look at shame, guilt, and stuttering. In: Ratner BN, Healey EC (eds), Stuttering Research and Practice: Bridging the gap. Mahwah, NJ: Lawrence Erlbaum, pp. 131-143.

Murphy B (2000) Speech pathologists can help children who are teased because they stutter. International Stuttering Awareness Day 2002 Online Conference - Reach Out to Children Who Stutter. Mankato, MN: Mankato State University.

Murphy WP, Quesal RW (2002) Strategies for addressing bullying with the school-age child who stutters. Seminars in Speech and Language 23: 205-211.

Neilson MD (1999) Cognitive-behavioral treatment of adults who stutter: the process and the art. In: Curlee RG (ed.), Stuttering and Related Disorders of Fluency, 2nd edn. New York: Thième Medical Publishers, pp. 181-199.

Newman D, Horne AM, Bartolomucci CL (2000) Bully busters: A teacher's manual for helping bullies, victims and bystanders. Champaign, IL: Research Press.

Newman L, Smit A (1989) Some effects of variations in response time latency on speech rate, interruptions and fluency in children's speech. Journal of Speech and Hearing Research 2: 635-644.

Nicholas A, Millard S (2002) A study investigating the effectiveness of parent-child interaction therapy. In: Baker KL, Rustin L, Cook F (eds) Proceedings of the Sixth Oxford Dysfluency Conference. Windsor: Kevin L Baker, pp. 145-147.

Nippold M (1990) Concomitant speech and language disorders in stuttering children: a critique of the literature. Journal of Speech and Hearing Disorders 55: 51-60.

Nippold M (2002) Stuttering and phonology: is there an interaction? American Journal of Speech-Language Pathology 11: 99-110.

Nowicki S, Strickland BR (1973) A locus of control scale for children. Journal of Consulting and Clinical Psychology 40: 148-154.

O'Hanlon W, Weiner-Davis M (1987) In Search of Solutions. New York: Norton.

Ollendick TH, King NJ (1991) Fears and phobias of childhood. In: Herbert M (ed.), Clinical Child Psychology: Social learning, development and behaviour. Chichester: John Wiley, pp. 309-329.

Onslow M (1996) Behavioral Management of Stuttering. San Diego, CA: Singular Publishing Group.

Onslow M, Ingham RJ (1987) Speech quality measurement and the management of stuttering. Journal of Speech and Hearing Disorders 52: 2-57.

Onslow M, Packman A (1999) Treatment recovery and spontaneous recovery from early stuttering: the need for consistent methods in collecting and interpreting data. Journal of Speech, Language, and Hearing Research 42: 398-402.

Onslow M, Andrews C, Lincoln M (1994) A control/experimental trial of an operant treatment for early stuttering. Journal of Speech and Hearing Research 37: 1244-1259.

Onslow M, Costa L, Rue S (1990) Direct early intervention with stuttering: some preliminary data Journal of Speech and Hearing Disorders 55: 405-416.

Onslow M, Packman A, Harrison E (2003) The Lidcombe Program of Early Stuttering Intervention: A clinician's guide. Austin, TX: Pro-Ed.

Onslow M, Costa L, Andrews C, Harrison E (1996) Speech outcomes of a prolonged-speech treatment for stuttering. Journal of Speech and Hearing Research 39: 734-749.

Oviatt S (1995) Predicting spoken disfluencies during human–computer interaction. Computer Speech and Language 9: 19-35.

Paden E, Ambrose N, Yairi E (2002) Phonological progress during the first 2 years of stuttering. Journal of Speech, Language and Hearing Research 45: 256-267.

Paden EP, Yairi E, Ambrose NG (1999) Early childhood stuttering II: Initial status of phonological abilities. Journal of Speech, Language and Hearing Research 42: 1113-1124.

Paul R (2001) Language Disorders from Infancy through Adolescence: Assessment and Intervention, 2nd edn. St Louis, MO: Mosby-Year Book.

Paulsen AS, Crowe RR, Noyes R, Pfohl B (1988) Reliability of the telephone interview in diagnosing anxiety disorders. Archives of General Psychiatry 45: 62-63.

Perkins W (1973) Replacement of stuttering with normal speech: II Clinical procedures. Journal of Speech and Hearing Disorders 38: 295-303.

Perkins WH (1992) Fluency controls and automatic fluency. American Journal of Speech-Language Pathology 1: 9-10.

Peters HFM, Starkweather CW (1990) The interaction between speech motor coordination and language processes in the development of stuttering. Journal of Fluency Disorders 15: 115-125.

Peters HFM, Hulstijn W, Van Lieshout PHHM (2000) Recent developments in speech motor research in stuttering. Folia Phoniatrica 52: 103-119.

Pfiffner LJ (1995) Off to school on the right foot: managing your child's education. In: Barkley RA (ed.), Taking Charge of ADHD: The complete authoritative guide for parents. New York: Guilford Press.

Porfert AR, Rosenfield DB (1978) Prevalence of stuttering. Journal of Neurology, Neurosurgery, and Psychiatry 41: 954-956.

Preus A (1981) Attempts at Identifying Subgroups of Stutterers. Oslo: University of Norway Press.

Preus A (1990) Treatment of mentally retarded stutterers. Journal of Fluency Disorders 15: 223-233.

Priestly P, McGuire J, Flegg D, Hemsley V, Welham D (1978) Social Skills and Personal Problem Solving. London: Tavistock.

Prins D (1993) Management of stuttering: treatment of adolescents and adults. In: Curlee RF (ed.), Stuttering and Related Disorders of Fluency. New York: Thième Medical Publishers, pp. 115-138.

Prochaska JO, DiClemente CC, Norcross JC (1992) In search of how people change: applications to addictive behaviors. American Psychologist 47: 1102-1114.

Quine S (1985) Does the mode matter? A comparison of three modes of questionnaires completion. Community Health Studies 9: 151-156.

Ramig P (1999) The School Clinician: Ways to be more effective (video). Available from The Stuttering Foundation of America, 3100 Walnut Grove Road, Suite 603, Memphis, TN 38110-749, USA.

Ramig P, Bennett E (1995) Working with 7- to 12-year-old children who stutter: ideas for intervention in the public schools. Language, Speech and Hearing Services in Schools 26: 138-150.

Ramig P, Bennett E (1997) Clinical management of children: direct management strategies. In: Curlee R, Siegel G (eds), Nature and Treatment of Stuttering: New directions, 2nd edn. London: Allyn & Bacon, pp. 292–312.

Reeve D (2002) Negotiating psycho-emotional dimensions of disability and their influence on identity constructions. Disability and Society 17: 493–508.

Reid R (1999) Attention deficit hyperactivity disorder: effective methods for the classroom. Focus on Exceptional Children 32: 1–20.

Reid R, Maag JW (1994) How many 'fidgets' in a 'pretty much': a critique of behavior rating scales for identifying students with ADHD. Journal of School Psychology 32: 339–354.

Reilly S (2004) The move to evidence-based practice within speech pathology. In: Reilly S, Douglas J, Oates J (eds), Evidence-based Practice in Speech Pathology. London: Whurr Publishers, pp. 3–18.

Renfrew CE (1988) Renfrew Action Picture Test, 3rd edn. Oxford: Language Test Publisher.

Riley G (1994) Stuttering Severity Instrument for Children and Adults, 3rd edn. Austin, TX: Pro-ed.

Riley G, Riley J (1979) A component model of diagnosing and treating children who stutter. Journal of Fluency Disorders 4: 279–293.

Riley G, Riley J (1984) A component model for treating stuttering in children. In: Peins M (ed.), Contemporary Approaches in Stuttering Therapy. Boston, MA: Little, Brown, pp. 123–171.

Riley G, Riley J (2000) A revised component model for diagnosing and treating children who stutter. Contemporary Issues in Communication Sciences and Disorders 27: 188–189.

Roberts H, Liabo K, Lucas P, DuBois DL, Sheldon TA (2004) Mentoring to address anti-social behaviour in childhood. British Medical Journal 328: 512–514.

Rommell D (2000) The influence of psycholinguistic variables on stuttering in children. Journal of Fluency Disorders 25: 212–212.

Rothke S (1986) The role of interpersonal feedback in group psychotherapy. International Journal of Group Psychotherapy 36: 225–240.

Runyan C, Runyan S (1986) A fluency rules program for young children in the public schools. Language, Speech and Hearing Services in the Schools 17: 276–285.

Runyan C, Runyan S (1999) Therapy for school-age stutterers: an update on the fluency rules programme. In: Curlee R (ed.), Stuttering and Related Disorders of Fluency (2nd edn). New York: Thième Medical Publishers, pp. 110–123.

Rustin L (1987) The treatment of childhood dysfluency through active parental involvement. In: Rustin L, Purser H, Rowley D (eds), Progress in the Treatment of Fluency Disorders. London: Taylor & Francis, pp. 166–180.

Rustin L, Kuhr A (1983) The treatment of stammering: a multi-modal approach in an inpatient setting. British Journal of Disorders of Communication 18: 90–97.

Rustin L, Kuhr A (1999) Social Skills and the Speech Impaired, 2nd edn. London: Whurr Publishers.

Rustin L, Botterill W, Kelman E (1996) Assessment and Therapy for Young Dysfluent Children: Family interaction. London: Whurr Publishers.

Rustin L, Cook F, Spence R (1995) The Management of Stuttering in Adolescence: A communication skills approach. London: Whurr Publishers.

Rustin L, Cook F, Botterill W, Hughes C, Kelman E (2001) Stammering: A practical guide for teachers and other professionals. London: David Fulton.

Ryan B (1971) Operant procedures applied to stuttering therapy for children. Journal of Speech and Hearing Disorders 36: 264–280.

Ryan B (1974) Programmed Therapy for Stuttering in Children and Adults. Springfield, IL: Charles C Thomas.

Ryan B, Van Kirk B (1978) Monterey Fluency Program. Monterey, CA: Monterey Learning Systems.

Ryan B, Van Kirk Ryan B (1983) Programmed stuttering therapy for children: A comparison of four establishment programmes. Journal of Fluency Disorders 8: 291-321.

Ryan B, Van Kirk Ryan B (1995) Programmed stuttering therapy treatment for children: comparison of two establishment programmes through transfer, maintenance, and follow-up. Journal of Speech and Hearing Research 38: 61-75.

Sabatino DH, Vance HB (1994) Are diagnoses of attention deficit/hyperactivity disorder still meaningful? Psychology in the Schools 31: 188-196.

Sackett DL, Rosenberg WMC, Gray JAM, Haynes RB, Richardson WS (1996) Evidence based medicine: what it is and what it isn't: it's about integrating individual clinical expertise and the best external evidence. British Medical Journal 312: 71-72.

St Louis K, Durrenberger C (1993) What communication disorders do experienced clinicians prefer to manage? ASHA 35: 23-31.

St Louis K, Hinzman AR (1988) A descriptive study of speech, language and hearing characteristics of school-aged stutterers. Journal of Fluency Disorders 13: 331-355.

St Louis K, Lass N (1981) A survey of communicative disorders students' attitudes toward stuttering. Journal of Fluency Disorders 6: 49-80.

St Louis K, Murray C, Ashworth M. Co-existing communication disorders in a random sample of school-aged stutterers. Journal of Fluency Disorders 1991; 16: 13-23.

St Louis K, Ruscello DM, Lundeen C (1992) Coexistence of communication disorders in school children. ASHA monographs 27: 1-57.

Schiavetti N, Metz D (1997) Stuttering and the measurement of speech naturalness. In: Curlee R, Siegel G (eds), Nature and Treatment of Stuttering: New directions, 2nd edn. Boston, MA: Allyn & Bacon, pp. 398-412.

Schlanger BB (1953) Speech measurements of institutionalized mentally handicapped children. American Journal of Mental Deficiency 58: 114-122.

Schooling T (2003) Lessons from the National Outcomes Measurement System (NOMS). Seminars in Speech and Language 24: 245-256.

Schwartz HD, Conture EG (1988) Subgrouping young stutterers: preliminary behavioral observations. Journal of Speech and Hearing Research 31: 62-71.

Scott C, Windsor J (2000) General language performance measures in spoken and written narrative and expository discourse of school-aged children with language-learning disabilities. Journal of Speech, Language and Hearing Research 43: 324-339.

Scott Trautman LA, Healey EC, Norris J (2001) Effects of contextualization on fluency in three groups of children. Journal of Speech-Language-Hearing Research 44: 564-576.

Selekman M (1993) Pathways to Change. New York: Guilford Press.

Seligman M (1990) Learned Optimism. New York: Pocket Books.

Semel EM, Wiig EH, Secord W (2003) Clinical evaluation of language fundamentals, 4th edn. San Antonio, TX: The Psychological Corporation.

Shames G, Anderson N (2002) Human Communication Disorders: An introduction, 6th edn. Boston, MA: Allyn & Bacon.

Shames GH, Florance CL (1980) Stutter-free Speech: A goal for therapy. Columbus, OH: CE Merrill Publishing Company.

Shapiro DA (1999) Stuttering Intervention: A collaborative journey to fluency freedom. Austin, TX: Pro-Ed.

Sheehan JG (1970) Stuttering: Research and therapy. New York, NY: Harper & Row.

Sheehan J (1975) Conflict theory and avoidance reduction therapy. In: Eisenson J (ed.), Stuttering: A second symposium. New York: Harper & Row, pp. 121-126.

Shine R (1988) Systematic Fluency Training for Young Children, 3rd edn. Austin, TX: Pro-Ed.

Shriberg L, Austin D (1997) The speech disorders classification system (SDCS): extensions and lifespan reference data. Journal of Speech, Language and Hearing Research 40: 723-741.

Shriberg L, Tomblin JB, McSweeny J (1999) Prevalence of speech delay in 6-year old children and comorbidity with language impairment. Journal of Speech, Language and Hearing Research 42: 1461-1481.

Siegel G (2000) Demands and capacities or demands and performance? Journal of Fluency Disorders 25: 321-327.

Skinner BF (1953) The Science of Human Behavior. New York: Macmillan.

Slome C, Brogan D, Eyres S, Lednar W (1986) Basic Epidemiological Methods and Biostatistics. Boston, MA: Jones & Bartlett.

Smith A, Kelly E (1997) Stuttering: a dynamic multifactorial model. In: Curlee RF, Siegel GM (eds), The Nature and Treatment of Stuttering: New directions, 2nd edn. Boston, MA: Allyn & Bacon, pp. 204-217.

Spielberger C, Edwards C, Luschene R, Montuori J, Platzek D (1972) STAIC Preliminary Manual. New York: Consulting Psychologists Press.

Spielberger C, Gorsuch RL, Luschene RE, Vagg PR, Jacobs GA (1983) STAIC Manual for the State-Trait Anxiety Inventory. New York: Consulting Psychologists Press.

Spinelli E (1994) Demistifying Therapy. London: Constable.

Stallard P (2002) Cognitive behaviour therapy with children and young people: a selective review of key issues. Behavioural and Cognitive Psychotherapy 30: 297-309.

Stansfield J (1990) Prevalence of stuttering and cluttering in adults with mental handicaps. Journal of Mental Deficiency Research 34: 287-307.

Stansfield J (1995) Word-final disfluencies in adults with learning disabilities. Journal of Fluency Disorders 20: 1-10.

Stark C, Lees R, Black C, Waugh N (2004) Altered auditory feedback treatments for stuttering in childhood and adolescence (Protocol for a Cochrane Review). In: The Cochrane Library, Issue 3. Chichester: John Wiley & Sons.

Starkweather CW (1987) Fluency and Stuttering. Englewood Cliffs, NJ: Prentice Hall.

Starkweather CW (1993) Issues in the efficacy of treatment for fluency disorders. Journal of Fluency Disorders 18: 291-321.

Starkweather CW, Givens-Ackerman J (1997) Stuttering. Austin, TX: Pro-Ed.

Starkweather CW, Gottwald S (1990) The demands and capacities model II: clinical applications. Journal of Fluency Disorders 15: 143-157.

Starkweather C, Gottwald S (1993) A pilot study of relations among specific measures obtained at intake and discharge in a programme of prevention and early intervention for stuttering. American Journal of Speech and Language Pathology January: 51-58.

Starkweather CW, Gottwald R, Halfond MM (1990) Stuttering Prevention: A clinical method. Englewood Cliffs, NJ: Prentice-Hall.

Starkweather W, Ridener-Gottwald S, Halfond MM (1991) Stuttering Prevention: A clinical method. Englewood Cliffs, NJ: Prentice Hall.

Stein MB, Baird A, Walker JR (1996) Social phobia in adults with stuttering. American Journal of Psychiatry 153: 278-280.

Stewart T, Brosh H (1997) The use of drawings in the management of adults who stammer. Journal of Fluency Disorders 22: 35-50.

Stewart T, Turnbull J (1995) Working with Dysfluent Children. Bicester: Winslow.

Taylor RM, Morrison LP (1996) Taylor-Johnson Temperament Analysis Manual. Thousand Oaks, CA: Psychological Publications.

Tetnowski J, Damico J (2001) A demonstration of the advantages of qualitative methodologies in stuttering research. Journal of Fluency Disorders 26: 17-42.

Thordadottir E, Ellis Weismer S (2002) Content mazes and filled pauses in narrative language samples of children with specific language impairment. Brain and Cognition 48: 587-592.

Throneburg R, Yairi E (1994) Relation between phonologic difficulty and the occurrence of disfluencies in the early stage of stuttering. Journal of Speech and Hearing Research 37: 504–510.

Tiffany WR (1980) The effects of syllable structure on diadochokinetic and reading rates. Journal of Speech and Hearing Research 23: 894–908.

Turnbull J, Stewart T (1999) The Dysfluency Resource Book. Bicester: Winslow Press.

Tutuncuoglu S, Serdaroglu G, Kadioglu B (2002) Landau–Kleffner syndrome beginning with stuttering: a case report. Journal of Child Neurology 17: 785–787.

Van Borsel J, Vanryckeghem M (2000) Dysfluency and phonic tics in Tourette syndrome: a case report. Journal of Communication Disorders 33: 227–240.

Van Borsel J, Dhooge I, Verhoye K, Derde K, Curfs L (1992) Communication problems in Turner syndrome: a sample survey. Journal of Communication Disorders 32: 435–446.

Van Borsel J, Dhooge I, Verhoye K, Derde K, Curfs L (1999) Communication problems in Turner syndrome: a sample survey. Journal of Communication Disorders 32(6): pp. 435–444.

Van Riper C (1971) The Nature of Stuttering. Englewood Cliffs, NJ: Prentice Hall.

Van Riper C (1973) The Treatment of Stuttering. Englewood Cliffs, NJ: Prentice Hall.

Van Riper C (1982) The Treatment of Stuttering. Englewood Cliffs, NJ: Prentice Hall.

Vanryckeghem M, Brutten G (1997) The speech-associated attitude of children who do and do not stutter and the differential effect of age. American Journal of Speech-Language Pathology 6: 67–73.

Vanryckeghem M, Hylebos C, Brutten G, Peleman M (2001) The relationship between communication attitude and emotion of children who stutter. Journal of Fluency Disorders 26: 1–15.

Wall MJ, Myers FL (1995) Clinical Management of Childhood Stuttering, 2nd edn. Austin, TX: Pro-Ed.

Wall MJ, Starkweather CW, Cairns HS (1981) Syntactic influences on stuttering in young child stutterers. Journal of Fluency Disorders 6: 283–298.

Wampold B (2001) The Great Psychotherapy Debate: Models, methods, and findings. Mahwah, NJ: Lawrence Erlbaum.

Waters TL, Barrett PM, March JS (2001) Cognitive-behavioral family treatment of childhood obsessive-compulsive disorder: preliminary findings. American Journal of Psychotherapy 55: 372–387.

Watkins RV, Yairi E (1997) Language production abilities of children whose stuttering persisted or recovered. Journal of Speech and Hearing Research 40: 385–399.

Watkins RV, Yairi E (1999) Language production abilities of children whose stuttering persisted or recovered. Journal of Speech, Language and Hearing Research 42: 398–409.

Watson N (2002) Well, I know this is going to sound very strange to you, but I don't see myself as a disabled person: identity and disability. Disability and Society 17: 509–527.

Webster R, Wohlberg GC (1992) The Precision Fluency Shaping Program: Speech reconstruction for stutterers, Volumes I and II, 4th edn. Roanoke, VA: Communications Development Corporation.

Weiss AL, Zebrowski PM (1992) Disfluencies in the conversations of young children who stutter: some answers about questions. Journal of Speech and Hearing Research 35: 1230–1238.

Wells A (1997) Cognitive Therapy of Anxiety Disorders: A practical manual and conceptual guide. Chichester: Wiley.

Westbrook J (1994) Jacob's Secret Speech Bracelet. Garland, TX: Staff at Aaron's Associates.

Westby C, Cutler S (1994) Language and ADHD: Understanding the bases and treatment of self regulatory deficits. Topics in Language Disorders 14: 58–76.

Whalen CK, Henker B, Collins BE, Finck D, Dotemoto S (1979) A social ecology of hyperactive boys: Medication effects in structured classroom environments. Journal of Applied Behavior Analysis 12: 65–81.

Wilkenfield JR, Curlee RF (1997) The relative effects of questions and comments on children's stuttering. American Journal of Speech–Language Pathology 6(3): 79–89.

Willcox A (1988) An investigation into non-fluency in Down's syndrome. British Journal of Disorders of Communication 23: 153–170.

Williams D (1971) Stuttering therapy for children. In: Travis L (ed.), Handbook of Speech Pathology. New York: Appleton–Century–Crofts, pp. 1073–1093.

Williams D (1984) Prevention of stuttering. In: Perkins W (ed.), Stuttering Disorders. New York: Thième-Stratton, pp. 21–27.

Williams D (1994) Discovery: the nuts and bolts of therapy. In: Stuttering Therapy: Practical ideas for the school clinician. Workshop sponsored by SFA and the University of Colorado.

Williams K (1997) Expressive Vocabulary Test. Circle Pines, MN: American Guidance Service.

Williams R (1995) Personal construct theory in use with people who stutter. In: Fawcus M (ed.), Stuttering: From theory to practice. London: Whurr Publishers, pp. 105–129.

Wingate ME (1988) The Structure of Stuttering: A psycholinguistic analysis. New York: Springer-Verlag.

Wolk L (1998) Intervention strategies for children who exhibit coexisting phonological and fluency disorders: a clinical note. Child Language Teaching and Therapy 14: 69–82.

Wolk L, Edwards ML, Conture E (1993) Coexistence of stuttering and disordered phonology in young children. Journal of Speech and Hearing Research 36: 906-917.

Woods J, Shearsby M, Burnham D (2002) The psychological impact of the Lidcombe Program of Early Stuttering Intervention: eight case studies. International Journal of Language and Communication Disorders 37: 31–40.

World Health Organization (2001) International Classification of Functioning, Disability, and Health: Short version. Geneva: WHO.

Wright L, Ayre A (2000) WASSP: The Wright and Ayre Stuttering Self-Rating Profile. Bicester, Oxon: Winslow Press.

Yairi E (1993) Epidemiologic and other considerations in treatment efficacy with preschool children who stutter. Journal of Fluency Disorders 18: 2–3, 197–219.

Yairi E (1997) Home environment and parent–child interaction in childhood stuttering. In: Curlee R, Siegel G (eds), Nature and treatment of stuttering: New directions, 2nd edn. Needham Heights, MA: Allyn & Bacon, pp. 24–48.

Yairi E, Ambrose N (1992) A longitudinal study of stuttering in preschool children. Journal of Speech and Hearing Research 35: 756–760.

Yairi E, Ambrose N (1993) The early months of stuttering in children: a preliminary report. Journal of Speech and Hearing Research 35: 755–760.

Yairi E, Ambrose N (1999) Spontaneous recovery and clinical trials research in early childhood stuttering: a response to Onslow and Packman. Journal of Speech, Language, and Hearing Research 42: 402–409.

Yairi E, Ambrose N, Cox N (1996) Genetics of stuttering: a critical review. Journal of Speech and Hearing Research 39: 771–784.

Yairi E, Ambrose N, Paden E, Throneburg R (1996) Predictive factors of persistence and recovery: pathways of childhood stuttering. Journal of Communication Disorders 29: 51–77.

Yalom ID (1983) Inpatient Group Psychotherapy. New York: Basic Books.

Yalom ID (1995) The Theory and Practice of Group Psychotherapy, 4th edn. New York: Basic Books.

Yaruss JS (1997) Clinical implications of situational variability in preschool children who stutter. Journal of Fluency Disorders 22: 187–203.

Yaruss J (1998a) Treatment outcomes in stuttering: finding value in clinical data. In: Cordes A, Ingham R (eds), Treatment Efficacy for Stuttering: A search for empirical bases. London: Singular, 213–242.

Yaruss J (1998b) Describing the consequences of disorders: stuttering and the international classification of impairments, disabilities, and handicaps. Journal of Speech, Language, and Hearing Research 41: 249–257.

Yaruss JS, LaSalle LR, Conture EG (1998) Evaluating stuttering in young children: Diagnostic data. American Journal of Speech–Language Pathology 7: 62–76.

Yovetich W, Leschied A, Flicht J (2000) Self esteem of school age children who stutter. Journal of Fluency Disorders 25: 143–153.

Zeaman D, House BJ (1979) A review of attention theory. In: Ellis NR (ed.), Handbook of Mental Deficiency: Psychological Theory and Research, 2nd edn. Hillside, NJ: Erlbaum, pp. 63–120.

Zebrowski P (1995) The topography of beginning stuttering. Journal of Communication Disorders 28: 75–91.

Zebrowski P (1997) Assisting young children who stutter and their families: defining the role of the speech-language pathologist. American Journal of Speech-Language Pathology 6: 19–28.

Zebrowski P, Conture E (1998) Influence of nontreatment variables on treatment effectiveness for school aged children who stutter. In: Cordes A, Ingham R (eds), Treatment Efficacy for Stuttering: A search for empirical bases. London, Singular, pp. 293–310.

Zebrowski P, Kelly EM (2002) Manual of Stuttering Intervention. New York: Singular.

Index